# KING COBRA

## Mekong Adventures
## in French Indochina

*For Asia —*
*I daresay that I would rather*
*embark on odysseys such as*
*this — some fabulous tale,*
*rich as brocade and unreal*
*as a fairy story — condemn*
*me not for this dereliction*
*and believe me —*
*Your friend*
*Harry Hervey*

"...there came a King from the West
who married a cobra's daughter;
and their children were the gods
of ancient Kambodja...."

Cambodian Legend

# KING COBRA
## Mekong Adventures in French Indochina

by

## HARRY HERVEY

Foreword by

**Pico IYER**

Edited by

**Kent DAVIS**

Featuring

## *HARRY HERVEY:*
## *The Charmer Behind the Cobra*

by

**Harlan GREENE**

DatAsia Press

MMXIII

## About the Cover

Award-winning cover artist Yuehui Tang is widely recognized for his stunning depictions of Asian women. His vision captures the feminine mystery of the Mekong River, the giver of life to countless millions of people from its source on the Tibetan Plateau to its delta in Vietnam. The river's name—derived from Sanskrit, Khmer, Thai and Lao origins—means the "Mother of Water."

## DatASIA Press
### www.DatAsia.us

Copyright ©2013 DatASIA, Inc. Holmes Beach, Florida

All rights reserved. No part of this book may be reproduced, stored in a retrieval system, or transmitted, in any form, without prior permission in writing from the publisher.

### Production Credits

Editor – **Kent Davis**

Hervey Biographical Consultant – **Harlan Greene**

Cover Artist – **Yuehui Tang**

Cover Design – **Becca Klein**

Text design – **Surendra Gupta** and **Daria Lacy**

Indochina Image Consultant – **Joel Montague**

Literary Consultant – **François Doré, Librairie du Siam et des Colonies**

With special thanks to the **Georgia Historical Society** (www.georgiahistory.com) for maintaining the Hervey archive and for use of the author's portrait.

Additional blessings to **Sophaphan Davis, Jon Dobbs, Tom Kramer, Jenny Hua** and **Duffy Rutledge** for their special contributions.

### ISBN 978-1-934431-82-5 (paperback)

Library of Congress Control Number: 2013934933

Printed simultaneously in the **United States of America** and **Great Britain**.

### First Edition

## *To Carleton*

*The tropic sand is pale as foam,*
*Is pale as lilacs brushed with dusk;*
*And deep the tracks of naked feet*
*Make bruises on the sand...*
*Quick! Follow them...*
*A wind is near...*
*Gray flurries rise in saraband*
*To fill these footprints left by dreams....*

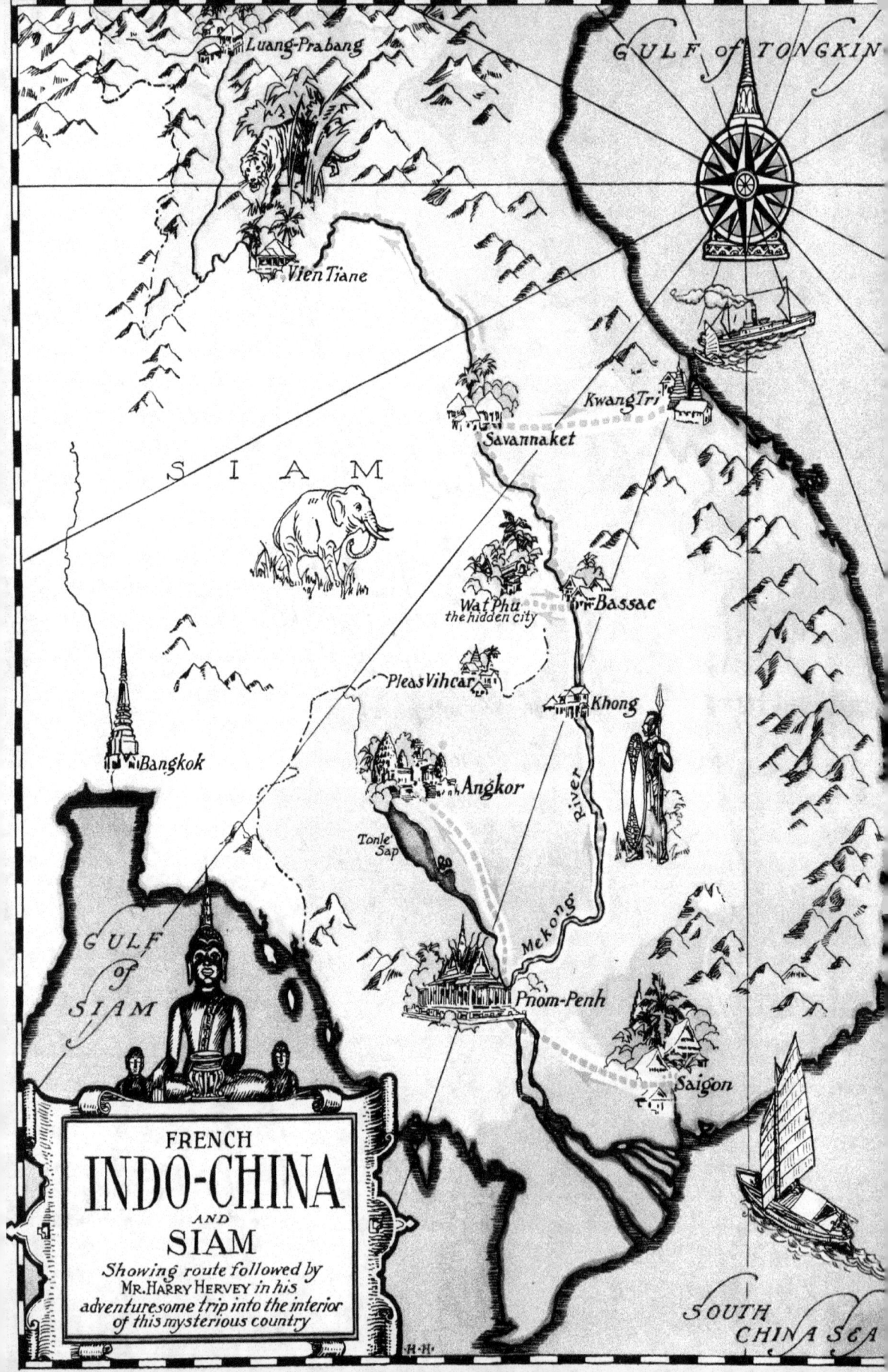

# Table of Contents

**FOREWORD:** *The Lure of Hidden Treasure* by Pico Iyer ......... IX

I     **Bayonets in the Sun** .................................3
Tells of a Dark Lady and Her White Master

II     **The City of the Serpents** ..........................47
Tells of the Indiscretions of a Cobra

III     **Saramani** .........................................101
Tells of a King and a Few Concubines

IV     **Green Serenade** ..................................129
Tells of Profane Beauty

V     **Laos** ..............................................149
Tells of the Land of Tattooed Men

VI     **The Twilight of the Khmers** .....................183
Tells of a Dead City

VII     **Sun-Weary Town** ................................205
Tells of a Prince and the Fortress of Santal-Trees

VIII     **River and Drum** ................................227
Tells of the Gentle Moods of Mother Mé-Kong

IX     **I Am the Forest** ..................................243
Tells of Nham and the Suitors of Madame Guillotine

X     **The Chinese Inn** .................................273
Tells Why This Book is Called King Cobra

**Appendices**

    *Harry Hervey: The Charmer Behind the Cobra*
    by Harlan Greene ................................. 287

    Harry Hervey Bibliography ......................... 308

    *King Cobra* 1928 Review by Margaret Mead ............. 318

    *The Lover of Madame Guillotine* by Harry Hervey ......... 321

    List of Illustrations ................................ 334

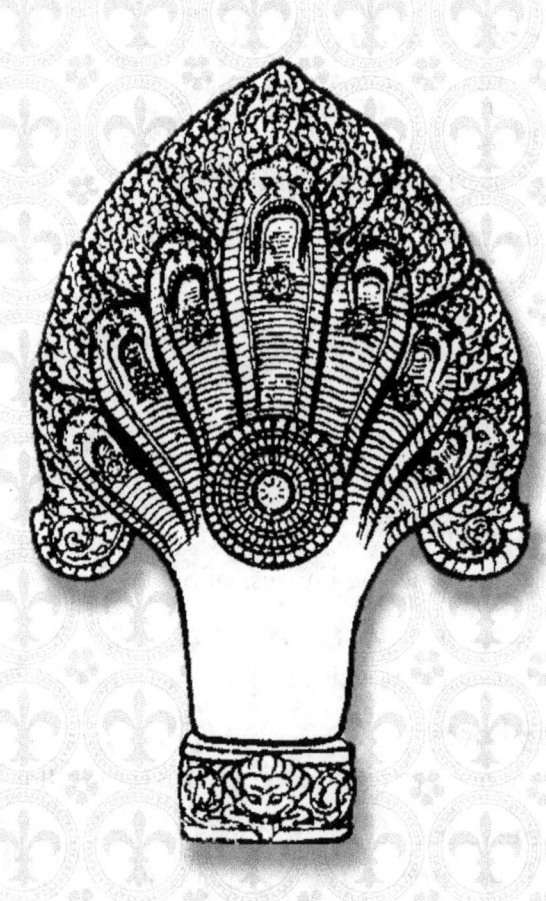

# The Lure of Hidden Treasure

## By Pico Iyer

At 26, I had a rich—and dangerous—sense of knowing it all. I was living in New York City and I had a 25th-floor office in Rockefeller Center, from which I could look out on a jungle of other high-rises. I'd only recently emerged from college and I hadn't seen much of the world, though my job, implausibly, called for me to write palpitating, first-hand accounts, every week, of places I'd never visited (worked up from colleagues' reports) for *Time* magazine. I had no dependents and few responsibilities and, though I'd traveled widely in South and Central America and grown up between England and California, I knew next to nothing about the East.

Then I made a near-fatal mistake, which probably saved my life. I decided to take a three-week holiday to Thailand and Burma and Hong Kong. I got into a Japan Air Lines plane and, a couple of days later, I was bumping through the joss-sticked darkness in Bangkok, red lanterns banging against storefronts, dancers of indeterminate sex fluttering their palms in roadside temples, barely-dressed girls slinking out of bars along little neon-lit lanes raucous with the thump of rock 'n' roll.

I'd never seen anything like this—so charged and beyond my reckoning. The day I came back from my trip, I made plans to return, five months later. And then again, five months after that. And then, the next year, for another four months. And, the following year, this time for life. There was something in both the beauty and the darkness of the area that kept pulling me, beyond the limits of my understanding, into places in myself (and in the world) I hadn't taken the trouble to uncover yet. I couldn't say what I found would be consoling—or flattering—but I knew that not looking behind the door would be a kind of death.

That sense of near-compulsion has never left me, though by now I've been to Thailand more than 60 times, gone back again and again to Vietnam and Cambodia, even written stories, and articles and film-scripts set there. One day, along the Mekong River, a couple of hours out of Luang Prabang, in Laos, I went into a cave full of Buddhas and found I couldn't leave.

Anxious, my longtime Japanese sweetheart came over and told me it was time to go. I stayed where I was. "Our boat is about to depart," she said.

"I don't want to go."

Finally she pulled me out. But when we were out in the daylight, I said, "I have to go in again."

Later I would learn that these caves had sheltered thousands of Laotians during the bombings of the Vietnam War. They were rich with ghosts and unburied spirits for the locals. But what I was responding to was something more alluring: the Buddhas that stood at the back of the opening, whose tapered arms and unswerving gazes seemed to beckon me.

Finally my companion came in to where I was standing again, recited the Heart Sutra in Japanese at high speed and dragged me out. To this day, in 26 years of friendship, she's never seen me, she says, in such a state of possession.

I thought of all this when I met one of the startling discoveries of my recent life, secreted in plain sight like a temple in a jungle: Harry Hervey. I'd never heard of the precocious American traveler and prolific novelist until Kent Davis, the publisher of this volume, brought him to my attention earlier this year. I'd barely known, in fact, that Americans were traveling in Southeast Asia in the 1920s, even though Bali was filling up with foreign artists eager to record their discovery of Paradise and British novelists were fanning out to Mexico and Ethiopia and Tibet.

But once I began to surrender to Hervey's spell, I started—as, perhaps, he did—to lose all sense of where fact ended and fiction began. I found myself drawn by his vision, for all its occasional clunkiness and excess, much as I'd been drawn by a temple I once saw, unforgettably, in a dream in 1987. In certain moods and moments, I found, few writers could transport you more potently. You begin to succumb to the drift of a river Hervey describes, the lure of a sleepy afternoon in the sun. You can all but taste the stillness atop a temple in Angkor, towers rising "like guttered candles." You can virtually inhale the dust as you begin to sweat. "A drum was beating in a monastery somewhere in the thickets along the river and it made a ghost prance on the silence."

Hervey at his best gives you a dreamy, wide-awake sense of an Indochina where white-suited Frenchmen were carried in rickshaws through the streets of Phnom Penh at mid-day, it took 14 days from Saigon to Vientiane by "the swiftest travel possible," and six weeks to sail from Vientiane to Luang Prabang and back. But more than showing you a world that has disappeared, he gives you a world that will surround you if you're in those streets tomorrow (the public park in Saigon "after nightfall alive with prowlers innocent and otherwise"). And, most of all, he has the rare traveler's gift of evoking for you all that you can't quite see and urging you to join him on a journey towards what you'll never quite touch.

Great travel books give you journeys from which the traveler (perhaps the reader) comes back transformed, a mystery to himself. Suddenly you can no longer trust what you knew so firmly a day ago; suddenly all sense of "home" and "abroad"—of "you" and "I"—dissolves. A real trip turns you around so that you leave behind the person you were—and maybe the one you wanted to become.

Hervey may have embellished his real experiences, and drawn liberally from books that fired his imagination before he left home—as Marco Polo and Ibn Battuta and Bruce Chatwin did—but the young American who loved to devour exotic romances transforms himself (and so perhaps his readers) by giving us a traveler venturing so deep into the heart of Southeast Asia that soon he's almost describing it from the inside out.

The man who so casually wrote of Saigon as a "half-caste lady" when he began, and who described the Vietnamese city as a "pseudo-French hussy," turns, before our eyes, into a man who seems to have left most judgments behind as he lies out on his pirogue, heading toward the unknown, reflecting on "immortality" and feeling "very close to something I had always wanted to understand." He's not an English traveler, like Norman Lewis a generation later, giving us droll and beautiful descriptions of Indochinese culture and customs; he's not simply recounting what he saw, as Helen Candee did in her exuberant *Angkor the Magnificent*, published two years earlier. Rather, Hervey feels like a man possessed, someone who's lost his heart (perhaps his mind) to what's around him, and has given himself over to the new world he's discovering. The result is that we feel something at stake in every sentence and gain an exhilarating sense of not beginning to know what Hervey will find next in Indochina (or what Indochina will find in Hervey).

This goes with a peculiar mix of brusqueness and lyricism that gives one a sense of a narrator in motion, "fluid" (in one of his favorite terms), and always ready to be converted into something else. Put differently, he's a poet who's never lost his common sense—or a healthy skepticism about his own romanticism. A river "is burnished gold," he writes early on, "which is to say, it is exceedingly muddy." A woman he sees in a shop is "more than enchanting…she might have been some priestess of the Khmers." But "As we left the shop the divine Apsaras followed us with a proprietorial gaze, then snatched the money from the dealer and sat down to count it." Hervey is always eager to surrender to the sensual tug of a foreign culture, but he's not allergic to the spiritual, and it's often hard to tell one from the other. This means that we never know, from one moment to the next, if we're going to meet a rhapsodist or a fury of disenchantment: "One of Indo-China's dreamy and disconcerting charms," he writes, "is its abundance of misinformation."

I'll confess that when I began King Cobra, I formed quite a distinct impression of its author: a senior political intelligence officer, I decided, or a slightly withered Asia hand who was favoring us with his unvarnished impressions of a continent he'd been crisscrossing for decades. A strongly opinionated figure who could be a bit of a pain to travel with, though was undeniably compelling in his forays into the unknown. You can imagine my surprise when I learned that he was in fact in his mid-twenties when he wrote *King Cobra*. His book wasn't the summation of a long acquaintance but rather an excited torrent of first impressions, during which we actually see its unseasoned author move beyond his summary judgments to something more open and agnostic.

It may well be his descriptions that grab hold of you first—whether of the "dusk-frail" scarves he sees in Cambodia or of trees enfolding the temple of Preah Khan, as they do to this day. Hervey's verbs and insects alone show you what a natural writer he was, for all his sometimes purple prose and green perspective: "Fireflies stitched the dusk like luminous needles"; "Insects rasped about a yellow-shaded lamp." And, true to his sensibility, he is always as alert to what's in the soil as to what's up in the air—a romancer, you could say, who hasn't turned his back on real life: "Water-buffaloes lie nostril-deep in the pools along the way; butterflies wheel drunkenly over the piles of dung."

He's never slow to pass reckless and sweeping judgments and, ninety years on, most readers will notice how much manners and customs have changed since his time. No one today would dream of writing, "Most Cambodians are pleasantly lazy" (even if they think it) or averring that the "natives" (as they so often are in Hervey's prose) are "gentle and with no complexities—yet capable of terrible things." The air of *King Cobra* is thick with words like "indolent" and "primitive" and Hervey has no hesitation in writing, of a woman in Laos, that she was "a soft, wild thing, warm as her golden skin."

It's not that visitors don't entertain the same thoughts and impressions today: we've simply learned to dress up our responses differently or to keep them to ourselves. Yet the more I read in Hervey, the more I felt that he might not always be a subtle writer, but he was certainly an intuitive one: his claims are large ones, but that does not always make them wrong. And what's most striking today is not all the ways in which he sounds like any traveler of his time, but all the ways he doesn't.

To a powerful extent, the young American in French Indochina refuses to play along with the prevailing attitudes of his time; he mocks those Frenchmen who condescend towards the people they're ruling and, again and again, he refuses to say that either race is "Superior." Although he often falls into the local habit of talking of "savages" and writing of local Buddhas, say, as "barbaric little images," he more often delights in admiring those colonizers who admit to having been taken over—remade—by the culture they're so confident they're remaking. "Man is at his worst," Hervey writes, in one of his bracing moments, "in the role of altruist."

He wasn't anyone's fool or subject, in other words, and he wasn't about to find all good either in the locals or in their European rulers. This gives his writing an unusual freshness—it does not run along predictable lines, even if it has familiar moments—and its author seems always ready to be surprised. He's not a seeker after "esoteric truths," he asserts at one point, but he's clearly not a defensive cynic either. Everything is up for grabs in his path, and we're in the hands of a real explorer who has traveled all the way to Indochina to see what he can learn from its largely untracked open spaces.

I love the uncensored directness and candor of his writing, which gives it at times the quick pungency of a Paul Theroux, to cite a more recent, very American traveler in these parts. Hervey thinks nothing of frankly admiring the local beauties that he passes or admitting, when he comes to a climax in a trip, that he's "tired and sore." He openly notes that the romance between the cultures of East and West often comes down to a matter of sex and he doesn't fall victim to either the elegant evasions of the Brit or the philosophizing of the Frenchman. Here is a man who will call a spade a spade, yet nonetheless be willing to drift into the spirit of acceptance and indirection he so admires in the cultures around him.

Unlike most travelers, Hervey never forgets what a presumptuous act he's embarked upon; imagine, he notes at one point, how a Laotian would be treated if, arriving in America, he started examining the make-up on a local woman's face. And his relative youth gives him a freshness and vulnerability you won't find in the contemporaneous Southeast Asian travel accounts of Somerset Maugham, say. "Generalizations upon a nation are not only banal but futile," the young American asserts without qualification—only to give us a whole rush of new generalizations upon a nation.

At the heart of his journey, I always feel, is a quest, and around it is a question that still haunts many a traveler today: to what extent do the cultures we visit have something that we, in all our seeming affluence and mobility, lack? And how much are and should we be "conquered" by the places we're so sure that we're conquering? It's no coincidence that Hervey shows us so many white men stealing Buddhas. Or that he was so consumed by Southeast Asia that he turned out six books on it in a few years, not least the novel, *Congai*, that he wrote as soon as he completed *King Cobra*, and to which he seems to allude near the conclusion of his travel book.

In the end, it's his very openness, his eagerness to learn from the places he visits, and to be taken out of his comfort zone, beyond what he knows, that gives Hervey's story such a pulsing vitality. One feels he really has come more as pilgrim than as a master. For all the historical and archaeological facts he includes in his narrative, it's consistently what he doesn't understand that lends his story charm and vivacity.

As I followed, with him, young monks stepping by candlelight through the temples of Angkor; as I watched, through his eyes, a dance by torchlight among the ruins; as I followed his intuition—and his intuitions are often as strong as his passing judgments may be questionable—of a "vast drowned city" in the jungle, I came to feel something of what draws many a foreigner into the depths of Angkor and Southeast Asia today. A sense of imminent discovery, of wonder, is in the air.

*King Cobra* imparts all the tremendous excitement of coming upon a hidden treasure in the jungles of Indochina. And as you begin to advance through it, you realize you're holding another kind of hidden treasure in your hands. His knowingness may put you off at times; but his sense of all he doesn't know, his readiness to travel even deeper into uncertainty can turn Hervey into a grand discovery, as he was for me— and one who deserves his place in the annals of important and undeservedly forgotten travel writing. *King Cobra* is one of the rare books of its time to give us an outsider's glimpse of Indochina at a pivotal moment. Just embrace the lurid title and dive into the unexpectedness within.

**Pico Iyer**
Santa Barbara — July 2013

---

Pico Iyer has been called "arguably the greatest living travel-writer" by *Outside* magazine and "one of 100 visionaries worldwide who could change your life" by the *Utne Reader*.

A traveler since birth, he has ventured throughout Asia for more than 30 years, as chronicled in his books including *Video Night in Kathmandu, Falling Off the Map, Sun After Dark, The Lady and the Monk* and *The Global Soul*. Since 1987 he's been based in western Japan, though often making forays from Laos to Bali and Ladakh to Bangkok.

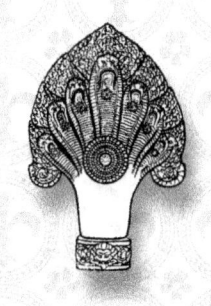

# KING COBRA

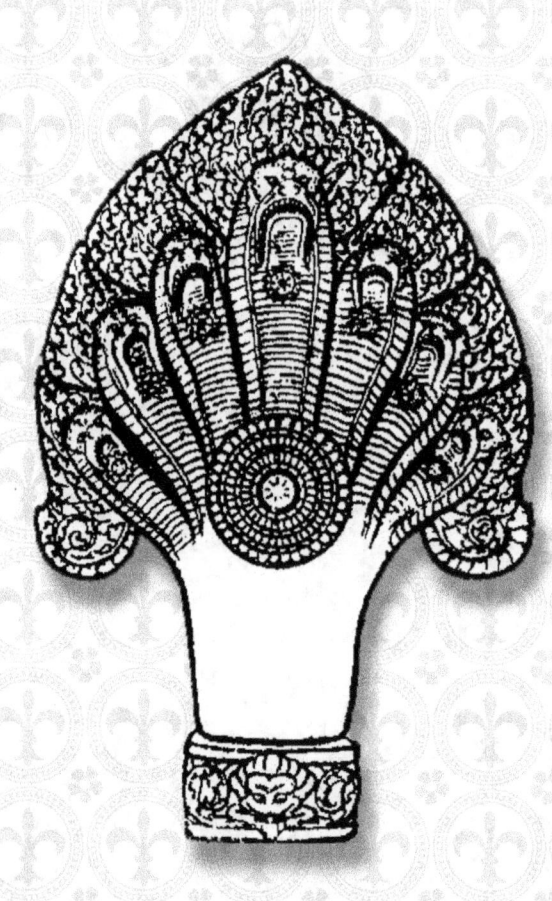

# Chapter 1
# Bayonets in the Sun
*Tells of a Dark Lady and Her White Master*

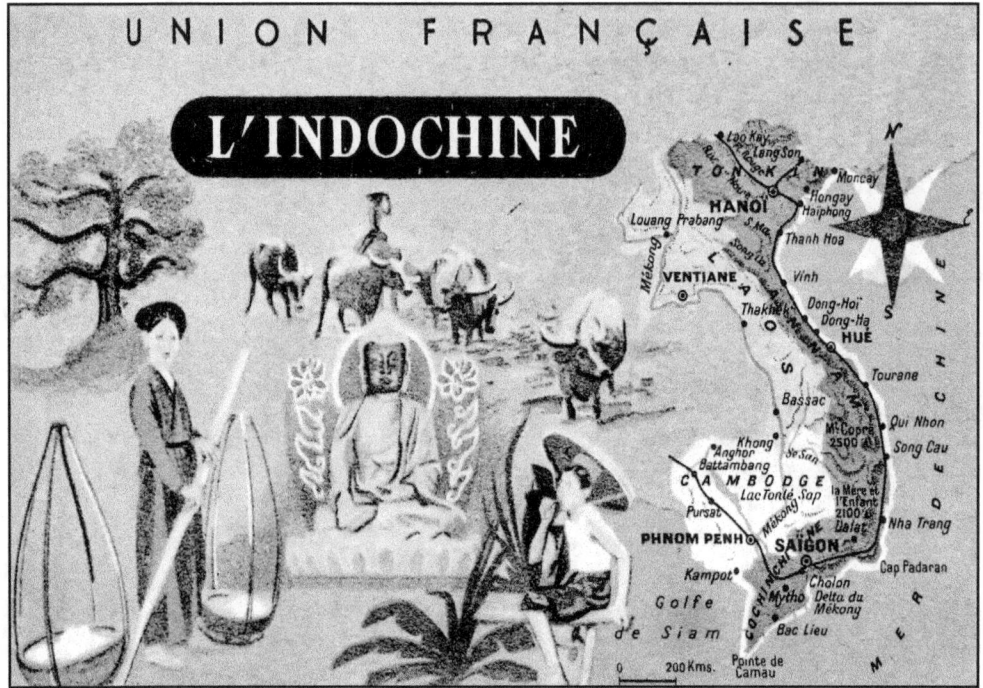

"On the map of Asia, Indo-China forms an argus-pheasant whose plumes are the jungles that undulate over the states of Cambodia, Laos, Tonkin, Annam and Cochin-China."

"A ghost of the rue de la Paix has wandered down to the equator."

# Saigon

## 1

ROM THAT gallant and casual fellow the Tired Cavalier I heard this parable: Once while out strolling in Peshawar he saw a young Mussulman lying beside the road, dust-streaked and bleeding; and when he asked a bystander what had happened, the native shrugged in that insolent manner hillmen have and retorted, "The fool told the truth...."

## 2

Inasmuch as this is a book of personal reflections on that corner of Asia where France has planted her bayonets, it should begin with a glimpse of the coast as it crawled lazily out of the South China Sea. But, considering it is also a narrative in which individuals as well as the country are involved, it must begin with the Tired Cavalier.

A ghost of the rue de la Paix has wandered down to the equator, derisively haunting that city of half-breed impulses, Saigon. One sets out from his hotel in a rickshaw and sees, on either side, numbers of Annamites in sloppy trousers drifting along in the midst of Frenchmen in trousers equally sloppy, all pausing now and again to gaze into windows displaying the latest styles from Paris. Overhead, signs in French laugh soundlessly at the tamarind trees and other languid proof that Saigon is in the tropics. Finally, bewildered by the incongruous scene, one takes refuge in some sidewalk café which, like the French signs, jokingly taunts this Cochin-Chinese city.

It was at such a café on the rue Catinat—that ghost of the rue de la Paix—that I met the Tired Cavalier.

He attracted me not by his person—which, on inspection, was sufficient to merit a second glance—but by a prismatic drink on the table before him. As this table was directly beside mine, I was close enough to observe the charms of this particular drink as well as his satisfaction when he sipped it. A layer of green in the bottom of the glass melted into a haze of gold and clouded upward into cherry-red.

I was entranced.

In my stumbling French I told the Chinese "boy" I desired one like it, but he failed to understand until I pointed to the glass and pronounced "*Encore*" Then the owner of the drink, amused rather than annoyed by my vulgar display, smiled and said, "*Arc-en-ciel.*"

I confess to an immediate admiration for him.. He was... well—impeccable. A faultless white suit—something of an achievement in a country where the tailors are Chinese—scarf of delicate azure and handkerchief to match, with his black hair pomaded to the sheen of lacquer. It was not until he invited me to join him that I noticed the dark half-moons under his eyes and his skin, sallow as old white silk. Yet for all these outward signs of his inward and spiritual weariness he maintained a cavalier manner. And he spoke English with the exquisite precision of one not born to it.

"You are a tourist," he said; and it was not even a question.

I replied that I was a writer; for, aside from my perfectly healthy dislike for the word tourist applied to me, it would be technically incorrect because a tourist, in spite of popular opinion, travels to tell other countries about his own.

I was, I added, looking for some ruins called Wat Phu.

"Never heard of the place," he announced in the tone of one dismissing a trivial thing. "But I do know that back there"—he gestured—"in the jungle, are the remains of a civilization as great as China's or India's—and the world knows extraordinarily little about it."

He paused introspectively. But I did not speak. I could see he was a man who enjoyed uninterrupted discourse.

**Harry's personal photo of "the rue Catinat—that ghost of the rue de la Paix."**

"And here we are, we French," he continued presently, "with Versailles and a few other feeble pieces of architecture to our credit, imposing our civilization on their descendants."

By the gleam in his eyes it was evident that, being French himself, he could cast scornful criticism at his government and be very emotional about it. "We call it civilization, my friend." Whereupon he halted to ask if I objected to being called his friend, and without waiting for an answer, hurried on: "But it is *business*. Business. Attend, my friend—the Frenchman is just as much a business man as the American, although the Frenchman may play a violin after hours whereas the American usually plays golf; and the American is more successful. Yes, at heart we are just as much a merchant nation but more impractical." Then he sighed and looked vaguely tired. "I suppose if my mother had not been Russian I would not say that...."

As we talked, a concourse of life took itself past in the street: numerous *pousses* as rickshaws are called in French possessions, drawn by lithe Annamites, turbaned or wearing cone-shaped straw hats; small Cambodian ponies harnessed to equally small victorias;[1] a few French motorcars; and a motley of beings, brown, yellow and white, whose faces, so diversified, seemed to roll by like varied coins poured into a common smelter.

Indeed, the night was not unlike a vat, welding about us iron-dark and close. In this heat the tamarinds seemed to droop, and the people in the café, busy with handkerchiefs and fans, appeared determined to enjoy themselves in spite of the climate.

Close by, an orchestra was playing "Tea for Two." Little Annamite boys, black-trousered and bare-chested, moved along the curbing with brass gods and post-cards to sell; and other natives, gathered in groups across the street by the opera-house, watched the people at the tables with an expression of perplexity. I could not help wondering what they thought, if they thought at all; whether they felt resentment or merely animal curiosity.

The Tired Cavalier, following my gaze, smiled that charming, fatigued smile of his.

"You are pitying the natives," he divined. "They all do at first. Then they grow tired of them. They end by ignoring them. This is no climate for emotions as strenuous as pity or active dislike. Except, of course, Official Compassion, which is the duty of every good colonial government.... We are not unkind to the natives; and they are clever, these *indigenes*. They are—what do you say?—passive? Yes, they are passive—and they make a good living, which is all a native wants. Also," he added with the expression of one who enjoys a profound secret, "I think they understand a very ancient truth...."

I waited for him to divulge that truth, but instead, as an afterthought, he remarked it was very interesting that I had come hunting for some ruins.

"I shall dine with you tomorrow night and hear about it," he informed me.

# 3

Saigon turns a tawny cheek to the sun.

Along the rue Catinat, which strays from the river up to the cathedral, the shops are a pale buff-color, as are most of the buildings in those intersecting

---

[1] A victoria (not capitalized) is a light, four-wheeled carriage for two with a folding top and an elevated driver's seat in front. Later the term was applied to touring cars with a folding top that usually only covered the rear seat.

boulevards and avenues that make up the French and Chinese business section; and in the rue Taberd, the rue Pelerin and adjacent shady streets where small plaster dwellings are smothered in tropical luxuriance, this same mellow tone pervades, as though the sun had smitten the city and left it to take in the equatorial glare.

Instead of becoming depressing, this predominance of one hue lends a certain inconspicuousness to the whole city, and one's sense of color is never violated by a sudden Staring white or an anguished blue, as often happens in other towns of the East. Immediately Saigon becomes friendly, familiar, and one soon realizes he can ride about and safely allow the populace to engage his attention, never fearing he may miss some innovation in the color-scheme of the background.

However, Nature is not so contented with this tyranny of yellow. Mold spreads upward from the bases of the houses, it tongues the walls and introduces a sickly malarial pallor into the otherwise healthy sunburn of these dwellings.

From Rond Point, the rue Paul Blanchy idles along in verdant shadow, ambling past barracks and red-tiled public buildings until, after skirting the Place de la Cathédrale, it reaches a quarter where lush, exuberant gardens unload their fragrances upon the green quiet. Here, during the day, the silence is undisturbed except by the soft pad-pad of rickshaw coolies and the stridulations of insects. After dusk the air is no less somnolent: from verandas come the clink of ice and glasses, little trickles of laughter, and other sounds indicative of languid amusement. It is an atmosphere of dignity and well-bred indolence. To live "beyond the cathedral," while not actually a privilege, is at least an advantage, inasmuch as one's neighbors are sure to be the very best colonials.

Personally, I find that part of the city below the Boulevard Norodom much more amenable. Particularly the streets where neat French letters on the barracks walls announce it is forbidden to post bills there. A ghost of childish fancy in me is stirred by even the suggestion of colonial troops. It takes me back to those luxurious days when I read *Le Roman d'un Spahi* and *Rarahu*.[2] Consequently, these barracks drowsing in sensuous shade

---

[2] Published in 1880, *Rarahu* was a semi-autobiographical novel by French author Pierre Loti describing his (fictionalized) romantic liaison with an exotic Tahitian girl of the same name. Though only his second book, it won him recognition among readers, launching his literary career. The title

bring to life pages of romance, and wandering past them I am able to invest the stupid Annamite sentinel with the dignity of an iniquitous rascal or to find in the glimpses of khaki-clad soldiers, permitted by open doors and windows, a hint of something decadent and definitely improper. I am convinced, for the moment, that all of them have native mistresses—for haven't I read and believed "Le Roman d'un Spahi" and "Rarahu"?—or, if not, at least they go every night to the Botanical Garden, which is conveniently, near the barracks, to tryst with rice-powdered *congaies* who do not blacken their teeth with betel.

It is not a perverted imagination that suggests such possibilities, nor is the suggestion extravagant or unnecessary. In a city where the soil bursts with amazing plant life, where the very air is heavy with the breath of prolific earth, it would be surprising if the human beings dwelling there remained unaffected. Such fecund surroundings undoubtedly have a tendency to dilate every sensation. For instance, boredom in a place like Saigon can amount almost to madness; and an emotion as violent as indignation, generally so brief in an atmosphere less intense, becomes a devastating event requiring hours or an entire day to exhaust itself.

Walk along the rue Taberd, which crosses the rue Paul Blanchy. Except for the bare, dry area surrounding the cathedral, this street lies in the same damp shadow that immerses all of Saigon. On the sidewalks are thickly leaved tamarinds, and in the gardens—each compound is a garden, sometimes cultivated, but just as often natural—cycas-trees, traveler-palms, papayas, pomegranates, agaves and other growths almost inundate the mossy red-tiled dwellings. Here, in extensive grounds, is the governor's palace, and behind it a public park, usually deserted during the day, but after nightfall alive with prowlers innocent and otherwise.

I remember a certain midnight stroll when, purposelessly following the rue Taberd, I reached the end and turned into another street. I could hear the clatter of Annamite sandals nearby, thrice loud in the dark stillness; far away—it might have been at the end of the world, so remote it sounded—a voice shouted "Kaol" followed by the smothered crunch of wheels as a rickshaw answered. Without realizing it, I had drifted into another road—a

---

was republished as *Tahiti*, and then *Le Mariage de Loti* (*The Marriage of Loti*). In 1881, Loti followed with *Le Roman d'un spahi*, a sad account of a French soldier serving in Senegal. Loti's adventures fueled Hervey's exotic dreams from childhood, and he credits Loti's book about his trip to Cambodia, *Un Pèlerin d'Angkor* (1912) as his inspiration to travel to Asia.

road so pale it seemed powdered with star-dust. It had a look surprisingly chaste. All the houses were white, so white they seemed to speak in the dimness. Only a few lights cast gleams athwart the road, and no one was astir. As I moved by open doors I could see through one red and gold memorial banners hanging on the walls within, and through another an altar laden with gods and tablets to the ancestors. In the air was a vague sweetness —I doubt if it came from any shrub or flower or if it existed at all outside my own imagination. For suddenly I realized this street was the East as I wanted it to be: infinitely composed, quiet with the stillness of centuries, and dreaming beneath a multitude of stars.

This quarter unravels into sections less poised. Any one of a number of dusty highways leads eventually to the market-place. I have browsed about this immense square by day and by night, and I find it has greater charm after dark. Then it seems to take on a carnival aspect. Under the many arches of this vast shed are the stalls, piled with every variety of merchandise from the lowliest native vegetable to exquisitely wrought ornaments in gold. The place swims in a veritable stink. Salted fish, spoilt fruit, offal ... In the early evening sooty lamps and naphtha-flares, the warm, curdling air filled with liquid syllables and throaty cries, and the numbers of people shifting back and forth combine to give an effect of feverish activity to a scene where in reality business is carried on with a truly admirable disregard for time and speed.

Facing the market-square are many Chinese shops. Ideographs announce that inside are silks or meat and fowl or a miscellany of leather goods such as belts and shoes. Smells of spices and teas breathe out warmly from dim interiors. Groups of Chinese are always gathered on the sidewalks in seemingly endless conversations, but never too engrossed to pause and stare at a foreigner, following these looks with humorous gutturals, which one suspects are not altogether complimentary. Lithe-flanked rickshaw-men go swinging through the street, drawing little girls in brocaded jackets or pompous and obese merchants. Nondescript boys, naked from the waist up, drift about aimlessly. One thinks of Canton or Foo-chow.

Not far from the market is a canal that empties all the refuse of Cholon, the Chinese suburb, into Saigon River, and along its east bank is the Quai de Belgique, a small section which might be called the "financial district."

Here and in adjacent streets are most of the banks and consulates. Rickshaws and bullock carts creak along, almost touching wheels with a Fiat

Mailboat of the Messageries Maritimes arriving in Saigon in 1921.

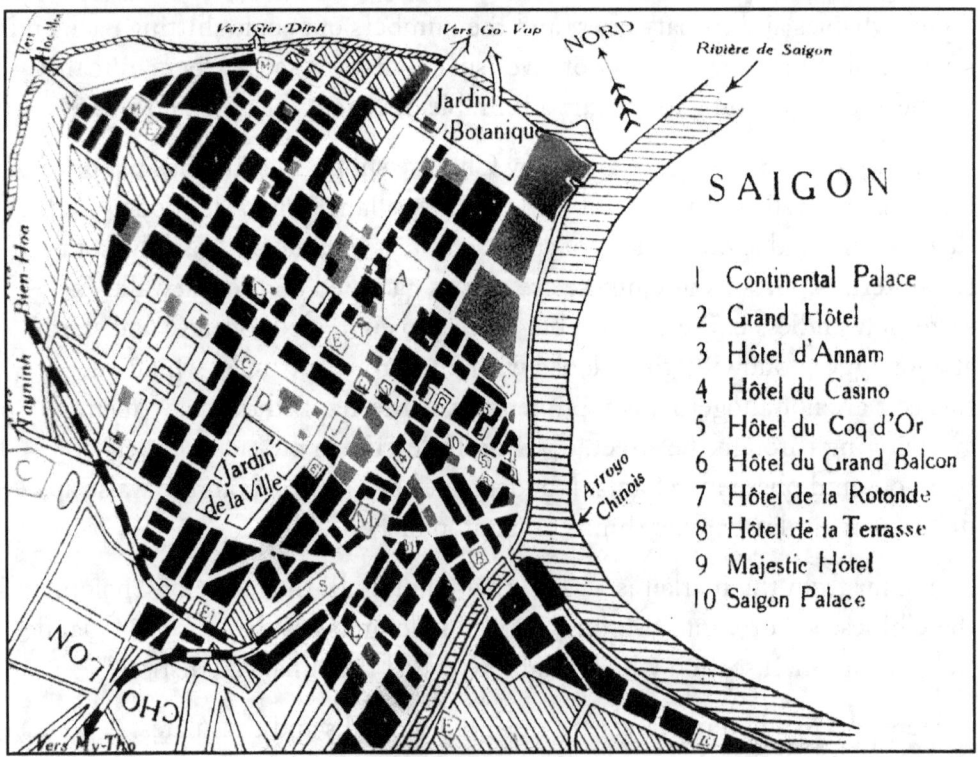
Downtown Saigon, circa 1930.

or a Renault; and in and out of the banking-houses move Chetties,[3] caste-marked and white-robed, brushing arms with Frenchmen, immaculate in ill-fitting suits and preposterously large hats.

A bridge conveys one across the arroyo to the docks where the ships of the Messageries Maritimes and other big companies come into port. The river, as though submitting to the color-scheme of the town, is burnished gold; which is to say, it is exceedingly muddy. On a bright morning the sunlight seems to concentrate on its surface, shimmering hotly about the vessels riding at anchor—lousy freighters harlequined with paint, sailing-ships lying like sea-birds with folded wings, and sampans and junks under ragged, ill-patched canvas. On the wharves, where the heat makes a thick essence of the odors of fruit, copra, oil and hemp, coolies move in and out of the sweltering hatches, bent under loads that press their muscles into sinuous play.

From the southwestern end of the water-front, a road running parallel with the river follows a casual course past the foot of the rue Catinat, past the Marine Barracks, to the other end of the harbor, where the Botanical Garden slumbers in its own miasmal vapors. A series of elegant names designates the streets. Quai Francis Garnier, Quai de la Grandiere, Rond Point Rigault de Genouilly, Quai Primaguet. One is impressed.

As a matter of fact, there is something hilarious about all these names with which the French have garnished Saigon. To be walking along a street obviously tropical—a street where the buildings are touched with green rot, where the gardens drip with moisture and lie suffocated in hot fragrances—and discover it is called the Boulevard de l'Abattoir or the rue de l'Avalanche, is like encountering a tawny and slightly disreputable Asiatic lady who suddenly thumbs her nose at you and shouts: "*Vive la France!*"

But there is an ominous note in these names: they sound an echo of the clash of arms. Catinat... Rigault de Genouilly... de la Grandiere... Was it not the French warship Catinat that in 1856 was dispatched to Tourane on the coast of Annam to impress upon the Emperor Tu-Duc the advisability of complying with France's demands? Did not Admiral Rigault de Genouilly bombard and finally subjugate Saigon? And did it not fall to the lot of

---

[3] Indians from Ceylon.

Admiral de la Grandiere to lay out a new town after the old one came into the hands of his government?

It is not my intention to become excessively historical, but considering Saigon as the half-caste lady she is, it would be unnatural not to go poking about in her past in an effort to discover the means by which she became this pseudo-French hussy.[4]

# 4

On the map of Asia, Indo-China forms an argus-pheasant whose plumes are the jungles that undulate over the states of Cambodia, Laos, Tonkin, Annam and Cochin-China; a proud creature poised upon Siam, with its throat pressed against Yunnan and its tail sweeping out into the South China Sea.

Many bloods have mingled in its warm breast Shan, Chinese, Thai, Tibetan, Annamite, Indian, Burmese, Malay, Karen... and the blood of how many others?

The early people of Cochin-China were part Annamite and part Phonamese, that is to say, Cambodian. Later they came under the domination of the Karens and absorbed them. These Karens were a race remotely connected with the Chinese as indicated by the fact that they worshiped the ancient Chinese god Tien, and arrived in Indo-China by the same route from the west as the Chinese.

Annamite history began, technically, about 2879 B. C., when these people were known as Giao-chi, or They-of-the-Big-Toe; but it was with the Ly Dynasty that the events commenced which led to the intervention of France. Annam was fighting China, and realizing she would be defeated eventually, she compromised by accepting Chinese suzerainty. In 1610 a Jesuit mission was established—and politically speaking the first note of doom was sounded.

When about a hundred years later the houses of Ly and Nguyen were warring, a prince of the latter family fled to Siam, and there met the Jesuit

---

[4] Throughout the book, Hervey's accuracy with historical details—especially ancient dates—is often questionable and frequently wrong. Readers should refer to other sources for accuracy, instead relying on this text to gain anthropological and artistic insights into this complex society, as seen by an American traveler in the early 20th century.

bishop Monsignor Pigneaux de Behaine, who as is often the case was a diplomat as well as a priest. Immediately he persuaded the prince to go to France. A treaty was made between him and Louis XVI whereby he was declared Emperor of Annam, with the name Gia-long, and under the protection of the French—in return for which France would receive the Bay of Tourane and the island of Pulo Condore, off the Cochin-Chinese coast.

After regaining his kingdom Gia-long was tolerant of the French, but he wasted no love upon them. His successors gave full vent to his smoldering animosity.

The persecution of the Jesuits which followed offers a startling example of the barbarism of Annam at that period; and it also offers a survey of the most popular method by which Western nations have always acquired fat slices of the East.

From the very earliest times enthusiastic proselytes of religion have inadvertently, or otherwise, carried the banners of political influence into so-called savage lands. I am inclined to believe, even with the possibility of Heaven descending upon my head, that missionary work, whatever its sentimental pretensions, is the outgrowth of an acquisitive impulse and generally has more to do with man than God. Many a blundering cleric like some magic bean in a fairy story has turned into a prosperous colonial possession. In fact, if Western politicians would only admit it, they frequently owe the extension of their territory into regions below the equator to those very clergymen whom in view of their antithetical professions they regard with scorn—except just previous to elections.

This killing of missionaries has ever been a jolly pastime in the heathen countries, but a pastime with dire results for the originators. If these heathen would only look beyond their prejudices, or realize the public pride with which the enlightened countries take their religions, they would be less harried by crusades. Although I dare say if the West were robbed of this eloquent excuse for expansion it would find another and probably less dignified one.

Therefore, out of the martyrdom of the Jesuits crept the stealthy dawn of French power in Indo-China.

In 1858 Admiral Rigault de Genouilly landed his marines at Tourane and captured the city; and the following year his ships sailed past Cap Saint-Jacques, up the river, and opened fire on Saigon.

By 1860 French troops were massed there. It is doubtful which took the greater toll, the climate or the natives. Fever bedded with the soldiers like a vindictive courtesan; and intermittent warfare gnawed at the security of this new stronghold. The next two years were years of terrible drama for the French.

Without becoming excessively sentimental, one can understand the psychology of these white troops, exposed to the cruelty of the equatorial sun and to warfare in a country where Nature as well as the inhabitants threw up a malignant barricade.

I doubt if anyone can be as lonely in a foreign land as a Frenchman. And most of these soldiers who held Saigon during the sieges between 1860 and 1862 were simple fellows—men who had come out with some tenuous idea of adventure and had found themselves caught in the reality of building the foundation for a colonial empire. It is questionable if they realized their own tragedy. Of course when, during some night attack, a comrade fell, or when another, succumbing to malaria or dysentery, was dumped into the very ground that had slain him, they must have experienced a momentary contact with the truth. But they differed only slightly from the soldiers of our period, and undoubtedly their greatest complaint was against the climate, the hardships of the campaign and the lack of decent wine and eminently acceptable women.

Judging by the consequences, one might suggest that after twenty or thirty years of fighting, the French and the natives discontinued hostilities for the common good of a new generation who jabbered a strange patois and ate *foie-gras* with chop-sticks.

Miscegenation either as a pastime or as the result of necessity is not peculiar to the French, although they have' shown themselves now and then singularly adept at it. Nor can they or any other nation be blamed for it when the scene is on or near the equator. Not that I would impute a relaxation of racial integrity to that imaginary line which divides the hemispheres. The reason is much more subtle than a matter of geography or climate. Indeed geography and climate have a great deal to do with it, but the main factor, it seems to me, is the unconscious willingness of darker races to insinuate themselves into the graces of those nations that make no secret of their superiority. And what surer means than sex?

There is, I find, something delightfully tolerant about the French, as evidenced by their willingness to take over the vices as well as the virtues of those they conquer. When they acquire new territory the act becomes, so to speak, a marriage in which nothing is withheld; and the result except in individual cases is-that the progeny can be depended upon to be representative.

In looking over sundry books of travel I have discovered that in the majority the element of sex is entirely absent, whether because of genuine modesty on the part of the writers or fear of personal publicity I am unable to say. However, it seems a deplorable lapse of fidelity with the reader. Being at times a reader myself, I resent it: if I am to have an authentic view of a country I desire nothing withheld, except perhaps those minor habits which we suspect everyone of practicing, even foreigners.

Should one care to explore the past of Indo-China, he will come upon hints of certain religious festivals that may momentarily upset his sense of propriety. Particularly if he realizes the same festivals are today celebrated in countries not so pagan, although these recent variations are carefully disguised to conform with the standards of a civilization not publicly interested in sex except where maternity and statutory crimes are concerned.

History itself is not necessarily distressing, but the suggestions behind history invariably startle the illusions. Quite frequently the cynical snoopers of our literature and sciences disclose facts proving that now and again in the past, behind the tragic gesture of slaughter and battle, the actual victory was gained when a queen slipped down the back stairway to meet some yokel from the enemy camp.

A few glances at the history of French Indo-China convince one that, figuratively speaking, a dusky lady slipped down the back stairway there....

It happened in a very simple and natural manner; and we cannot censure these first colonials, who found an acceptable gentleness in the native *congai*, or the *congai* herself, who submitted to these men as she had been taught to submit to all men.

Consider the scene....

It is sometime between the years of 1860 and 1862, in Gia-Dinh-Thanh, or the Great Market, as Saigon was called then....

On the river, muddy with the silt discharged from a swampy delta, is a floating village: sampans, junks and bamboo rafts lashed together, all slumbering in the hot effluvium of their own swill. Along the bank, in dense vegetation, the brick and mortar shops of the Chinese, their walls plastered with strips of ideographs and soiled with the mold that seems to steal up from the earth. Behind this pretense of a town, the jungle holds carnival about a village stewing in malarial vapors: a village of thatch and bamboo huts, a few shrines and pagodas, and rows of stalls where food is exposed to the insect-ridden sunlight and the reek lifting from gutters dark with slime. In the midst of all this, a comparatively small garrison of white men quartered behind primitive fortifications and in barracks uniformly crude.

Each day is the same: sunlight and routine, given a certain hysterical emphasis by intermittent bugle-calls. In the air a silence that glitters. Hot soil and hot sky. Flies buzzing in the stillness. Smells of garbage and half-sweet odors from the jungle. The very earth seems to yawn and sink into a torpor as midday smothers the world. A few white helmets glare in the downpour of torrid light. That same light runs a malevolent tongue along the gun-barrels of sentinels. Flies buzzing in the stillness. Guttural native voices. In the hospital, a fever patient shouts; another is covered with a sheet, and preparations for a hasty burial are made.... The commandant sits beneath an indolent *punkah*, thinking of France when he should be thinking of Indo-China. A young major, becoming actively indignant about the climate, gives his orderly a kick in the posterior. Soldiers lie half asleep in even rows, sweating and breathing the odors of their musty bedding. The sentinels, most of them limp from dysentery, return the stare of the sunlight with a look glazed and full of hatred.

In this garrison are hundreds of minds dry as gunpowder-dry and inflammable. Hundreds of tunics tainted with perspiration, hundreds of boots spotted. with mildew, hundreds of bayonets and bores flecked with rust. Damp, damp, damp. A terrific fecundity of earth and brain. In some bodies, wounds; scars on the hands and faces of many.... They wonder, these men, when the stone will be rolled away from the sepulcher and they will be free to walk forth and show France the marks of their crucifixion....

Evening fills the town with a hint of coolness. The river seems to sigh and give up a silver breath. Reed-flares burning in the floating village. From a Chinese brothel the insinuating scraping of zither and guitar. In the French barracks the troops are stirring impatiently. Perhaps there will be an attack tonight. Meanwhile, some are writing home, others are gambling, while the majority prepare to go out and wander through the *ville indigène*....

In the roadway that parallels the river a ghost of opium fumes haunts the air, mingling with the fragrance of blossoms that open at dusk.

Several legionaries drift into the street, falling in with the shifting groups of natives. The lanterns in the Chinese shops flaunt their brilliant orange, and spills of hot light clot the darkening air. Suddenly the night becomes a spotted clown, dancing to the music from the brothel. To these white men it is derisive revelry. Nevertheless, they begin to sing boisterously. The Annamite girls passing give them half-startled, half-amused glances. One girl smiles openly. A young Breton trooper follows her with an appraising look, taking in the black bandeau of her hair, her black lace tunic and the tiny black sandals that drop from her heels as she walks. He wonders if her teeth also are black. But that possibility is dispelled as she turns and smiles again.... The night is very soft.... He will go to her father and make a bargain; then there will be someone to keep his clothes in order, to brush away the mildew....

Very simple.... And the map is changed.

Thus a brief glimpse of Saigon as Admiral de la Grandiere found it when he took over the town and laid out plans for a new city.

In 1862 a treaty was made in which the provinces of Saigon, Mytho and Bien-Hoa were ceded to France; and five years later Admiral de la Grandiere declared Vinh-Long, Chaudoc and Hatien annexed. The whole of Cochin-China had been stamped with the French seal.

Insurrections followed, with cholera, fever, dysentery and other tropical maladies as their deadly allies, but France survived, somewhat emaciated but triumphant; and from the homeland came voyagers who explored the hinterlands, acquiring new territory and bringing back stories of tremendous natural resources that burned the ears of ambitious settlers. These men in turn penetrated into the interior, planting the fleur-de-lis in the midst of jungle-flowers, with the result that soon a new blossom luxuriated in the sun.

"...we cannot censure these first colonials,
who found an acceptable gentleness in the native *congai*,"

This blossom had its roots in rubber and copra plantations, in rice-fields, in mines, and in soil that burst with wealth; and it became known as the Piaster, symbol of the Frenchman's power in Indo-China.

At the beginning of the twentieth century Saigon emerged from her questionable past, carefully powdering her skin and scenting her hair with essences imported from France—an insinuating little cocotte who quickly woos the traveler to her bosom.

## 5

The second evening in Saigon, as I dressed to dine with the Tired Cavalier, a faint odor drifting in from the hall carried my memory back to the afternoon the Angkor, bringing me from Shanghai to Cochin-China, steamed up the river. From one of the upper decks I watched the low, marshy banks slip by, while ahead the twin spires of the cathedral lifted out of a welter of green. Below, in the steerage, one of the Chinese passengers was smoking opium, tainting the air with a half-nauseating, acrid smell.

"Is that permitted?" I inquired of a Frenchman at my side.

He looked at me in surprise, then smiled and shrugged....

On that evening two nights later, as the Tired Cavalier and I sat at a table in the Café de la Rotonde, I remarked: "Do you know, a few minutes ago, in my room, I thought I smelled opium."

He stared at me. "I suppose you did," he said finally.

"But..."

He laughed. "You consider it a dreadful vice?"

And then I understood his sallow skin and the dark half-moons under his eyes.

"I take only fifteen or twenty pipes a day," he volunteered. "It's no worse than the whisky you Americans drink. Many people in Saigon use it—more women than men."

I asked where they got it.

"Anywhere," he replied elaborately. "There are a number of houses close by—and about half a hundred in Cholon, the Chinese city. You find that

"Over on the rue Paul Blanchy is the Régie d'Opium where the government manufactures it."

"The Tired Cavalier informed me that very few white men frequent the opium-houses of Cholon."

astonishing? ...Over on the rue Paul Blanchy is the Régie d'Opium where the government manufactures it."

"The government?" I repeated.

"Certainly. It is a monopoly. And why not?" He smiled. "If the government did not regulate the price, we poor exiles who find pleasure in the poppy would be cheated outrageously by the Chinese. You have never used it? ...Then you have an experience.... Suppose we go to one of the houses some night...."

Our table was on the sidewalk, just outside the café itself, and beyond ragged greenery lay the Quai de la Grandiere and the river. A charming spot, this Café Rotonde. Social Saigon frequents the Café Continental, but there is a genial air about the Rotonde that invites intimacy. During the day a rattan shade allows only a pale ghost of the sunlight to steal in, and at the noon hour —all shops and business houses close between eleven and two—a pleasantly noisy crowd of civilians and soldiers luxuriates in the cool gloom, drinking and enjoying the innumerable courses of dejeuner. At the hour of the aperitif, when a gray-lilac coolness prowls through the streets, this rattan curtain is rolled up, and the same crowd gathers again. Until long after midnight the tables are occupied, and quite frequently, when a group of officers drifts in, lusty and ribald songs send their echoes out over the river.

One of the most amiable attractions of the Rotonde is its proprietor. A small man, with curly black hair, an illustrious mustache and owlishly wise eyes that survey life through bifocal lenses. I am certain that in the past this preposterously courteous and unreal gentleman wandered out of the pages of a Conrad book, became lost, and finally, rather tired of the world of actualities, became resigned to it in this city just across from Conrad's archipelago.

A very elegant sign outside the Rotonde announces: "*Tout confort moderne, prix modères....*" Monsieur Walthausen, the proprietor, is not boasting. Often, finding myself tangled in passport difficulties or those other endless details by which the French support a myth of efficiency, I would seek him, and always, with elaborate politeness and in that inimitable manner of his—one finger lifted mysteriously, a wise little smile lurking behind his gaze—he would take me in hand, saying: "Come wis me."

No matter how simple the mission, his air was that of one admitting another into a conspiracy, and it made the routine of interviewing prosaic officials an affair of utmost intrigue. In consequence, I found myself going to him for

Harry gave us no photo of the "Tired Cavalier" but the French gentleman in Saigon to our right offers a credible facsimile.

"...there is a genial air about the Rotonde that invites intimacy... '*Tout confort moderne, prix modères*'..."
as seen below in this 1920 photo.

the slightest reason, merely to enjoy that secretive gesture, that knowing little smile, and to hear him say: "Come wis me...." He had a hacking cough, this chivalrous proprietor.... Perhaps when I return he will not be there. If so I shall know he has somehow managed to steal back into the pages of that book from which he came. But a ghost will hover at my elbow—a ghost that lifts one finger in shadowy beckoning and whispers: "Come wis me...."

On this particular evening as the Tired Cavalier and I sat in the Café Rotonde, Monsieur Walthausen appeared with a benignant and satisfied smile. "I have prepare' a surprise," he announced.

The "surprise" followed in many courses.... Soup thick with *oignons* and *fromage, foie-gras en gelée, langouste a l'américain, poulet rôti, pommes naturelles, haricots verts, salade de saison, crème chocolat, petits fours*.... All this made even more acceptable by the addition of a bottle of Chateau Rose, a bottle of sparkling Burgundy, and cherry brandy afterward.

The Tired Cavalier discoursed entertainingly about nothing. After the meal, looking rather drowsy as he inhaled a heavy Turkish cigarette, he glanced around the café and became vaguely annoyed.

"Sixty men and women," he said suddenly, "or perhaps seventy—and all here for a definite purpose."

I suggested that we also were there for that same purpose, and considering the amount of food we had consumed without protest we could not consistently be superior about it.

He fixed his weary, liquid-dark gaze upon me.

"I don't mean only here in this café," he explained with a hint of condescension. "I mean, in Saigon as well.... Look at them.... Every morning they rise at about the same hour, they bathe, they have *petit-dejeuner*, they go to work, they return home, eat, go to sleep, work again for a little while, bathe once more, then drink, eat, drink and go to sleep."

He seemed quite indignant about it all, which appeared to me a waste of energy after such a superb meal. And so, in a spirit of lightness induced by the blending of Chateau Rose, Burgundy and cherry brandy, I remarked that where the two baths daily were concerned I thought he was being unduly optimistic.

He did not even smile.

And incidentally, by way of intensely personal observation, I find that remarks intended to be humorous rarely have the desired effect upon a foreigner, perhaps because he is too busy translating the conversation to bother with being amused.

"It is depressing," he pronounced. "Everybody, everywhere for a purpose! Myself, I am here by accident—I stay until I get bored—I work merely to be able to live comfortably."

I told him that sounded very attractive....

"Are you interested in faces?" he demanded.

I confessed I was; and reminded him, as modestly as possible, that I wrote books—which I felt justified that interest.

"I suppose you are traveling for color," he said superciliously.

I was hunting for a dead city, I informed him; didn't he remember?

Ah, yes! He did remember; in fact, he had come this night to hear about it, hadn't he?

"What do you expect to find in this dead city?" he asked.

Ruins, I told him, and some records of a lost people.

"Strange," he mused. "You are looking for the things that are written, while I am hunting the things that aren't written—which are the truest, perhaps."

Perhaps, I admitted.

"Where is this dead city?"

I didn't know exactly.... He looked interested at that.

"Where will you go?"

To Angkor, and beyond ... up the Mé-Kong....

"Who built this city?"

The Khmers, I thought....

"The people of Angkor... yes.... From whom did you hear about it?"

From a man whose name I didn't know. ... It happened in Singapore, in a bar. The man asked me for a drink. ... A coin well spent, for he told me of his wanderings.... Once, somewhere in Laos, near the Siamese border, he had come upon a pile of ruins. There was a lake at the foot of the mountain, and from the lake to the mountain an almost obliterated causeway, and then a huge stairway climbing the mountain to a temple near the top. At the bottom of the stairway were ruins; maybe palaces, maybe more temples, all carved and roofless and covered with vines.... The big temple itself was a mass of sculpturing.... Native priests lived in a monastery nearby; and there was a village below, while some distance away was a town called Bassac.... He didn't know whether any other white man had seen it or not... He'd never been to Angkor, but judging from the pictures, this place—Wat Phu, the natives called it—was built by the same race....

And so, I concluded, I was going to find that dead city.

"Suppose your beachcomber friend lied," the Tired Cavalier suggested.

Well, I returned, there would still be the adventure of searching for something that didn't exist; which would be rather novel, wouldn't it?

"No, it wouldn't," he announced. "Every man does that... Tell me: if you get to these ruins, provided they exist, will you write a history of the people who built them?"

Hardly, I said.

"Then," he continued sarcastically, "undoubtedly you will do a book that is an arabesque of the country, with your own emotions and experiences superimposed upon it, and a little historical frieze running around the top?"

Undoubtedly, I agreed.

"And will your little historical frieze be made up of the regulation figures, the marionettes worked by the historians, who believe that every good history should be noble and glorious?"

Perhaps no, perhaps yes, I answered discreetly.

"History is a flame," he declared eloquently, "with bats circling about it.... Why not put some of those dark creatures into your book?"

But why, I asked, should one destroy the Myth of History? Moreover, I added, a maker of books must live....

"I should like to write a book," he said; and it was the first occasion I had to suspect him of being sentimental. "But after all," he reconsidered, "I think I should prefer to do nothing that comes so close to being constructive. Take me now, I have an advantage over you. I have no purpose, as purposes go; I have no destination... and I am searching for something I shall probably never find...."

And that? I prompted.

"Well, perhaps you might call me the pilgrim of a glance... the glance from a stranger's eyes.... Consider ! Think of the interesting faces you see that you will never see again! There's a certain exciting mystery about seeing people you don't know, about being in love with faces.... And there's something behind it all—the something I'm hunting for...."

But why, I asked, was he looking for it in the East instead of the West, where it might be found just as easily?

"Not just as easily," he contended. "In the West one has first to break through the plaster of Paris in which emotions have been cast—and why use unnecessary effort? Too, there seems to be a greater intensity in people of darker skins—perhaps because they live closer to the earth and in the sun, which makes them darker physically and penetrates even to their emotions. Or perhaps it is because they have learned to listen to the music of death."

What, I inquired, did he mean by the "music of death"?

He smiled. "You are going into the jungle; listen, and perhaps you will hear it."

We drank another Martel-Perrier. ... It was growing late, for the crowd in the café was rapidly thinning. Rickshaws were lined up at the curb, waiting for the remaining revelers. A few prostitutes and painted boys wandered by on the quay, all watching the Frenchmen at the tables.

The Tired Cavalier's mood expanded.

"Think, my friend," he said with feeling, leaning across the table. "Here we sit, you and I, two men talking under a lamp in the Café Rotonde. But we are more than that. We are two impulses, each sufficiently free of any provincial or racial complications to be symbolical of a human urge, brought together under the common illumination of a restless intelligence. Why, it is like the meeting of two odysseys, one searching for the earth and the other for the fire under the earth!"

I agreed with him enthusiastically; and added that evidently we both were very drunk.

"You are right," he returned somberly. "But it is a privilege to be intoxicated and yet remain intellectual."

So we drank a toast to the Khmers, the colonial government and the dead city of Wat Phu, not failing to include the Music of Death and the Fire under the Earth.

The following night we visited Cholon, some six kilometers from Saigon.

A motor-car whirled us through darkness heavy with the humidity rising from the rice-fields; and overhead the stars were like drops of moisture purling from a glazed bowl.

From silent, lamp-riddled country roads we plunged into the streets of the Chinese city, into a sphere of such noise and confusion that I felt as though we had been hurled back hundreds of years. The flares of gaslights made medallions upon the houses and shops, woven into an amazing luminous design by the beadwork on countless smaller lamps; and moving against this tremulous pattern were the shapes of men and vehicles, all shifting back and forth in the mingled light and shadow like the figures of an animated tapestry.

Ideographed signs hung from balconies; over some doors were carved panels, moldy and shedding their gold-leaf. In the shops half-naked yellow men were busy with mysterious tasks, while other Chinese, some bare-chested and some in long robes slit at the sides, thronged the streets. Among them were little girls in brocaded coats and trousers, hair clasped with jeweled pins, faces whited and lips vermillioned; and a few older women staggering along on "golden-lily" feet. All this set to the bewildering discord of auto-horns, the rattle of rickshaw wheels and the muffled beat of many soft-shod feet, and given a certain peculiarly Eastern flavor by the blended smells of perfume, spices, cooking food and dung that seemed to float through the hot air in visible waves.

Images like Newell Convers Wyeth's 1913 painting, "The Opium Smoker," almost certainly fueled Harry's curiosity about the drug.

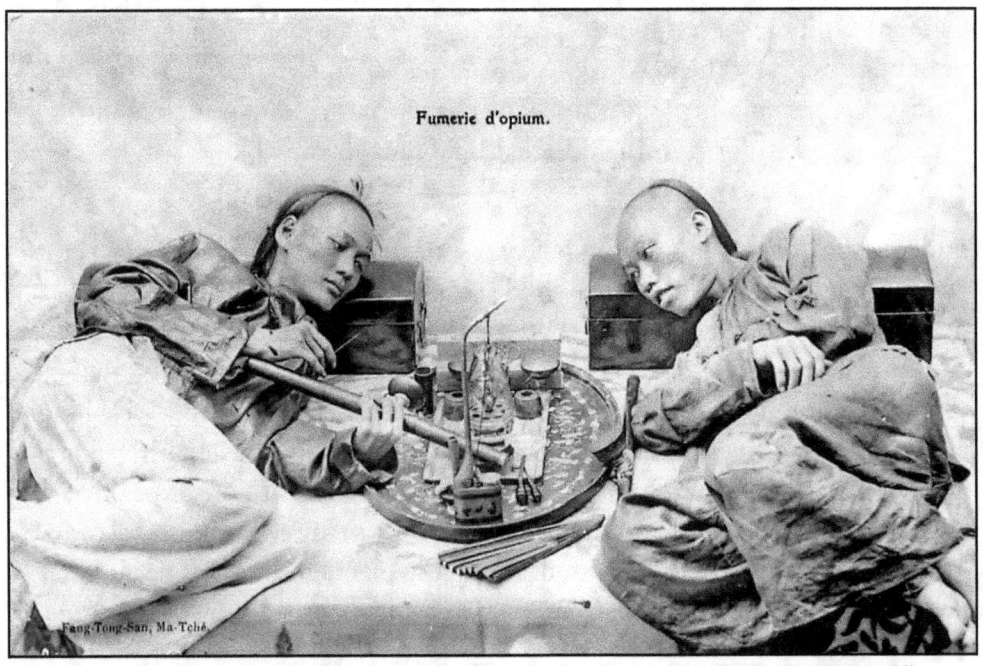
"...one lies on his side, with his head resting upon a small block of wood."

We stopped at a particularly iniquitous-looking street and followed its crooked darkness until the Tired Cavalier, in the lead, made a sudden turn and stopped before a little door that resembled the entrance to a safe. Above it was written "Hop Ky—Tmong An." Inside was a barred enclosure similar to the box-office of a theater. This was occupied by an ancient Chinese who, after a conversation in French with my host, led us upstairs into a low, gas-lit room where, sprawled upon long wooden slabs, a number of yellow men were smoking opium. The place was fairly clean, but the thick fumes from the poppy-treacle made it almost unendurable. I tried to realize I was in an "opium-den" and that I should feel rather vicious, at least desperate, but I was too nauseated to do other than desire clean air.

From this first place we went to a second and larger establishment. Here, as at the other house, there was the customary barred cage below, the narrow stairs that led up to a large room, but the bunks were fenced off, thus giving a certain privacy to the smokers. However, privacy did not seem what they desired, for over half of the forty-odd customers were leaning upon the "partitions and chatting between pipes. All were Chinese, all were stripped to the waist; and in the drifts of blue smoke made faintly luminous by two wavering lamps their oily bodies formed a weird, indeterminate fresco.

As we left we met two white men entering, obviously Frenchmen; and they did not appear in the least disconcerted, as was I, but raised their hats politely, as Frenchmen do, and murmured a genial *"Bonsoir, messieurs."*

The Tired Cavalier informed me that very few white men frequent the opium-houses of Cholon, but prefer those of Saigon. The most fashionable establishment, he added, was on the rue Tabert, near the American Consulate.

At the third place, just off one of the main streets of Cholon, my host suggested that I try a pipe. It was the largest opium-house we had visited, with an arrangement of cages upstairs and down, and a few private rooms partitioned off. Evidently I had become accustomed to the smell of opium, for the fumes no longer sickened me, and I was beginning to feel that awareness of adventure I so utterly lacked at the start.

A pitted Chinese conducted us upstairs and to a room at the front, all with a ridiculous air of secrecy which was explained when the Tired Cavalier

"As an attendant prepared two pipes,
I watched the other patrons through the doorway."

told me foreigners were not allowed to smoke opium at these places without a permit.

As an attendant prepared two pipes, I watched the other patrons through the doorway. A single lantern reclaimed from the shadows what appeared to be separate members, a bare arm or a leg, a shaven skull, or a corded throat concave below a relaxed chin. The effect was bewildering unreality. In the vaporish gloom the tiny lamps of the smokers made flowers of flame; and in a dark corner a half-naked figure was twanging a moon-guitar. As though to italicize the unreality, the mingled noises of motor-cars and strident voices came up from the street.

One cannot carelessly smoke an opium-pipe as one first smokes an ordinary tobacco-pipe. It is a matter of great technique. The Tired Cavalier had to repeat his illustration twice before I was successful. It is done in this fashion: one lies on his side, with his head resting upon a small block of wood, while the attendant twists a bit of viscid gum on a needle, holds it over a lighted lamp until it bubbles, and dips it in a small cup of dark liquid; then the smoker takes the pipe—usually made of bamboo, with a metal bowl in the center—and inhales while the opium sizzles and cooks over the flame. Four or five long puffs and the pipe is finished.

After my first pipe I waited in anticipatory delight. But nothing happened. The Tired Cavalier recommended another. Again I waited, expecting a stealthy drowsiness to glide over me and unfold purple dreams. I smoked three pipes. Then my head began to swell; vertigo pranced before me; I became violently ill....

When my stomach regained its equilibrium we left; and the stairway seemed to careen beneath me, while outside the lights of Cholon were mad moons that reveled and mocked.

As we rode back to Saigon, and the rush of wind cleared my head, I felt extremely vicious—and disappointed. I had smoked opium. And another illusion had gone to the scaffold.

## 6

A few days later, just before the hour of the aperitif, I drifted with the late afternoon crowd in the rue Catinat.

Overhead, a roll of clouds, like rose-dyed smoke in the aftermath of sunset, reflected a luminous gloom among the tamarinds, and above the ruddy-tiled roofs, a sky flawlessly blue seemed to take fire where it met the horizon.

In this soft, blushing twilight, Saigon became beautifully decadent. The houses, so starkly yellow through the day, acquired a red-gold tone suggesting those old Portuguese doubloons dug up from the Spanish Main.

As I left the Rotonde, there was a great clamor across the street, outside the shop of Ly Binh, *tailleur*. The shout of a native brought others out of nowhere, and a crowd gathered at a safe distance about the trunk of a tamarind, staring up excitedly. One, bolder than the others, darted into a doorway, returning immediately with a long bamboo pole. Followed a splintering pop as he struck into the branches, and a writhing green snake dropped to the pavement. The crowd scattered, crying with fright and glee, but the bold one remained, beating the serpent to a pulp....

Farther along, numerous little Annamite boys were gathering outside the office of the evening journal waiting for the last edition. Dark Madrassees sat cross-legged in their stalls; these fellows are the local moneychangers, and they also sell everything from Abdulla cigarettes to corn-cutters. From the Chinese *épiceries* came whiffs of cellar-damp air, aromatic with the scents of wines, coffee and sweets. Silver-plate and Parisian jewelry gleamed in the windows of many *bijouteries*. Antiseptic odors escaped from a pharmacy. Inside a shop bearing the legend "*charcuterie*" a red-faced Frenchman was disjointing a goat....

Still farther along, I paused to look into a window where pictures of Angkor were displayed. "*Tourisme de l'Indochine*" said the lettering on the glass. These photographs, so carefully catalogued and in precise rows, frightened me. Was this a hint of what I should find at Angkor?

The Boulevard Bonnard.... Here stands the municipal opera-house, evidence of France's determination to be thoroughly cultured even though thousands of miles away from Paris; and here, at irregular intervals disreputable troupes of singers torture Puccini and Verdi for the benefit of bored colonial audiences....

As usual, taxicabs with native drivers were lined up in the square before the opera-house. In the parkway of the boulevard groups of Annamites were collecting to enjoy the cool of the evening, and, incidentally, the tea-music at the Hotel Continental. The many people, the lights, the noise of vehicles and voices gave the street an air of festival....

A white and crimson banner out in front of the Saigon Cinema announced that Hugette Dufloss was playing in "*Koenigsmark*" by Pierre Benoit....

The rue Catinat settled into quiet beyond the Hotel Continental. A certain dignity in the atmosphere proclaimed the fact that I was passing government buildings, among them the office of the chief of police. Suddenly the street opened into a vast square, in the center of which the cathedral raised its twin spires. This is an edifice convincingly French, and its red bricks offer stubborn defiance to the mellow, sunburnt walls of the rest of the town. Turning back, I sought a table on the sidewalk outside the Continental....

The orchestra was jazzing "*Chanson Indoue.*" Automobiles and rickshaws, pausing momentarily at the entrance, poured a stream of men and women into the café. Among these French colonials were the usual Russians, one or two Englishmen, an American or so, and the inevitable Japanese merchant in the company of a painfully pleasant white man who wanted to sell him something.

Presently the Tired Cavalier joined me....

A little later, when dusk had thickened and the *thé-dansant* threatened to end, I observed a very opulent limousine that glided alongside the curb and stopped. Immediately a woman came out of the café. Even had I not seen her face, I should have noticed her because of her bearing as she descended the steps and got into the waiting car. If the limousine had suddenly turned into a golden palanquin I should not have been surprised, for surely Balkis of Sheba on her way to conquer the young Solomon could not have moved with more proud assurance.

Several Frenchmen at the next table laughed as she drove off. "I wonder how long that will last!" said one....

A pallor as warm as though golden smoke had been breathed over it; lips daringly red; a hint of short blue-black hair beneath a small gray hat; and a gown of soft pearl that seemed incongruously chaste on this creature of ivory and flame. The barbarity of the woman made me catch my breath. Yet, strangely, in that glimpse her poise was super-civilized. It was as though the naked figure of Annam just walked past, half hidden beneath Parisian clothes and manners.

"Who is the lady?" I asked the Tired Cavalier.

"She is not a lady," he replied lazily. "At present she is making life happy—or at least interesting—for a certain elderly gentleman who is both rich and indulgent.... Some of the chaps here in Saigon jokingly call her '*Madame la Panthère.*' ... To be truthful, I think the joke is on them.

"You noticed the way she walked? If you had not looked well you would have said she was French, is it not so?... Well, she is—except in her heart. And in her heart she is just a *congai*, a native woman—not the sort you see standing belly-deep in the rice-fields—but the powdered, smiling little devil who insinuates herself into the graces of her masters—I say 'masters' because usually they have more than one—and who gives willingly while she is a mistress, but who when it is finished goes back to her native hut as chaste, spiritually, as when she left....

Femmes fumant la Pipe

"Who is the lady?" I asked the Tired Cavalier.
"She is not a lady," he replied lazily.

"Paradoxical, is it not?... But they know something we do not know, these *congaies*. And *Madame la Panthère* is wiser than most....

"Consider, my friend: she began life in some little village—perhaps at Mytho or Bien-Hoa, or maybe back in the jungle—where she slept on mats, ate with chopsticks, and had no technical knowledge, of life. But what she did know was the *technique* of living—which is quite different from a technical knowledge of life.

"Undoubtedly her mother lived with a Frenchman, one or more—and the result, *Madame la Panthère*.

She must have been a good business woman, that mother; she knew enough not to let her daughter disfigure herself by chewing betel; and she taught her French—and men.

"Perhaps the girl's first 'husband' was some *délégué*—or a soldier. Who knows? Many followed.... And look at her now. She cannot be thirty—yet on the surface an evolved Frenchwoman.

"A curious fact about her history is this: she has never been deserted by any of her men. Not one! Always she left them first! Ironic, eh? No 'Madame Chrysanthème' or 'Butterfly'! She was too wise! And, believe it or not, she has always helped those with whom she lived.

"I know of one instance—an officer who had her for some time. She got him a promotion, helped him make investments, then when she saw a chance for her own advancement she departed—just as if she had performed a mission and was ready for the next experience!

"Now she is with that senile idiot who gives her limousines.... You heard what that fellow at the next table said? Well, I wonder. Perhaps she has reached the top, perhaps not....

"After all," he concluded, smiling, "what does it matter now whether you find your dead city or not? You can write a book about *Madame la Panthère*. Doesn't she tell the story of Indo-China eloquently?"

# 7

I once heard an editor remark that writers who traveled in foreign countries—that is, writers who were not temporary beachcombers in search

"...she began life in some little village — perhaps at Mytho."
The market at Mytho seen above.

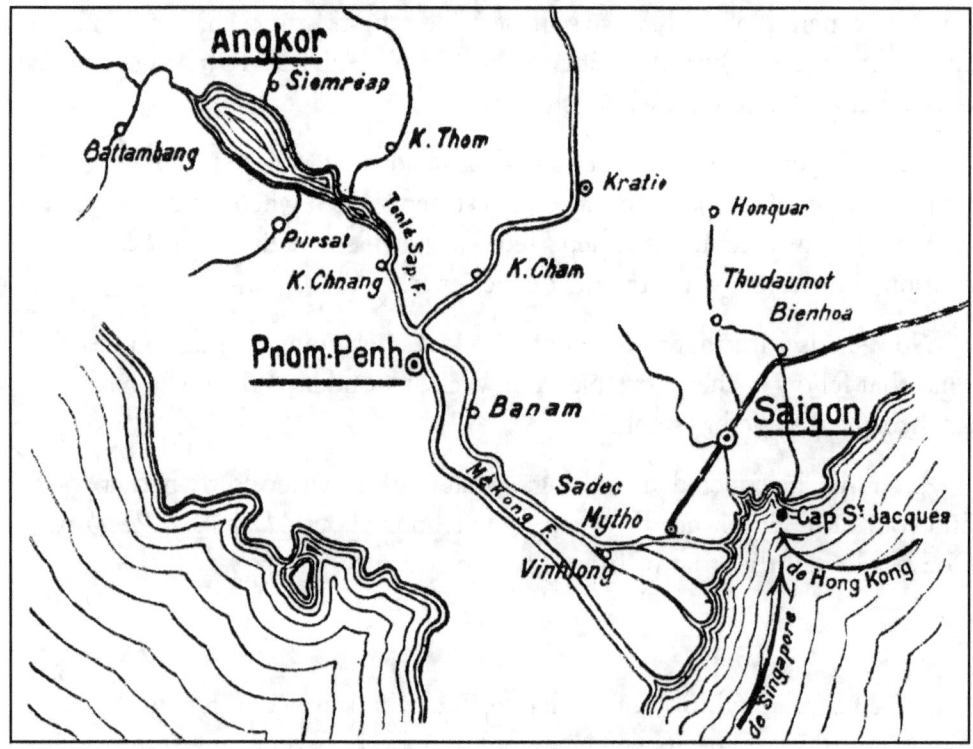

Harry's route from Saigon to Angkor.

of robust adventure—never went into the houses of the natives but spent their time drinking champagne with the officials and discussing politics and women; both of which might be attractive as personal experiences, but were utterly useless when transposed to paper.

Remembering this remark, I made it a point, after drinking champagne with the officials and discussing politics and women, to visit, not only one Annamite house, but several. And I found these natives of Indo-China a genial and courteous people. Of course, to declare that all Annamites are genial and courteous would be as stupid as to say that all Japanese are quaint. Generalizations upon a nation are not only banal but futile. The Westerner, particularly if he be a traveler, can never see the inside life of the people; he may be invited only to the houses of the higher caste and rudely force his way into the huts of the poor. The middle class, that is to say the people, remain a mystery, or if not a mystery, at least unknown to him.

One of the most colorful native customs I encountered was an Annamite wedding ceremony. In Indo-China marriage is too much of a social institution to be left to love or fancy. While the children are quite young the parents settle the matter, and usually the marriage takes place when the boy is about sixteen and the girl fourteen.

The first important ceremony is the betrothal, which occurs after the "go-between" (generally a friend of both families) has arranged the date of the wedding. On this occasion the young man goes to the house of his fiancée with gifts which, if accepted, consummate the affair. These gifts consist of betel and areca nuts, bracelets, silks, two red tapers, rice-wine and a small roast pig. All the participants are dressed in gala costume, and flute-players make music. The gifts are placed on the family altar (ancestor-worship is the native religion of the Annamites), the candles are burned, and the alcohol divided into two cups. Then, after the families have prostrated themselves before the altar, there is a feast, which concludes the betrothal.

On the wedding-day the bridegroom, accompanied by family and friends, and a train of servants carrying presents, goes again to the house of the girl. Upon entering, he prostrates himself before the altar, and then offers wine and betel to his parents-in-law. After that the couple are taken into another room where there is an altar dedicated to the Gods of Marriage. Candles and incense are lighted. The parents wish them prosperity and command that they remain wedded until death. Then the girl prostrates herself four times before the boy, the boy prostrates himself once, and all repair to another room where a feast is waiting.

Polygamy is a custom among the Annamites, and as in the Turkish harem, the *vo-chanh*, or head-wife, rules. Unlike the Chinese code, the Annamite Ly-Hi or Memorial of Rights states that "*the gia te ra*" ("the wife is an equal"). To a certain extent this is true. Certainly in Indo-China, and particularly among the Annamites and Tonkinese, the women have more privileges than in most Far Eastern countries; although I hold no stock in the popular myth that Oriental women are oppressed and mistreated. In theory they may be, for thus by code and ritual does the man maintain what he calls his self-respect; but actually, as investigation has shown me, the women rule very subtly by pretended submission.

There appeared to be very little even pretended submission among the Annamite women I observed; in fact, one of the first sights I witnessed in Indo-China was a wrathful native lady hurling stones at the retreating figure of her master. I do not mean to say the men are always gentle; indeed, that very retreating husband turned upon his wife when her supply of stones was exhausted and dragged her along the street by her hair. But I do mean to say this Annamite woman did what a Japanese or East Indian wife would never think of doing.

And, to finish the incident, after the husband had dragged his wife by her hair for fully fifty feet, three Frenchmen jumped upon him and beat him unmercifully. Which, I suppose, was chivalrous. However, I cannot help wondering if it would not have been more chivalrous if only one Frenchman had done it. Certainly it could have been done easily; for the Annamite was small; and Orientals, unlike the men of the West, are not proficient in fist-fighting.

I should not mention this instance if it were uncommon. But it is typical. Not that all or even many Annamite women hurl stones at their husbands and are dragged by their hair along the streets of Saigon; nor is it an ordinary sight to see three Frenchmen thrashing an Annamite. But it is an ordinary sight to see a Frenchman strike a native, and for the slightest offense.

After witnessing this thing in many tropical countries, I have reached the opinion that it is an expression of Racial Pride; and of indignation in the white man against the existence, except in extreme servility, of those darker people whom priests and politicians call his brothers. One of its current forms is slapping. This is provoked when a stupid native is slow to obey an order. Or when a rickshaw coolie tries to overcharge one of the Superior Race.

I would make it plain that this is not peculiar in Indo-China. It is also practiced by the Americans and British in China, the British in India, and the Dutch in Java. It is used, I am told, "to put the fear of God into the natives." Evidently it succeeds. But it does something else; for I have seen the eyes of natives who have been struck or thrashed. It is a singular fact that the conqueror rarely if ever absorbs the virtues of the conquered. Thus, in Indo-China for instance, one never hears of a white man cultivating the gracious politeness of an Annamite mandarin, while almost invariably he acquires the average Easterner's disregard for human suffering; and not infrequently he adopts polygamy, though of course under another name.

I must, as one of the Superior Race, admire the French for their method of ruling the natives. What their government lacks in efficiency, it makes up for in strength. No dilly-dallying. An iron rule. That is why. there is never any trouble there as in other Asiatic colonies. The guillotine, prison, the penal colony; these are the tolls of treason.

But, as a human being, I can but see the ridiculous irony of its pretensions.... To prevent the promiscuous sale of opium, the government makes it a monopoly, manufacturing it and regulating the price, with the result that this particular vice becomes legally a virtue. For, paradoxical as it may seem, is this not a kindness to the natives, who otherwise might be overcharged? ...And many weary exiles condemned to live in this abominable climate make their banishment easier by yielding to the poppy. Always "to the victor belong the spoils." And after all a vice in others is vicious; in ourselves it is merely a habit... The soldier who beats a coolie for trying to cheat him may, if the chance presents itself and he is disposed, take the woman of that same coolie for his own. This, I suppose, is Human Nature....

So the hand of iron falters to enjoy the pleasures of the conquered. But this is true of all countries where the Dominant Race asserts its superiority through commercial enterprise and calls it, with exquisite humor, altruism.

The day of the supremacy of the East is ended. Never, I believe, will it become the power that it was; for if it does not wear itself out in natural and borrowed vices, it must eventually through association with its masters acquire a sense of humor, and when it does, it will appreciate the elaborate pretensions of white men, and laugh itself to death.

## 8

Facing a discussion of French colonial policy, I find myself faltering. Generally when one discards the primitive belief that politicians are benefactors he becomes either a skeptic or a politician himself. Unfortunately, I am of the former class. However, it is apparent, even to the skeptic, that the French have a very efficient government in Indo-China; certainly as efficient as one could expect in an equatorial climate. Witness the regulation that makes it compulsory for every native who lives in or enters the country to have a card of identification bearing his photograph and finger-prints; this and many other thorough ordinances. I know also that the government is divided in this manner; a Governor-General, a Governor of Cochin-China, a Resident Superior of Laos, of Cambodia, of Tonkin and of Annam; followed by numerous local residents, chiefs of cabinet, commissioners and delegates. And I know, too, that politics there is filled with the usual bribery and corruption which rusts political machinery everywhere. One of these rust-spots is visible in Saigon.

Go to the rue Paul Blanchy where a great tawny wall encloses the Régie d'Opium, and you will see it. Candor is a virtue of the French; for over the entrance a sign announces "Manufacture d'Opium." Underneath, an arched gateway admits one past offices into a palm-grown court, around which are the various buildings where the opium is made and stored.

I visited the Régie d'Opium one early morning while the shadows of the palms were still cool in the quadrangle. A courteous French official conducted me to a large' building facing the gate (a formidable structure with barred windows), prefacing the tour of inspection with the information that much of the poppy-juice came from Annam, Tonkin and Laos; while a great deal was sent from Yunnan; and some from India. It was impossible, he said, to raise enough in the country.

As he talked I could picture the raw treacle being pressed from the pistils of poppies; millions of white poppies that lay in spotless drifts throughout Asia. I could picture it being made into gummy balls like coconuts, covered with poppy-leaves and packed in bales; then shipped down to the coast by caravan, by coolie, by pirogue and steamer; there to be poured into the great reservoir of the Régie d'Opium.

Within the building the fumes nearly stifled me. In coils of steam, naked muscular torsos strained over copper pots, over troughs and great metal vats. A pallid vapor ascended to the dark beams that supported the roof.

We paused by a row of kettles, and my conductor explained that the process required three days. The raw opium was first steamed, and then stirred with wooden spatulas until it reached the consistency of dough; after this it was spread thinly in brass bowls and placed over ovens where the heat caused it to separate, and it was pulled off in tissue-like layers. The third stage was a matter of refining. The substance was put with water into deep receptacles and soaked for about twenty hours, during which time the impurities rose to the top and the opium settled in the bottom. Then it was filtered through pith (an ancient Chinese method) and the impurities boiled and refiltered, so that not a drop would be wasted. After that it was placed in immense vats to boil again for many hours, thus removing the remaining water. Finally, it was poured into drums and stored for three or four months.

My guide informed me that the opium was kept in the upper story of another building until needed, then released from the drums into pipes which discharged it, with absolute accuracy, into boxes holding 100, 40, 20, 10 and 5 grams respectively. These boxes were then sent to the collector of customs, who sold the finished product to licensed dealers. One kilogram, he stated, was worth 180 piasters. And he added that from 80,000 to 100,000 kilograms were produced a year. Later, from a different source, I learned certain figures that will give some idea of the yearly profit to the French government. From January to June of 1923 the proceeds from the sale of opium were 9,537,051 piasters; and from January to June of 1924 they were 7,126,079 piasters.

It is, perhaps, impertinent for a visitor to criticize a country, particularly when his sojourn there was a matter of months instead of years. But this is not intended entirely as a criticism of France's policy in this Asiatic colony. It is broader than that. It is giving a specific example to illustrate the policies of all nations who maintain colonial possessions. France is no worse than the other countries who control foreign territory, and she is better than most. But her principle, as proved by the Régie d'Opium if nothing else, is the principle of one who offers protection and substitutes exploitation.

We of the West are humanitarians outside theory until the skin changes color, then we are altruistic; and our weapon is conversion through acquisition.

French Naval personnel relaxing in Saigon.

The 1912 staff of the Résidence Supérieur in Cambodia, with Résident Luce seated front center. Even more intriguing is the presence of the impeccably dressed young man seen at upper left. This is none other than Roland Meyer, then 23 years old and already working on the manuscript of his epic book, *Saramani, danseuse khmèr*...the plot of which Harry liberally sampled 13 years later as the basis for the third chapter of this book!

In every country where the white man is "protector" I have found that democracy, the gallant cry of those of paler skins, is a mere rhetorical term, to be recited by children and used by politicians. In Indo-China it is not a matter of physical violence, for that is no longer necessary, so much as it is an injustice more exquisite and subtle: the suppression of racial individuality, the usurpation of natural resources, and the imposition of laws in which the natives themselves have no part. It is the eternal brutality of the conquerors to the conquered; which, it may be argued, is the price of defeat. But this feeble defense among nations pretending to be just is a paradox of justice. I was not only in Cochin-China, but also in Cambodia, Laos, Tonkin and Annam; and everywhere I found prosperity and progress—and the haunting servility of a vanquished people.

Man is at his worst in the role of altruist. And it is as silly to say that France maintains a protectorate and colonies in Asia for the betterment of the natives, as it is to assert that, actually, the Puritans were pioneers of religious tolerance. It is commercial enterprise flowering in a servile State. And the myth that Frenchmen are the chivalrous defenders of liberty is as absurd as the idea that England is made up entirely of asses and America of wealthy rowdies. Patriotism, when it emerges from the peasant class and that group of aristocrats who emotionally are peasants, is a genteel name for anything that politicians wish to foist on an unsuspecting people. France, instead of being a nation of gay legionaries as popularly assumed, is in fact a nation of shrewd, militant merchants. Thus the acquisition of Indo-China was not a great adventure, although the voyagers who brought it about were adventurers, but a serious business enterprise that proved most successful.

In our country, the victory of the North over the South in the Civil War was not the abolition of slavery; it was simply the abolition of the technical term of slavery applied to the Negro. It was in reality the triumph of Northern capitalism over Southern agriculture. The black man ceased to be a slave; but in the North, where white labor continued and increased, the clank of chains augmented the grim song of progress. And that King of Annam who, surrounded by yellow foes, appealed to France for succor, simply changed the color of his masters. Slavery in its original principles was patriarchal and a custom; and just as some fathers are cruel to their children, so were some slave-owners cruel to their slaves. But "colonization" is commerce and has no reverence for tradition or man, except in individual instances. Slavery in any form is inhuman. But, it seems to me, it was less inhuman in the past when it was recognized slavery than in the present when, although technically abolished except in remote corners of the world, it has merely been dissembled and dignified by the term "colonization."

I do not mean that the French make actual slaves of the natives of Indo-China any more than some organizations in the Enlightened Countries make slaves of their laborers, but I do mean that the French (and all white men of whatever nationality who assert physical mastery over darker races) are destroying the racial individuality of the people whom they rule, and harnessing them to the plow of their own peculiar form of progress.... And the tread of the oxen grows heavy.... And the end? At present the Glory of Freedom is supplanted by the Survival of the Fittest; and human beings, content with having merely ripped the shackles from the slaves, satisfy themselves by contemplating, in odd moments, the strange Divine Evolution which creates men unequal.

# Chapter II
# The City of the Serpents
*Tells of the Indiscretions of a Cobra*

Picture map of *Cambodge*.

Harry's personal photo of his iconic "King Cobra."

# Angkor

## 1

I REMEMBER that autumn afternoon so well; a dusk of faded amber crept like smoke between the flaming trees in the street; and in a great, dim living-room a little boy sat turning the pages of an illustrated book.

Suddenly he paused before a picture. What a startling thing! Rugged cone-shaped towers piling up from diminishing tiers of terraced courts and colonnades, of enclosed galleries and insolent stairways; all imposed in brutal relief upon a palm-sown sky. Under the picture was written "Angkor."

Angkor! A word that wheeled in his brain like a brazen eagle.

His eyes drew away from the picture to the opposite page where one phrase seemed to emerge and meet him with disconcerting familiarity. "In the depths of the forests of Siam, I have seen the star of evening rise over the ruins of Angkor...."

Many years afterwards, riding out of the moist greenness of Siem Reap—that little Cambodian village which is the gateway of Angkor—I beheld the towers of Angkor Wat thrusting up in the rain like guttered candles; and after so long a time of dreaming I felt I was merely gazing at an enlargement of the picture that had begun its thrilling tyranny in my boyhood.

It would be picturesque and fitting to recount the hardships of my journey through the jungles to Angkor; but, impelled by an innate veraciousness,

"I must admit the trip was made in a French motor-car..."

I must admit the trip was made in a French motor-car, and that in the late afternoon of the second day after leaving Saigon, I was installed in the *sala*, or government bungalow, separated by only a road and a wide moat from Angkor Wat itself.

The rain had ceased, the sky was gray, overcast with a burnished haze; a reflection that seemed to run fluid from the west where the clouds were smoky gold. It was like some weird crepuscular light. In it Angkor Wat was fabulous and pagan. The moat, drinking in the sunset, was tawny metal while the towers of the temple, great irregular tiaras crowning those bewildering terraces, seemed chased in old gold upon the rain-colored sky.

As I watched, the light died from it, swiftly, like the last breath from a living thing, and then it was dead stone, its towers ghosts that haunted the dusk.

In the roadway, a bullock cart creaked by; gleaming half-naked figures seemed to glide past with spectral litheness. Across the way, the broken obelisks of Angkor Wat stood dark beneath a single ascending star.

## 2

"Wait until daylight; at night the Wat is dangerous."

But how could I wait, with those black towers inviting me across the moat?

And so after dinner I followed the road to the causeway.

That causeway, unrolling magnificently across the moat, plunging through the great outer portico and past the gardens to the temple itself, is one of the glories of Angkor Wat. It lost none of its grandeur seen at night. On either side were broken balustrades that reared up into fan-shaped embellishments. Although I could not see the detail, I knew they were *nagas* or seven-headed cobras, replicas in stone of those demigods who were reputed, in mythology, to be the ancestors of the Cambodian people.

Beyond this fantastic balustrade the water of the moat shone darkly. And such a moat! Over six hundred feet wide, and encircling a space nearly three miles around. Surely fitting for a temple of such extravagant splendor. Indeed, it is more than merely a moat; it is a natural sacred basin; for lotus-flowers encumber its shallows and offer up incense to the gods of the High Penetralia. That evening the fragrance of those blossoms seemed to leave a poignant bruise on the soft air.

"I was installed in the *sala*, or government bungalow, separated by only a road and a wide moat from Angkor Wat itself."

"But how could I wait, with those black towers inviting me across the moat?"

Before the outer portico were pallid, crouching shapes. Lions; stone lions. *Nagas* were there, too, spreading gracefully in plumed fans below the steps of the entrance. Above, a tower made a torn pile among the stars.

The steps were so narrow and slippery I was forced to mount sidewise. Inside I found a damp, roofless chamber, with another doorway opposite the one through which I had entered. On either side long colonnaded galleries seemed to go on endlessly into gloom. There was a sharp, musky smell in the air.

A moment after I entered there came a stir in the darkness overhead, followed by the kissing whir of wings. Bats! One hurtled so close I felt it fan my hair.

I hurried on, almost plunging down another stair that descended to the continuation of the causeway. On it went, that mighty stone approach, past tall inclining palms, past ruins formless in the gloom, to the looming mass of the temple. Now and then I splashed through pools of water that had collected between the irregular flagstones; at times I imagined I could see the black glide of a snake, but these shapes were only scars on the stone. And how deep were some of them! Ruts made by chariot wheels in the days of Angkor's glory?

As I approached the temple a drone of sound trailed across the stillness. Suddenly I remembered the book I had read in my boyhood. Bonzes, or Buddhist priests, chanting in the ruins of Angkor.

A sense of exquisite fulfilment settled upon me.

I stopped at the very foot of the terrace which spreads its broad plateau before the temple. Up there among the tall palms that gave the illusion of growing mysteriously out of the stone were the owners of those voices. Listening carefully, I could distinguish the Pali words: "*Namu Thatsa Thakha vato ara Hato Sam ma Samp hout Thatsa...*"

"Veneration to the Illuminated Who is delivered from the enemies, Who alone discovered the Way...."

When I moved up the steps there was sudden silence. I could make out several forms seated on the flagging, and I sensed eyes upon me. I walked on, still conscious of those eyes, and wondering if hostile gazes followed me or merely curious looks.

"The *Apsarases*, according to legend, were dancers and consorts of the gods."

"...*Tevadas* were their earthly reproductions, attached to the various Brahmin temples"

At the doorway where I hesitated, facing the black interior, I heard the thud of bare feet behind me and a hand touched my arm. It was one of the bonzes. He made a gesture for me to wait and moved inside. A moment later there was a flickering reflection in the darkness, and he reappeared with a light, one of those fragrant torches made of palm-leaves and sweet gum. The priest was a young fellow, very solemn-looking with his shaven head and saffron robes.

He held the torch high as I entered, and the wavering light showed me a small, damp chamber similar to the one in the outer portico. The bats were there, too, whirling uncomfortably near. In the corners, carved upon the walls, were figures that caught the torchlight and smiled. *Apsarases*, the sacred courtesans of the Hindu heaven. Slim, exquisitely chiseled creatures, clothed only in girdles and elaborate necklaces, and wearing three-cone tiaras that resembled the towers of the Wat.

The *Apsarases*, according to legend, were dancers and consorts of the gods; and the *Tevadas* were their earthly reproductions, attached to the various Brahmin temples. Once an *Apsara* fell in love with a human. Their daughter, a child flower—lovely and graceful as the wind, danced before the gods and won such favor that she was given into the hands of high-caste Brahmins to be educated. When she married, her sons became the sacred musicians and her daughters the *Tevadas*.

Those figures carved on the walls smiled cryptically, as though they possessed the secret of the vanished people who built Angkor, and were pleased to mock the searcher.

The young bonze led me up narrow steps into another chamber where long galleries went out from both sides. He started along one of these colonnades, but still another stairway, mounting mysteriously into the dark heart of the Wat, tempted me.

These steps ascended to a corridor that ran between square columns. Beyond the pilasters lay what I supposed were sunken courts; later I learned they were sacred basins. On the opposite sides of these empty pools, peering from gloomy colonnades, were numerous figures of all sizes; evidently Buddhas and other holy images.

Another stair, this one more perilous than the others and mounting past windows barred with carved stone; and then I emerged into starlight, in a court of the third terrace, staring up at the prodigious mass of sculptured rock that was the fourth and last terrace. The five towers shaped like inverted fir-cones seemed to scale grandiosely to a remote and impossible ideal. All around the court was an enclosed gallery, and in the open space rugged piles of stone clustered about the tremendous plinth that reared from the center with crushing magnificence.

After a pause, the bonze led on in silence. This last stairway, the mightiest of all, was so worn I had to use both hands and feet to climb; and at the top, having breathlessly counted thirty-eight steps, I sank upon the stones, soaked with perspiration.

The young monk gestured toward the penetralia, a black maw gaping upon the portico, but I shook my head. I was tired; and I wanted to be alone. I gave him a coin and motioned him to leave, and although bonzes are forbidden by their religion to receive money he accepted it silently and descended the precipitous stairway with miraculous ease, vanishing with his torch and yellow robe into the sprawling labyrinth of the lower galleries.

From my seat I could look down upon tiers of dark courts and cloisters, over a descending terrace of roofs, to the causeway and outer building. Beyond the moat were dusky undulations of forest, and to the north an ominous depth of black where an immense surf of creepers and tortuous limbs crashed silently over Angkor Thom, dead city of the Khmers.

Khmers. A word to inflame the fancy. Name of a race half god, half man that appeared suddenly in Phonam (Funan), or ancient Cambodia, built Angkor and other cities, and then disappeared as mysteriously as they had come, leaving no history except a few meager inscriptions and these ruins that now lie forest-strangled and rotting.

Legend has it that a certain king of Arya-Deca, that is to say India, wandered into Phonam and took refuge in a cavern inhabited by *nagas*, or seven-headed cobras, who ruled the land. This king, called Kambu, made friends with the *nagas*, and later married the daughter of the king of the cobras; and from them descended the Cambodians, or sons of Kambu.

But that does not explain the Khmers. It merely points out, strengthened by the racial characteristics of the people, that they came from India. Brahminism was their religion; indeed, the very temple beneath whose towers I sat was dedicated to Siva the Destroyer. If it is true that the Khmers originated in India, then they must have migrated sometime before Christ, for it was after that their development commenced.

But how had they come? Marching across Manipur and Arakan, through Burma and Siam? Or had they traveled by sea, pushing in from the coast of Cochinchina to the fertile Cambodian plain?

In the thousand or more years following, their history was less nebulous. ...A line of kings whose names are barbaric music.... Wars with the Karens, the Chams, the Chinese and the Thai.... And after that?

Surely a history brazen as a scarlet poppy. And what sumptuous adventure to try to pluck it from the centuries!

## 3

Angkor Wat in the daylight is no less stirring than at night. I have seen it in the early morning when the sky behind it was wine-stained as though purple revelry had spent itself with the darkness; I have been there at midday, in sheening, glare-hot silence; in rain and in storm; and always it gives a sense of awe and bewilderment. But at sunset it is at its highest glory when the towers, inflamed with a ruddy-mauve light, have an air of wild anguish, as though kindled with grief.

Go there in the late afternoon and mount the top terrace where those five main towers crouch against the sky. One must climb to this elevation to understand the elaborate construction of the Wat. There the intricate corridors, stairways and galleries become simpler. One sees that the main structure is a symmetrically built pyramid, rising in four mammoth tiers, each graduated in size, to the central cone. Under this, the greatest tower, is the penetralia, that holy chamber, to enter which meant death in the days of Siva's tyranny.

This terrace is surrounded by a windowed, roofed gallery, whose four corners are helmeted with towers. One mounts from the court of the third terrace and passes under a carved portico into the gallery. Here, through windows with bars of turned stone, a twilight creeps in, making gossamer threads of the spider-webs that weave between numberless Buddhas. They stretch in endless rows, those Buddhas; silhouetted in doorways and windows; some of the greened stone, some painted red, some covered with gold-leaf; many broken; figures without arms, legs or heads; sitting in lotus flowers

"Tall palms that gave the illusion of growing mysteriously out of the stone..."

"Angkor Wat in the daylight is no less stirring than at night."

or under the curving fan of *naga*; and all powdered with the droppings of innumerable bats.

In the center of this enclosed gallery are four courts, in the past sacred basins, and four porticoes defining them, while in the middle, reached by these pillared approaches, are the penetralia, crowned with a tower, which like all towers of the Khmers ascends in diminishing ridges of carving to the apex, where in the time of Angkor's glory a golden lotus curled.

On the four sides of the penetralia are shrines, each containing large red and gold images and numerous smaller figures. And within the penetralia… vacancy. Perhaps while the Khmers were Brahmins it sheltered a replica of Siva, malignant patron of the Wat, which later, when the people became Buddhists, was supplanted by an image of the Master of Kapilavastu; perhaps even the famous Emerald Buddha. No one knows; many conjecture. When the French entered it after 1907 it was empty. But I have often wondered if the secret of the Wat were not an exquisitely ironic one. Today, wandering in the ruins, one comes upon phallic symbols; which, together with the fact that Angkor Wat was dedicated to the Destroyer, suggests that these penetralia might have been a shrine for the lingam of Siva.

Below the fourth terrace a great courtyard spreads itself in the ample enclosure of another gallery. Here again are countless Buddhas; the same windows with carved bars. A stairway plunges down from the center into a corridor with a peaked roof and square columns covered with elaborate and delicate chiseling. Figures of Siva, and designs that embroider the stone with patterns of leaves and flowers, of birds and gods.

Extending from both sides are short causeways, each running between two sacred basins and connecting the main intercourse with more galleries where, dimmed by a double colonnade, a bewildering number of stone images sit in the midst of dust and bat-guano. Always the air in these galleries is haunted by a ghost of incense burned by some bonze. On the walls are delicate figures of *Apsarases*, their breasts rubbed smooth by the hands of the devout, their limbs green with mold. The serrated sides of the empty pools, the corrugated terraces, the columns and carved roofs, the small towers that mount the tiers; all are scabbed with that mold, which seems to crawl over the entire temple like a devouring verdant rust. It is awesome to stand in these courts and gaze at that climbing mass of rock

"...staring up at the prodigious mass of sculptured rock."

which pierced by three enclosed parallel stairways ascends to the crashing pitch of the last coronaled gallery.

Another stairway, tortuous and slippery, descends to the first terrace. Those stairways! Gray, worn stones that seem to sag from so much usage. They are desolate grandeur itself.

In the lower gallery, which is more than half a mile around, is the tremendous bas-relief that tells the story of the Khmers and the gods who ruled them. It is a stupendous pageant, too immense to comprehend immediately; indeed, its enormity and opulence made me dizzy as I followed its intricate length for the first time.

If a symphony can be conceived in stone, surely the Khmers created delirious music on the walls of Angkor Wat. It begins its swelling rhythm southward from the entrance chamber. One hears the crashing dissonance of steel smiting steel, of armor ripped in sunder; of huge chariots locking their wheels in conflict; while accoutered elephants trumpet defiance and go undulating over shoals of dead. In an almost obscene mass of arms and legs one discovers warriors wearing strange helmets; armed with swords, spears and bows and arrows; some in chariots, some astride horses, and some riding scaly lion-like beasts. With them are armored monkeys, the troops of Hanuman, that simian deity. Here are the armies of both gods and men. One sees Vishnu in two incarnations: once as Varaha, a boar, another time in the form of a creature half animal and half man. Demons are fighting with angels. Kings, panoplied and in howdahs on elephants, are leading their armies. It is mythology and history poured into one stunning mold; the battles of the Ramayana mingled with the conflicts of the Khmers.

At each corner the bas-relief stops, to be resumed beyond a small chamber which itself is decorated with lacy carvings weaving from floor to ceiling. These chambers are like intermezzos between the acts of an opera. One pauses in them, breathless, then emerges into the next gallery, where the daylight gliding in between the pillars of a double colonnade suggests the regulated half-illumination of a stage setting. One thinks of "The Twilight of the Gods"; of music savage in its abuse of the senses....

In the southern gallery the motif is less violent. A frieze of winged gods sitting in shrines traces itself delicately over green-streaked stone. In places

"On the walls are delicate figures of *Apsarases*, their breasts rubbed smooth by the hands of the devout, their limbs green with mold."

On the four sides of the penetralia are shrines,
each containing large red and gold images and numerous smaller figures.

there are bits of gold-leaf; hints that perhaps this carving was once a thing of aureate splendor. Here also are sacred dancers, some dressed as birds. A god with twenty-four arms stands out in terrible relief. Royal carriages move in the midst of lions, tigers and demons. Armies are here, too; legions of soldiers in peaked helmets, bristling with bows and arrows.... Chariots rumble past drawn by leo-gryphs.... Then one has the feeling that viols are mounting dizzily to an attenuated pitch. For the theme has changed. Now it is the legend of the churning of the Sea of Milk. The *Asuras* and the *Devas*, gripping the body of *Naga*, are engaged in a tug of war above a sea filled with fish and monstrous marine animals, while Vishnu holding a sword and dancing on a turtle defines the center of balance.

In the rear of the Wat a plaque bearing Khmer script is inset in the bas-relief; and it leaps out like a challenge. For what do those curling characters mean? Do they tell some of Angkor's secrets?...

Now we reach the northern gallery; and the tympani rumble an introduction to Khmer court-life. One sees kings carried in palanquins or seated in the midst of royal ladies; court beauties attended by serving women; princes fanned by slaves; dancing girls in jeweled costumes and tall head-dresses. Suddenly there comes another change; the jarring clash of cymbals. There begins a double frieze picturing Paradise and Purgatory. The pleasures of Paradise consist mainly of being fanned and carried in palanquins. But the tortures of Purgatory are many. Dead bodies are held aloft by warriors or hurled through the air; others are trampled cruelly. There are figures on the rack, figures tied to trees.... Here we see the thirty-two hells of Brahminism... the Hell of Trees with Sharp Thorns... the Hell of Crippled Mountains... the Hell of Choking... the Hell of Tears... And in the midst of all this agony, sitting astride an ox, is Yama, judge of the dead....

Now comes the muffled basso of kettle-drums. One hears the throb of marching men, the cadenced clash of arms. It is the great migration of the Khmers. Elephants plunge above a sea of jungle bearing royal persons in all the panoply of state; palanquins sway in the crush of thousands of troops.... The tempo quickens, mounts wildly. ... Again the battles. Scream of elephants, crash of chariots; sweat and strain of grappling bodies; a mad whirl of arms and legs, of heads and torsos, from which seems to rise a roar that finally thunders to a climax as that prodigious bas-relief comes to an end....

1777. Ex-Cambodge - ANGKOR-VAT – Groupe de Tévadas,
Divinités bienfaisantes (Art Khmer)

One emerges upon the terrace exhausted. Here the palms that grow beside the grooved stone seem incredibly poised, and the causeway, unrolling to the outer portico and beyond, promises rest for the mind if not for the body.

In the daylight the flagstones of the causeway have a repose which they seem to impart to those who follow their seamed and haggard course. Flanking them, in the palm-tufted park, are twin pools. On the right as one leaves the temple is a little Buddhist pagoda with up-tilting, gilded eaves; and around it, peering from a cluster of palms, the pile-raised houses of the bonzes. Just this side of these monastic buildings, between the causeway and the jungle, is a ruin which Sinologues have designated as a library, with another facing it, in the opposite court of the garden.

At last one reaches that long, low building which the French call the *enceinte*. From the central chamber, upholding the melancholy ruin of a tower, long porticoes go out to arched entranceways, which, judged from the fact that they open upon the ground and have no thresholds, must have been used by elephants and chariots in the days of Angkor's arrogance.

One passes through this outer portico, through a room given grace and symmetry by *Apsarases*, and continues across the moat to the broad terrace from which the causeway begins. Here, in the midst of stone lions that seem to mourn the glory of the past, one lingers for a last look at that mighty sculptured pyramid which raises itself in desolate altars to the sky.

In the west a glow of vivid tangerine flares out of the forest, melting imperceptibly across space until it becomes visible again on the turreted mass of Angkor Wat. The towers are touched with orange, and rear like victorious flames from the purple ashes of the main structure. For a moment they stand thus, the apotheosis of glory; then dusk glides stealthily across the plain, and they grow dark, become charred cones against the evening sky.

## 4

The second night at Angkor (and I was not asleep and dreaming) the *Apsarases* came down from the walls and danced on the cruciform terrace where nearly a thousand years ago they danced before the emperors of the Khmers.

On the veranda of the *sala* I received the first hint that it was to be a night of enchantment. In the darkness toward Siem Reap appeared a swarm of lights, dancing like drunken stars. Nearer they came, accompanied by the murmur of many tongues.

"The torchbearers are coming now," said a voice at my side; "the dance will begin soon."

It was that excellent person, the host of the bungalow.

We descended into the midst of those dancing flames, into a shivering orange glare burdened with dragons of sweet smoke. There were fully fifty torches, all carried by little Cambodian boys, whose half-naked bodies gleamed like copper. What a procession they made, trailing off toward the causeway! I followed with a wild beating in my throat, drunk with the scent of burning gum.

Beneath the dipping, swaying torches the causeway became a concourse of living splendor. The little boys chattered and laughed, splashing fire upon the stones; now and then a bat hurtled up toward the rising moon.... I knew if I looked behind I should see a person dark and jeweled, his body anointed with sandal and musk, a girdle of gold about his waist, and a dazzling pointed head-dress flaunting up from his caste-marked forehead; followed by slaves and saffron-powdered women, all treading upon jasmine-flowers scattered before them by dancing *bayadères*.

At last the cruciform terrace was reached. There, at the very entrance of the temple, was a great circle of natives. The little boys filtered in among them, planting their torches on the flags against inclining sticks. A place was made for us, and as we sat down there came a clashing of barbaric music. This music rose from an orchestra half hidden in the crowd on the other side of the terrace. Tom-toms, primitive viols, and a long instrument that resembled a xylophone.

In the wake of the music came a low rumble, like the applause of the gods. The sound of approaching chariots?—or thunder? A passionate vein of lightning grew livid in the sky, and the palms shuddered.

In the glare of the torches, I could fancy these dark people were marked with spots of vermilion or yellow; and to make the illusion complete, several bonzes appeared above the stairs and hovered there, saffron-robed pontiffs awaiting the advent of the sacred dancers.

With no more than a soft clash of anklets to announce them they came, seeming to emerge magically from the gloom of the temple, and advanced into the center of the circle.

"They are from Siem Reap," my host whispered.

But I knew better; they were the *Apsarases*, made mortal for an hour.

They were eight, divided into double lines of four facing us. Their features were moon-white, their lips red with the stain of bits of Chinese paper. Above these etiolate faces tapered gilded head-dresses. They who were attired as men wore jackets drawn tight to the mold of their bodies; from their shoulders curved extravagant epaulets; while brocaded *sampots* were wrapped about their thighs and given dignity by embroidered panels. Over all was the glisten of jewels, of gold thread.... The dancers who represented princesses were draped in *sampots* that hung in pleated folds from the shoulders. Their throats were aflame with collars of jewels; and jewels flashed from their belts, from their arms, fingers and ankles. Their splendor, kindled by the torchlight, left me a little breathless.

At the first fluid pulse of music a tension stiffened their bodies. In perfect harmony each dancer stood poised on one foot, the other leg bent, toes upturned, and moved up and down on flexing knee, while the arms thrown out of joint at the elbows, described bewildering angular gestures that became liquid and melted into other gestures equally bewildering. Thus they stood, fearlessly balanced, while their bodies undulated and their limbs flowed into motions incredibly barbaric. Fingers were bent backward over hands, hands over arms in attitudes seemingly impossible. All seen in the shivering ghost-light of the torches and set to that wild jungle music made doubly savage by the cadenced clash of anklets.

After the dance they faded into the temple; no doubt to become stone again on those glorious friezes.

The moon mourned above the moat, weeping among the wind-stirred lilies. But the fractures of lightning were more frequent, and in the west a tumble of clouds poured down like black hydrangeas.

Suddenly, accompanied by a mad rumble of drums, a mailed figure leaped into the circle of the torches. This dancer was the King of the Garudas. She wore a hideous mask that tapered into a cone, and there was a fire of jewels on her exaggerated epaulets, on her tight girdle and dark *sampot*. From a moment she crouched on bent knees in the exact pose of the *Tevadas*, shoulders twitching, body undulating, and sword uplifted. Then she whirled

"They were the dancers of another century; the sacred courtesans of Angkor, resurrected and reveling on the terrace of their own tomb."

about the terrace in angular gyrations. It was a dance terrible and grotesque, done with such artistry I knew she could be none other than the *première danseuse*; the *Tevada* who nearly a thousand years ago danced before the secret splendor of the penetralia. The torchlight seemed to cling about her, kindling in the jewels of her costume and drawing added fire from her body.

With another crash of drums she vanished.

Often now the towers stood out in black relief as lightning veined the sky, and the palms shivered in successive gusts of wind.

Into the center of the terrace marched the eight dancers, led by the King of the Garudas. This time it was a fragment of the Ramayana they told in supple postures, in the gliding rhythm of trained muscles and unjointed limbs. Hands curved and unfolded; toes were upturned impertinently; rippling muscles made poetry emphasized by the impassive pallor of whited faces. They were the dancers of another century; the sacred courtesans of Angkor, resurrected and reveling on the terrace of their own tomb.

From the near-by forest, where the wind was dancing in the foliage, came quick, stealthy rustles, as though a ghostly army were astir, drawn from its grave by this echo of dead grandeur.

And then, the lightning cracked the sky with a last shattering blow, and the rain came down like a dark glistening curtain descending prematurely upon an incredible performance. The torches were guttered. The orchestra was drowned in the splashing of great drops. Where the dancers had been was a confusion of running figures.

A hand caught mine and led me down from the terrace, then disengaged itself mysteriously, leaving me to hurry blindly across the causeway; a drenched refugee fleeing from a dream.

The next morning I went early to the Wat; and they were there on the walls again, those stone *Apsarases*, smiling their distant, celestial smiles, as though they had never come to life for an hour to make real the dream of one who had traveled leagues—perhaps centuries!—to gaze upon their loveliness.

"Ong Kim Khouan, son of the Khmers."

# 5

"*Les dieux du crepuscule vert*; they are the gods that watch over Angkor Thom...."

Thus said Ong Kim Khouan, son of the Khmers.

At Siem Reap, that tiny village pulsing in the dead shadow of Angkor, I met him. I was in the market-place, looking for some of those dusk-frail scarves the Cambodian women wear about their throats, when I saw him smiling in the doorway of his father's shop.

He spoke French with perfect ease. Indeed, most of the natives of France's Far Eastern possessions do speak the language well, although not many with the ease of Ong Kim Khouan. It was a very poetic French. He had learned it in the school at Siem Reap, and he showed me his diploma. He must have thought my grammar very poor, for he offered to teach me French....

Did he intend to remain always in his father's shop? I asked.

Oh, no; he was going to take an examination for a position in the *Services Civils de l'Indochine*. At first he would work at Siem Reap, and then perhaps go to Saigon.

There was pride and hope in his tone; and I felt a little apprehensive. I had seen young natives working in the offices of Saigon, dressing and acting in pathetic mimicry of their masters. But, I reflected, it was the old story of the unspoiled Oriental and civilization; and this boy—he could not have been more than seventeen—was one of many. Yet there was a certain insolent grace in the poise of his head, a freedom in the utter relaxation of his body that made the prospect of his inevitable metamorphosis more tragic.

Was I a tourist? he inquired.

No; I was looking for a lost city somewhere in Upper Siam or Laos.

His face brightened. The name?

Wat Phu.

He had never heard of it. Was it built by the Siamese?

No. By the Khmers.

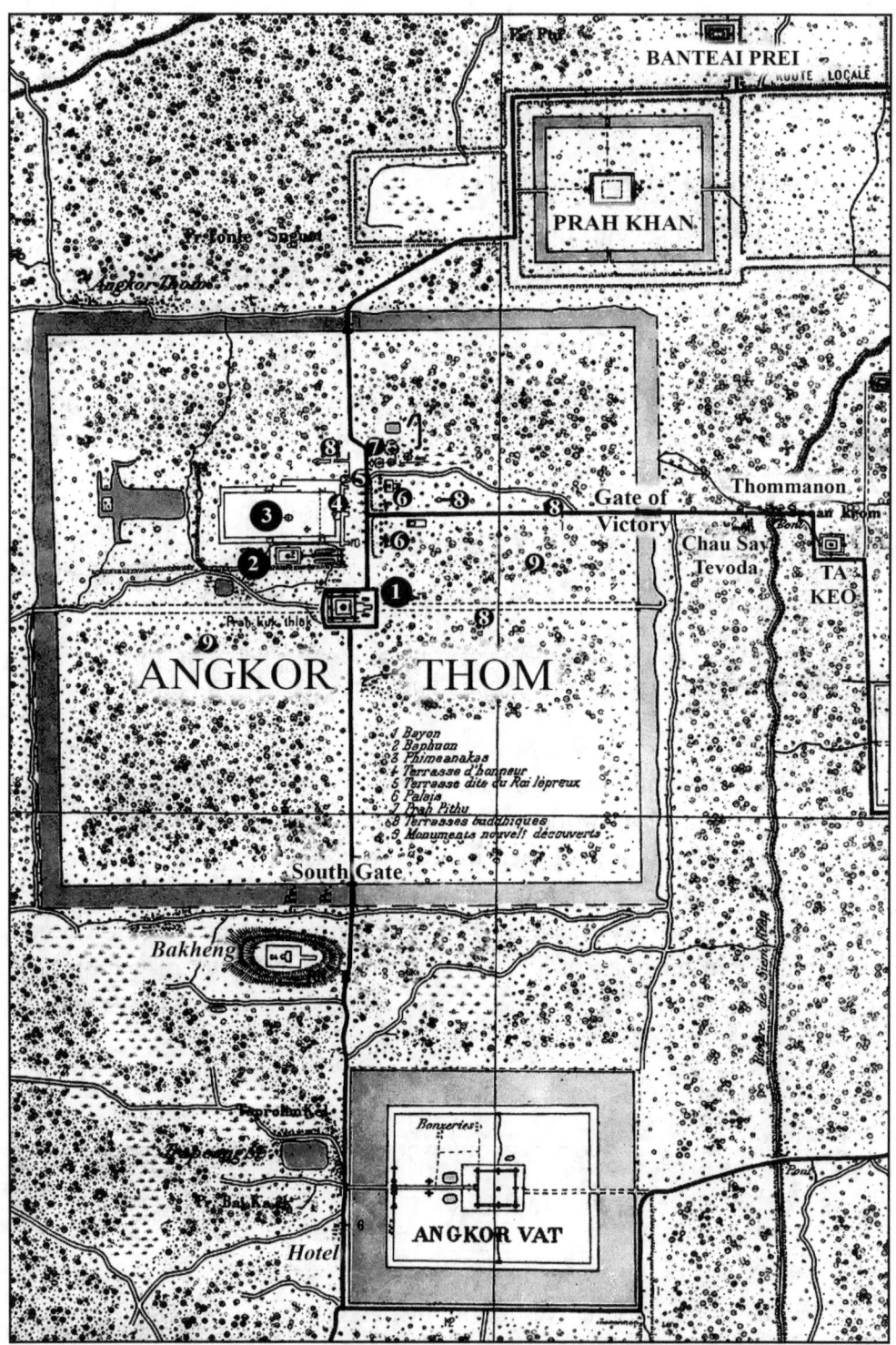

1926 map of Angkor showing sites Harry visited. Note his hotel lower left.

Again that bright look, this time with pride in it. "My ancestors were Khmers."

After that he asked many questions. ... I had met a traveler, I explained, a fellow little better than a beachcomber, who had wandered into the hinterland of Indo-China, and there, somewhere near a town called Bassac, stumbled upon the ruins of what had been a great city. The architecture was similar to that of Angkor. Was it not probable then, I suggested, that it was built by the Khmers—after Angkor was abandoned, or even before?

Near Bassac! Ah, he had a friend there. He would write him that I was coming. But had I seen Angkor?

Only Angkor Wat.

Then he would be my guide, he offered; he knew something of its history....

Of course, I should be delighted....

# 6

North from the bungalow at Angkor the road goes straight into a surf of jungle: here, like mighty foundered galleons, the ruins of Angkor Thom lie desolate.

We set out on horseback, my new friend and I, one early morning when the forest was still wet.

Many natives were astir, the women burdened with baskets of fruit and bags of rice, the men generally squatting beside the road rolling tobacco in green leaves to smoke or gathered in murmuring groups that invariably became quiet as we approached. Most Cambodians are pleasantly lazy without the feeling, so characteristic of indolent white people, that they are wasting time. They live entirely by the soil, and they would not raise more than necessary for their own needs if the French did not force them. Unlike the Annamites and Tonkinese, the Cambodians are not merchants by natural tendency, but some of the women have roadside stalls and shops in the bazaars; always the women, never the men. Their food is simple: fish, rice and fruit. And their dress is even simpler: a twist of colored cloth from loins to ankles (usually a sarong of some shade of red, purple or a plaid design) and a bright scarf about the neck. This lack of clothing is in keeping with their classic beauty and the unrestrained luxury of their bodies. When they move there is rhythm in the flexing of satiny muscles and agile joints. The women,

A. T. 58. – Voyage aux Monuments Khmers
ANGKOR-WAT. - Les Bonzes gardiens du Monument

"Always the air in these galleries is haunted by a ghost of incense burned by some bonze."

Porte de la Victoire - Angkor-Thom

Tourisme Vergoz.- Voitures Hotchkiss servant au tourisme en Indochine

The Gate of Victory with sacred *naga* serpent balustrades.

generally, are short-haired, while not a few of the men wear theirs to the shoulders; black hair, often wavy and shot with dull copperish tones.

With each slight curve of the road the forest seemed to grow thicker, greener, as though drawing together all its gloom in which to shroud Angkor Thom.

"Presently," announced Kim Khouan, "you will see the Gate of Victory. But before we go into the city we will stop at Phnom-Bakheng, an old pagoda."

Suddenly the palisade of jungle on the left fell into an indenture where a well-defined path ascended a hill, one of the very few in that vicinity. We dismounted, leaving our horses tethered at the foot of the steep incline. Two stone lions stood guard at the bottom of what was once a mighty stairway but now is only a difficult footpath over dirt and conglomerate. At the top, in a clearing among tall trees, rose a small brick structure, obviously new, which served as a shrine for an immense "footprint of Buddha."

Kim Khouan waved it aside with fine disregard for superstition, and we moved on past the remains of two towers, to the foot of a tremendous terrace mounting to five tiers like a mammoth altar flung up to the very face of heaven.

The steps were narrow and difficult, and vines and rank weeds grew over the terraces. On either side, crowning the two ends of each terrace, were piled stones that evidently had been towers. The usual stone lions were there, flanking the stairs. On the summit, rising from a broad esplanade, were the mournful masses of several towers, symmetrically placed; the central one, looming from the middle of the great platform, was in a fair state of preservation although roofless.

As we attained the top, breathless, nearly exhausted, a blue drone of sound flowed from the sanctuary. A moment later a Buddhist priest, or bonze, thrust his shaven head out of the doorway and, as he saw us, ceased chanting. He then emerged, followed by another, their yellow robes brilliant in the intense sunlight.

They did not appear cordial, even after Kim Khouan spoke to them, and they watched us with somber curiosity as we moved about the terrace.

From this elevation I could see that the main structure was built in the shape of a pyramid, rising in five many-towered tiers to the top platform where, surrounded by other, smaller towers, the central obelisk thrust its

Tower of Four Faces at the Bayon in Angkor Thom.

sculptured height into the air. Inside this tower was the shrine; at one time, Kim Khouan explained, it sheltered a golden Buddha. The encircling low walls and all the towers were ragged with foliage, beyond which, at the base of the pyramid, the earth melted down into an undulating profusion of surrounding jungle.

Some distance away, cresting the swells of green like gray pine cones, were the irregular towers of Angkor Wat, and around them the glazed silver of the moat. To the south the thatched roofs of Siem Reap swam on the green tide; and to the west, lambent in the bright tropical day, the Grand Lac shimmered and seemed to dissolve in smoke as the blue shapes of mountains swelled in a long, low roll beyond its shores.

In the rear of the tower, on a stone altar, was a phallic symbol which Kim Khouan designated as the lingam of Siva. "In the past, strange ceremonies occurred here," he remarked mysteriously....

We sat there for a while in hot silence and then after we had rested descended to the ponies.

The road continued for about three hundred yards from Phnom-Bakheng to the majestic southern portal of Angkor Thom. There the forest thinned, and the remains of a wide moat lay smothered in lily-pads beneath the city's crumbling walls. The road unrolled across a causeway smaller than that of Angkor Wat, to the irregular opening called the Gate of Victory. The balustrades were formed by the bodies of *nagas*, sacred serpents, each rearing up into seven heads, and held by shattered figures of *Asuras* and *Devas*, the angels and demons of Hindu mythology.

The gate itself was a mass of neutral-colored stone, veined and bearded with vines. Over the entranceway was a ruined tower ornamented upon its four sides with vague faces that smiled omnisciently from the strangling green of creepers. The faces of Siva or Brahma; who knows? Within the gate, opening into the broad walls, were two small chambers, perhaps guard-rooms, from which undoubtedly passages ran east and west to the angles of the walls and continued until they met on the other side of the city.

Beyond the wall the road went straight between thick flanks of jungle. A curve came subtly and unexpectedly, and suddenly there before us, developed with breath-taking swiftness upon the negative of green, a torn pile of galleries and towers scaled upward.

"It is the Bayon," pronounced Khouan. "But we do not stop there this morning."

"Why?"

"We go first to Prah Khan, outside the northern walls. It is there the Green Gods have been most cruel."

I sat fascinated as the road made a semicircle about that monster ruin. Its gaunt towers seemed to stab upward, tyrannical even in their desolation. And such a maze of towers! Towers large and towers small climbing the blue in an irregular pyramid, made more fantastic by the immense age-worn faces of Brahma that dreamed inscrutably in its haggard pile.

In the rear, across the road, was a Buddhist monastery and a small pagoda sheltering an image of the Master.

Another turn in the trail, and ahead was a clearing, very spacious, very bright—the great public square of Angkor Thom. On the left was a series of ruined terraces, uneven in height and bearing an intricate frieze of human and animal figures. Steps broke into them, evidently to meet with paths that stole into the challenging mystery of the forest. That silent rampart of foliage hinted at hidden palaces, temples. On the right rose an edifice similar to the Bayon but smaller, and a group of terraces, between which an intersecting road ran east.

"And do we stop here?" I inquired.

He shook his head. "We go to the temple of the green twilight."

Not far beyond the public square the road pierced another gate identical with the northern portal. Here again was the moat, the balustrade, the latter almost obliterated. After crossing the causeway the jungle was denser, and small bands of monkeys crashed noisily through the trees.

Suddenly Khouan turned off from the main road to follow an inconspicuous path. In answer to my questioning look he announced, "Prah Khan."

This path crossed an embankment between what appeared to be two long pools and curved to follow a dark, looming shape, which gradually became perceptible as the remains of a wall. Khouan indicated the embankment. "That was once a causeway."

Beside a green gap in the wall where broken pillars and blocks of stone lay submerged in spouts of ferns, we dismounted and followed a course parallel with the rampart. Gradually the path rose to surmount the battlements at a point where the stones had collapsed in a ragged breach. Beyond the wall the path plunged down into a tangle of wild growths that enclosed us with ghastly suddenness.

We had entered into a kingdom of twilight, a dank green twilight like the aqueous dusk close to the surface of the ocean, and the hush was vocal. The hot air seemed to rush out and inundate me. My lungs labored for breath. Strange rustles sounded a warning in the growths that sprang up breast-high on either side, and the stridulations of insects seemed to italicize the hidden menace. Deeper we went, crashing through limbs and grasping tendrils. I felt a sense of utter terror. I was drenched with perspiration; it stung the corners of my eyes and ran over my mouth. The smells of mossy stone, of wet earth, of decaying roots and innumerable varieties of fungi made the air close in with the effect of a palpitating thing that left a warm mucus over my lungs.

In the gauzy apparition of the forest appeared a wall and shattered pillars, all struggling out of verdant disorder. Dominating this ruin, their roots and limbs ghostly pale, were monstrous trees that seemed to dissolve overhead in that eternal green twilight. Some of the limbs were thrust cruelly into the walls; some of the roots sprayed out and imprisoned the pillars, looping down and slithering off into the gloom, as if to consort with other spectral, destroying things. In places, entire trees had broken through the crumbling ramparts or had seized upon some spot in the wall and shot up in vicious triumph. Ferns and plants with long tapering leaves took life in cornices and on the sills of empty windows. The moss was relentless in its desire to possess every inch of bare stone. Even the vines, generally so tender, seemed full of lust.

Kim Khouan gestured toward the giant trees.

"The gods..." he whispered. "Trees hundreds of years old—with the souls of gods in them—angry gods."

We paused, surveying the mournful spectacle. "They were a great people, the Khmers," he went on. "Some say they were gods.... And when they were defeated by Siam their souls entered the mighty trees and destroyed the

"Trees hundreds of years old—with the souls of gods in them—angry gods."

city they had built. . . He indicated the gloomy walls. "Once a great temple dedicated to Siva. There were four huge doors and three concentric galleries, each identical, guarding the sanctuary. They say it had more towers than the Bayon."

As we drew nearer the temple I could see the walls were extravagantly chiseled in lacelike designs, among which were figures of the *Apsarases*, or sacred courtesans, their carved bodies indistinct and smooth, like coins whose effigies are effaced. Kim Khouan moved ahead, stepping from rotted tree-trunk to crumbling pilaster, and climbing over the fallen walls. In the close hush our breathing was like scraping on dead husks. Dampness in the face, in the nostrils; the cling of sweaty clothes. And all about us that awesome tangle, into which rays of sunlight plunged, searching out the crawling green lava of eruginous roots and giving livid emphasis to the piles of rock that lay dark-stained as with verdigris.

The ruins seemed to stretch on interminably, like a vast drowned city. Its desolation was incredible. I remember the tragedy of broken columns in window-frames half crushed; battered-in parapets that lay beneath snarling roots; courtyards seeming sunk in fountains of plants; mold-green passages and chambers, dreadful as a subterranean prison; and over all, the dripping tallow of vines that melted down into dank twilight. In places, great trees lay felled in an agony of green, pressing deeper into the earth the stones that had fallen beneath them. Tower and rampart, gallery and colonnade, all lay in mute bondage—a terrible memorial to Angkor and its agonized surrender to the forest.

It is a ghastly punishment, the vengeance of the jungle.

## 7

Another day; and the sunlight glaring on the dead city of Angkor.

At seven o'clock Ong Kim Khouan presented himself at the bungalow, his slender hips wrapped about with a sarong of resplendent purple. A flower was stuck gallantly over one ear, and he wore a yellow towel thrown about his throat scarf-wise. That towel might have been ridiculous on another, but on him it had an insolent distinction.

This morning we rode straight under the Gate of Victory, past the torn pyramid of Bayon, and into the great public square. There was a certain glory

## 82 KING COBRA

15. - ANGKOR-THOM
Une des Tours à faces humaines du Bayon

"...we rode straight under the Gate of Victory, past the torn pyramid of Bayon."

in that spacious stretch of green, thrice brilliant in the violent downpour of sunlight. Immediately it gave me a feeling of imperial vastness. On the left, stretching for more than three hundred yards and plumed with the ragged planes of tall trees, was what Kim Khouan pronounced the Terrace of Honor. It was one great length of friezes, broken by five stairways; an intricate mass of sculpture that stenciled the brain with an array of Garudas, lions, gods and processions of howdahed elephants. Beyond, in the lacy verdure, rose the walls of Phimeanakas, the royal palace; and at the extreme northern end, after following its majestic length, we found a separate and smaller terrace, segregated from the larger by a narrow cleft of chiseled stone and literally covered with carvings of gods and other mythological figures. This, Kim Khouan explained, was called the Terrace of the Leper King.... And there he sat, behind the parapet, reproduced in stone; one of the mysterious and nameless rulers of Angkor.

From the center of the Terrace of Honor a path runs westward to the immense enclosure of Phimeanakas. The main entrance is a tall, four-sided gate, well preserved but, like all the other buildings, roofless, because the ceilings had been of wood or some other perishable material. The four little chambers that opened out from each side of the gate evidently were guard-rooms; and perhaps from the top of the tower a sentinel watched—a tall, swarthy fellow, oiled and anointed after the custom of the Khmers, and mailed in the barbaric regalia that one sees on the warriors of the bas-reliefs.

We were now within the walls of Phimeanakas. Deep courts wildly overgrown with jungle-grass; vine-wrapped stones piled in grandeur; and where the path ran into high foliage a pyramidal ruin of reddish stone, ridged and serried, with trees growing up from its parapets past dead windows and bursting in terrific green above roofless chambers. "It is the temple of Phimeanakas," said Kim Khouan.... At one time there must have been numerous other buildings about it. Now only broken walls and fallen rock kept visible the memory of spacious royal dwellings.

A path turns south from Phimeanakas into a tumble of forest. That forest is an undergrowth yielding unsuspected loveliness—a ruined gate and nearly obliterated walls; a deep, wide court that must have been a sacred tank or a sunken garden; and the Baphuon, splendorous temple rising like a stricken fortress from courts held in green bondage. There is something tragic and solitary about the Baphuon. Tragedy in the remains of a stone approach that lies matted in grass on the eastern side; in the refuse-filled windows that stare like sightless eyes; and an almost heroic anguish in the receding terraces that tumble into its roofless chambers.

To the parapet we climbed, sitting on the edge, with our legs hanging over the desolate courts below.

"This," said Kim Khouan, "was the palace of Jaya-Varmediaparamecvara, who was a great king of the Khmers...."[5]

For a long time he was silent, his eyes rheumy with dreams; then he swung his feet up to the parapet, rolled over on his belly and cupped his chin in his hands, gazing at me with a look that went through and beyond.

"My schoolmaster," he began, "once showed me a copy of the *Bulletin de l'École Française de l'Extrême Orient* in which there was an article by an ancient Chinese who visited Angkor sometime during the twelfth century. He was the ambassador of Kublai Khan—his name was Zhou Daguan.[6] His manuscript is the only detailed account of life in ancient Angkor.

"A strange city he found it, very magnificent and very terrible, ruled over by this king, Jaya-Varmediaparamecvara. It was a very rich city, too. In its center stood a tower of gold—probably very near where we are sitting now. One *li* from that was a copper tower.

"On the towers of all the temples were lotuses of gold.

All the palaces and houses of nobles, all the official buildings looked toward the east, and their roofs were of yellow terra-cotta, and the dimensions of each were determined by the rank of the dweller therein. The houses of the common people were not so fine—they were of wood or mud, and their roofs of thatch. In the palace the roofs were lead; and the building had many colonnaded verandas and long, open corridors. The Hall of Council, where the king received, was lighted by windows chased in gold, and decorated with square columns with many mirrors arranged about them. ... It must have been very gorgeous, much more than the Palace of Versailles, which the French boast of....

"In the center of Jaya-Varmediaparamecvara's palace stood the tower of gold, and it was there he slept. Legend says this tower was habited by the

---

[5] I.e. Jayavarman VII.
[6] I.e. Zhou Daguan.

soul of a serpent with nine heads, and if one night this soul did not appear it meant death to the king. Oh, it was a very jealous serpent! When the king missed a single night in the tower some misfortune befell the city. And not even the first wives of the king dared to enter.... He had five wives, this king; one for the private apartment, and one each for the four cardinal points of the compass. He had many concubines, too, for every family that had a beautiful daughter sent her to the palace. Only these and the women who did the work were allowed inside the palace. The rules were very rigid, and the guard very strong. And one dared not break them, for they were the law, and the law was the king, and the king, a god....

"All complaints were made directly to him, the sovereign, and while he was very just, he was also very severe in meting out punishments. Among other things, the bastinado was used, and for minor offenses members of the body were cut off. It was the law that one who captured a thief could punish him as he thought wise; and if a husband found his wife in adultery she was beaten and her lover's feet crushed between two huge stones. Outside the western gate the prisoners were put to death— Holes were dug in the earth and they were buried alive....

"No coffins were used for the dead, as now, but binding sheets and straw shrouds; and the corpses were left outside the walls to be devoured by dogs and vultures. There were only a few cremations, and those of royal persons, whose ashes were buried in state in tall towers. The funeral processions... they must have been very splendid. There was music, colored banners, and friends walked before the cortege throwing grilled rice, while the daughters of the dead, their heads shaven over their foreheads, and the sons, entirely shaven, walked beside the corpse....

"But it was not all so gruesome. The people had many beautiful customs. They anointed themselves with sweet oils and wore flowers, and each person did his or her hair in a chignon, and wore silks from Siam and Chiampa[7] about the loins. Only the king could use garments of feathers; and he dressed very splendidly, that king. On his head—I think it must have been a fine, dark head, with hair glossy as black lacquer—he wore a golden diadem like the crowns of the Vajradharas; and when he was without this diadem jasmine flowers were wreathed about his locks. On his neck were pounds of pearls. Bracelets were on his wrists and ankles; rings of cat's-eyes on his fingers.

---

[7] I.e. Champa.

He wore no shoes; and the soles of his feet were tinted with senna; and his hands, too. When he walked through the city he carried a golden sword, the Sword of Indra, while over him were held state umbrellas of gold,

"The umbrella was a very important thing among the Khmers. All the officials carried parasols of oiled green material with short fringes and silver handles. And some of them rode in palanquins of silver. These officials were designated *sseu-la-ti*. The men of higher rank, the princes, carried red silk parasols with gold handles and fringes that fell to the ground; and they rode in palanquins ornamented with gold. They were called *pa'ting* or *ngan-ting*. Imagine the sight of those umbrellas on a bright morning! And the silver and gold palanquins! And the nobles in rich silks, carried by naked slaves!...

"There were many of them, these slaves; thousands; a very low and degraded people, if they might be called people, who were treated as even less than animals. Their dwellings were beneath the houses of their masters; there they ate, slept and loved.... Yes, they must have loved, these creatures less than animals.... And if a master was so indiscreet as to take a slave-girl as his woman, great was his punishment if discovered. These slaves were supposed to have no relations except among themselves. And they were not permitted to express themselves in speech, they were only to listen when the master spoke. And yet the masters could not have been altogether cruel, for the slaves called them *pa-t'o*, which means 'father.' The master's wife they called *mi*, 'mother.' A barbaric language, this Khmer. I have heard it said that it sounded like the tongue of Champa— old Annam—and the letters were pronounced like Mongolian letters. But I do not know. It is known, though, that the writing ran from left to right, and that all the documents were done with a black substance on skins dipped in white fluid. Of course the bonzes wrote and spoke Sanskrit, and in the villages and cities the dialect was different. However, the base of the language was the same. *Mei, pie, pei, pan, pokien, pokienmei, pokienpie*... those were the numerals. Not ugly. And I like the sound, Khmer. It is—*mystérieuse*...."

He lapsed into silence, dreaming again; then, after a moment, he sat up, took the wilted jasmine flower from behind his ear and stuck it between his toes, examining it critically.

The courts below lay still in the windless, blazing morning. A lone dragonfly made a blue cicatrice upon the air and wheeled down to settle on an orchid's throat....

"I like to think of the eve before the final downfall of the city," said the boy suddenly. "It is my own fancy, what I think, but perhaps... Yes, I am sure it must have been a dark night, following a sunset also dark and very red. All the gates had been closed, and the king was asleep in his golden tower. The sentries were in their watch-towers along the walls. It was very quiet in Angkor Thom that evening....

"Then came the news: the terrible armies of the Siamese had swept upon the surrounding villages and were pressing nearer to Angkor. The king was aroused in his golden tower. Tall fires blazed in the streets. In the houses, mail and chain rattled as warriors prepared.... And then the dawn... The first stage of the great battle—perhaps beyond Prah Khan, or if the enemy approached from the south around Angkor Wat. Can you see the great armored elephants plunging over dead bodies, the war-chariots grinding to death those who lay wounded? And hear the sounds? The trumpeting of angry beasts, the cries and all the crashing noises....

"It must have lasted for days, that battle. And then, perhaps, the slaves given courage by the failing strength of their masters rose in rebellion. Fighting within and without. ... A last time the drums beat on the walls. After that, silence... and the forest growing, growing....

He sighed.

"It is always so, the triumph of the trees," he pronounced with somber wisdom. "My master told me that in the school. He is French—but he knows. Men are like the winds that rise up and die out, but the trees—they continue. Khmer, Thai, Annamite—and perhaps after the French—"

With a sudden kick he flung the jasmine-flower down upon the lower terrace, rose, stretched, unwrapped the yellow towel and fanned himself for a moment, then re-draped it in that cavalier manner.

"Let us go," he said. "Sometimes the trees frighten me...."

"Buddhas; silhouetted in doorways and windows…"

## 8

For two weeks now I had been at Angkor, climbing over the ruins, talking with the natives, visiting the bonzes, reading a few translated Sanskrit and Pali manuscripts and many books; and in consequence my mind throbbed with Khmer names, Khmer legends, bits of Khmer history, and visions that sagged under the opulence attributed to this vanished race.[8]

By day I wandered in the vine-grown cloisters of Ta Prohm, through the deserted courts of Neak Pean and Banteay Kedei, and amongst the fallen pilasters of Mebon and Pre Rup. In the evenings, when a dream-still silence dwelt over the dead city, I sought the lofty terraces of Ta-Keo or sat amidst the immense inscrutable faces of Brahma staring from the towers of Bayon, conjuring up in my thoughts moods of the past.

One midnight I ascended to the phallic altar of Phnom Bakheng. All about me, below the hill, the great Cambodian forest stretched away like some strange black sea hushed beneath the starry sky. Behind the roofless temple, on a block of stone, was a phallus; and suddenly, as I came upon that blunt, dark symbol, it seemed to open an unexplored dimension of Khmer history.

I had a new picture of Angkor—Angkor in the shadow of the lingam.

Even the legend of the king who married a cobra's daughter, thereby starting the Cambodian race, had a phallic aspect, I realized. Indeed, the entire growth of Indo-China had its inspiration in the visible symbol of procreation.

From the earliest times the various races drawn together in that country between Tibet, Yunnan and Siam marched in saraband[9] about the lingam,

---

[8] For the following section, readers are again gently reminded that many of Hervey's historical names, dates and "facts" are incorrect based on modern scholarship. Hervey, like Helen Churchill Candee in her 1925 book *Angkor the Magnificent*, could only rely on accounts available at the time. Still, there are seeds of truth in his story and its provides interesting reading, if only to realize how much historical understanding changes over time.

[9] The sarabande is a dance in triple metre first mentioned in a 16th century poem written in Central America. In 1539, the poet Fernando Guzmán Mexía mentions a dance called a *zarabanda* in a poem written in Panama. This dance apparently became popular in the Spanish colonies and then moved back across the Atlantic to Spain. In 1583, it was banned in Spain for its obscenity, however it was frequently cited in literature of the period, including works by Cervantes and Lope de Vega. In the late 19th and early 20th centuries, the sarabande form was revived by composers such as Debussy and Satie and, in different styles, Vaughan Williams (in *Job: A Masque for Dancing*) and Benjamin Britten (in The Simple Symphony, Op. 4).

"...courtyards seeming sunk in fountains of plants; mold-green passages and chambers, dreadful as a subterranean prison..."

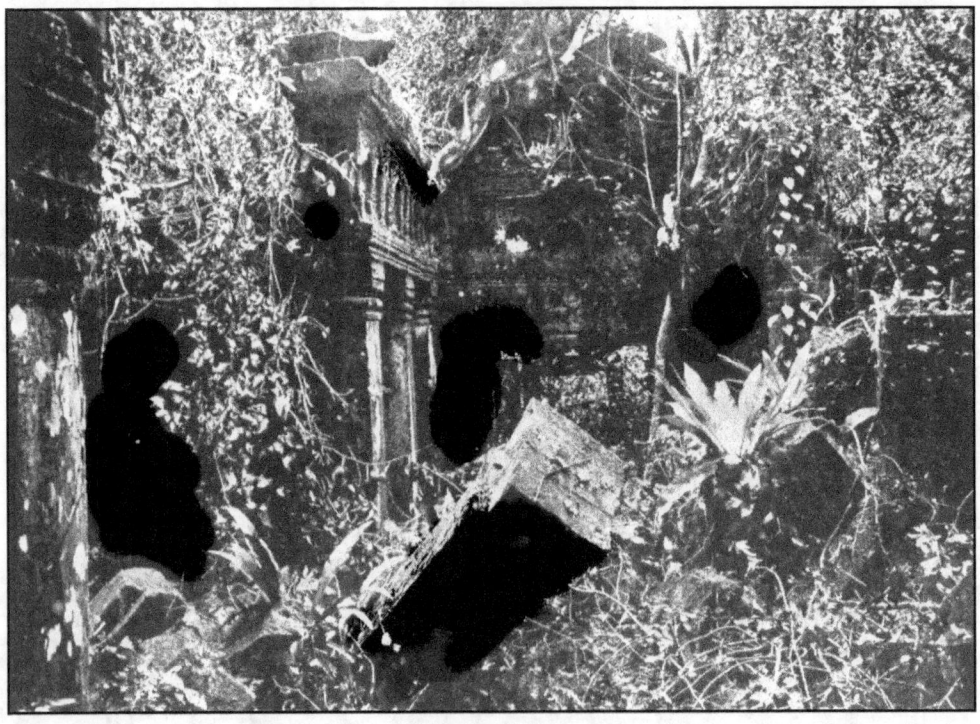

now moving slowly, now dancing hysterically, but always celebrating their allegiance to the phallic-stone.

In that period of nascence when Europe was divided into barbarian provinces, Indo-China loomed up in the haze of antiquity like a giant phallus, producing its brood: various aboriginal tribes of which the Lewas were the most important. In their midst appeared a tattooed, breech-clouted people, the Mon, one of the first races welded out of this conglomeration of tribes. Then another race arrived, marching across the country from the Kin-Lung mountains of China. Their religion was the religion of the soil, a natural phallism that included the creative powers of earth as well as man, but disfigured by a superstitious belief in devils.

Meanwhile, on either side of these people two other races were gathering momentum, very soon to plunge new life into this artery: on the east, the Annamites; on the west, the Thai or Siamese.

In a few years the Thai-Shan race emerged from this mingling of bloods. In the place of primitive altars dedicated to the genius of production, were temples shrining Buddhistic images; for that religion had crept in quietly from Tibet.

Then the Karens came, spraying the country like shrapnel. Their kingdom of Lin-y grew, later to be called Tchen-Tching and occupy the territory that is now Cochin-China; a kingdom very powerful in the fourth century.

All the while the Shan capital of Zimme farther north was rising in influence, conquering the surrounding territory. A dark insidious stream was seeping into Indo-China—the Indians, who according to Cambodian tradition migrated there about 254 B.C., mingling with the indigenous race. Cambodia was then called Funan (Phonam or Founan): a name it was known by as early as 1109 B.C. in Annamite chronicles.

About three hundred years after this migration of Indians, a Brahmin named Prea Thong married the Queen of Cambodia, instituting the religion and architecture of his race. At the time of Prea Thong's arrival, Cambodia was divided into seven provinces, each ruled over by one of the queen's sons. But the Brahmin quickly usurped all the power.

Travelers who visited Cambodia during that period—and the Romans were among them—described it as a place of swarthy, voluptuous beauty. The people were very dark and wore their hair knotted on the top of their heads; and the wealthy dressed in loin-cloths and robes of silk and gold. The women wore many ornaments of exquisitely wrought precious metals inset with jewels. They were an agricultural people; and proof that they were essentially honest is offered by a record which states that they had no prisons. The walls of the capital were made of tall tree-trunks, and the king lived in a palace raised high above the ground. When he went abroad he rode on an elephant, and the people burned incense before him. They were not a warlike race unless aroused to protect themselves.

This necessity soon came. The Karens attacked them, and later they were conquered by the Yun Shans. Like so many conquered people, the Cambodians absorbed the Shans; Cambodian religion, language and architecture dominated. It was then, after the blending of these races, that the Cambodians became known as the Khmers, and their kingdom called Chenla.

In 422 A.D., before, the pure Indian dynasty ended, a Buddhist preacher, Prea Ket Melia, was raised to the throne, and his religion was spread through the land. But it did not immediately exert a strong influence, for an ancient record, written about 600 A.D., recounts stories of human sacrifices made on Phnom-Bakheng. Brahma the Creator and Siva the Destroyer were still relentlessly chanting the creed of phallus.

With the beginning of the Shan dynasty, a new succession of kings began constructing the city of Angkor. In 800 A.D., or thereabout, Jayavarman II erected Prah Khan. Eighty-nine years later another king, Yacovarman, commenced Angkor Thom. Yacovarman was one of the youngest of the Khmer emperors and Angkor Thom was his dream. A city of limonite and sandstone, whose walls, floors, stairways and towers were fitted together cunningly without cement, and then, as though its builder was not satisfied with that feat, carved and embellished with such extravagance that even the baroque temples of Java seem simple beside it.

This citadel was called Yacodharapura; a place peacock-gay and fabulous. Its buildings bore fantastic names: the Tower of Gold, the Tower of Copper, the Terrace of Elephants, the Terrace of the Leper King.... Great trade caravans came from India and from China, bringing silk and sandalwood, gold-dust and musk. Jewels from all Asia enriched its temples. The Khmers flourished; for Yacovarman was successful in his conquests. Under him the empire included what is now Siam, Cambodia, Cochinchina, Laos and Annam.

It was Yacovarman who built the temple of Bayon; and it was he commenced the palace of Phimeanakas which later was completed by Hashavarman. Following that the Baphuon was erected by Jayavarman V.

Suryavarman II, some centuries later—between 1112 and 1160 A.D.—started work on the glorious Angkor Wat, largest of all the Wats. Out of the toil and death of thousands of slaves that mammoth edifice rose stone upon stone, tier upon tier until, its towers crowned with golden lotuses, it dominated the surrounding marshy jungle and even the torn pyramids of Angkor Thom, a monument to the cruelty and genius of the Khmers.

At the beginning of the thirteenth century the Thai, or Siamese, attacked the Khmers, but were held off with the aid of the Annamites; however, toward the end of the century, when the Mon Shans swarmed down, the kingdom was temporarily subjugated. This was in 1296. It was a year later that the Chinese Ambassador Zhou Daguan visited Angkor, writing the only record of the manners and customs of the people which has survived.

In his memoirs he draws a picture of prodigal splendor.[10]

Each individual, he says, had from twenty to a hundred slaves, and royal persons never walked but were carried in golden palanquins. The burnished lotus, emblem of Angkor's wealth, unfolded its petals from every tower; and in the temples were treasures to intoxicate the temperate Occidental gaze. Attached to the shrines were numerous *Tevadas*, or sacred dancers; and one can fancy those graceful creatures, lily-pale and flame-slim, dancing to the mounting rhythm of drums while swarthy priests, caste-marked with the colors of the trinity, heaped jasmine-petals about the lingam of Siva.

There were many of these dancers in the royal household. According to Zhou Daguan, in the palace of Phimeanakas alone there were from three to five thousand concubines. Under these imperial courtesans was another caste of women who also served the ruler. They were called *tchan-kia-lan*, and were distinguished by a shaven spot over their brows and a touch of scarlet on forehead and temples. All the nobility and the wealthy anointed their bodies

---

[10] As surprising as some of Zhou Daguan's revelations are, Hervey reports them accurately based on the translation available to him at that time. In 2008, Peter Harris completed the first direct Chinese to English translation of the work: *"Zhou Daguan: A Record of Cambodia"*. In 2010, Cambodian scholar Solang Uk published *"A Record of Cambodia's Land & Customs,"* offering a second direct from Chinese translation, adding refinements to Zhou's account based on the author's knowledge of Cambodian culture, language and tradition.

"...one can fancy those graceful creatures, lily-pale and flame-slim, dancing to the mounting rhythm of drums..."

with sandal and musk; and the women beautified themselves with saffron and henna and cassia, and glossed their hair with sweet oils.

The king received from a golden window in Phimeanakas , and when he went about the city, he carried the sacred sword which the god Indra is reputed to have bequeathed to the Khmer emperors. What processions they must have been! Courtiers announcing the royal advent with conchs and cymbals; then the soldiers, followed by priests; and last, surrounded by courtesans and dancing girls, by troops and officials, the king himself, carried in a jeweled palanquin and shaded by the numerous golden umbrellas to which his rank entitled him.

There is no mention in Zhou Daguan's memoirs of a pronounced homosexual element among the Khmers, but here and there, buried in Cambodian legends and in various historical records dealing with the surrounding kingdoms at that time, are evidences that in Chenla, as in many Far Eastern kingdoms of the past, this inverted social condition flourished. It is a singular fact, borne out by all historians who have graduated from provincial mythology, that this inversion, perversion or whatever one may choose to call it, has figured prominently in many a gallant history. Witness ancient Egypt, Greece and Rome, to say nothing of India, China and Japan.

Regardless of opinion or prejudice, this phase cannot be dismissed with a hurried blush. It has been, at intervals, a part of the rise of culture and art in every land; and invariably it has been the preface to doom. For, in addition to its unhealthy aspects, it cannot be said to encourage propagation.

On the great bas-relief stretching around the lower terrace of Angkor Wat is a section which shows Khmer warriors marching to battle, and the profile of each figure is rimmed with the profile of another, suggesting—and not fantastically—that there existed among the soldiers of ancient Cambodia a comradeship not entirely Platonic and similar to that of the Dorian Greeks.

Among the customs remarked by Zhou Daguan were those of courtship and marriage; customs, it must be admitted, not altogether commendable. Each mother, he says, prayed for her daughter as follows: "May you be desired by men! May a hundred and a thousand ask for you in marriage!"

The ages for betrothal were between seven and nine for rich girls, but generally not before eleven for the poor. It was customary for the suitor to present

*A. T. 98. -* **Voyage aux Monuments Khmers**
ANGKOR-THOM. - Galerie du Kedeï

"...I wandered in the vine-grown cloisters of Ta Prohm, through the deserted courts of Neak Pean and Banteay Kedei."

RUINES D'ANGKOR - TA-PROHM — Pavillon d'entrée de la 2ᵉ enceinte orientale - Façade intérieure

the maiden's family with gifts of silk, wine and silver worth one hundred *piculs* or more. Following the betrothal came a ceremony called *tchen-t'an*.

This ceremony was one eminently symbolical. According to the law, every girl belonged to the gods; therefore, when one desired to marry, it was necessary for her first to have her virginity taken by a priest, the earthly intercessor of the gods.

The procedure was very complicated: a girl about to be married applied to the local mandarin, who gave her a candle with a mark upon it. At dusk of the day set for the ceremony of *tchen-t'an* she would light this taper; when it had burned down to the mark it was time for the actual ceremony to begin.

That day a platform had been erected outside the girl's house, with a wooden phallic figure on it, and on either side of this platform, was a pavilion curtained with silk and decorated with flowers; one for the priest and one for the girl.

At the appointed hour, fires blazed in the street, incense was burned, and processions of half-naked Khmers, both priests and laity, marched about the pavilions, strewing the earth with mango-blossoms and jasmine-flowers. The girl was then taken to her pavilion, the priest to his. Following that came some religious rite, after which the bonze entered the maiden's pavilion and performed the ceremony with his hand, thereby taking her virginity without breaking his vow of celibacy. He then immersed his hand in wine, and the families and friends of the betrothed girl marked their foreheads with it. This finished, the bonze was carried back to his monastery in a palanquin. The girl followed, was blessed, and the ceremony ended.... For his services, the monk received between fifty and a hundred *piculs*, according to the wealth of the girl's parents.

Such were the conditions in Angkor at the time of Zhou Daguan's visit.

Golden rot was eating into the heart of the Khmer Empire. In one mighty gesture, spending their wealth and their strength, these people had built Angkor—and their own tomb. Internally, Cambodia was suffering. Arrogant Brahminism was struggling with the antithetical creed of Buddhism. The thousands of slaves were restless. The kingdom was attacked by the Siamese, the Laotians and the Karens. This was toward the end of the fourteenth century.

And after that?...

"It is a relief to reach Siem Reap."

In 1570, two hundred years later, Cristoval de Jacque, a Portuguese explorer, penetrated the Cambodian forests and found Angkor deserted, delivered over to the jungle, whose monstrous greenness had completely inundated it.

The Khmers had vanished.

## 9

It is my last day of Angkor.

Across the way Angkor Wat stands gray against the blazing sky. Even the consoling sun, which daily puts a flush upon its towers, cannot give this dread pile more than a transitory semblance of life.

I set out on horseback for Siem Reap, bound for the shop of Ong Kim Khouan.

Along the road, spirals of foraging butterflies ascend from the scattered offal like rockets. A few monkeys harass the branches overhead. The atmosphere is still and seems charged, as though about to deliver a shower.

The road winds through a depth of forest that is oppressive. No one is abroad at this hour, and even the bungalows packed away here and there in the greenery appear deserted.

It is a relief to reach Siem Reap. On one side is a brown stream turned to frothy chocolate where a water-wheel winds languidly. A few Cambodians are bathing, one a bonze, whose yellow robes are spread out on the bank. On the other side is a high fence of bamboo; potbellied children peep out as I approach.

I pass the Gendarmerie Coloniale. Two sleepy-looking native soldiers are slouching by the gate, and they stare dully. Ahead numerous matchbox houses rise on stilts beside the river.

At length I reach the market-place. Here shops are built in arcades on three sides of the square, the fourth side fronting the stream. Several young girls are parading lazily along the street, preening themselves for the benefit of a group of boys lounging by the bridge. Old women squat in front of their stalls, chatting and spitting betel-juice.

Arriving at the shop of Ong Kim Khouan, I inquire for him. There is a mild flurry among the people in the store; they call loudly for him and then giggle. It appears he is at this moment taking a bath. I sit down to wait, gazing with annoyance at the European wares on the shelves.

Presently he comes. His black hair is wet and drips little streams down over his smiling face. Instead of the usual sarong, he is wearing trousers, a pink shirt and a tight-fitting coat.

Immensely pleased, he announces that he thought *Monsieur le Américain* would be gratified to see him dressed in this manner.

*Monsieur le Américain* smiles feebly.

There is great excitement in the life of Ong Kim Khouan today. His schoolmaster, who has gone to Saigon, has telegraphed that he has obtained a position for him in one of the banks.

I congratulate him....

"I shall go to the cinema every night," he declares extravagantly.

We talk for a few minutes. I promise to send him some books when I return to America; he promises to write to me. Perhaps, he announces, he will even visit me some day!

He is too excited for ordinary conversation. He tells me of the things he will buy in Saigon: French shoes, a French hat....

I bid him good-by; I wish him luck....

"When you come back to Indo-China," boasts Ong Kim Khouan, son of the Khmers, "I shall be a Frenchman!"

... I am out in the square again. There is something depressing in the lucidity of the sunlight: it makes one aware of the exaggerated importance of people.

As I ride back past the Gendarmerie Coloniale, into the relentless green of the jungle, vultures are circling overhead.

There is death in Angkor.

# Chapter III
# Saramani
*Tells of a King and a Few Concubines*

# Pnom Penh

## 1

CTUALLY, it is some two hundred and thirty kilometers from Angkor to Pnom Penh. But it might be a thousand miles. Esthetically the change is more drastic than that. The difference between the magnificence of the Khmers, even after nine hundred years of isolation in the jungle, and the pretense of splendor that is Pnom Penh cannot be reckoned in distances.

Dusty and hot I rode in from Angkor one afternoon, leaving the dust on the road, but feeling in the town a heat more depressing because of the presence of so many people and houses. Pnom Penh dazzled, its yellow' plaster walls staring from the tremulous clarity of atmosphere that is intense heat. The hotel, separated from the Mé-Kong by only a road and a low embankment, lay as though stricken. A few Frenchmen rode past in rickshaws, returning to their offices after the customary noonday rest, and their white suits were cruelly bright in the glare. I retreated to the hushed dusk of a room guarded by rattan blinds, with that feeling of despair the equatorial midday sometimes brings.

There is a beautiful futility about dressing in fresh clothes in Indo-China. The very act is a sort of cynical defiance of a climate that restricts men's vanity to a series of gestures. The result almost encourages one to revert, or progress, to the form of dress which has had constant popularity with the natives for more than a thousand years. In fact this idea on a lazy torrid afternoon is

"The hotel, separated from the Mé-Kong by only a road and a low embankment, lay as though stricken."

Mailboat departing for France on November 7, 1924.
Perhaps some of Harry's letters and cards were aboard?

quite alluring, with no affront to the modesty, unless the extravagant fancy enlarges the thought and suggests the sudden vogue of sarongs among the whites of Pnom Penh. And even then there is no particular immodesty involved, but instead a rather alarming quiver of the artistic senses at the prospect of red-faced, whiskered Frenchmen sauntering along the rue du Protectorat, helmeted and in colored loin cloths; or, without being personal, say his Excellency the Resident Superior of Cambodia in a plaid sarong, riding along the Quai de Verneville with his wife, the latter barefoot and resplendent in a red *sampot*. The effect upon the intelligence, after all, is not a feeling of impropriety, but a faltering in the steadfast belief that we are the Superior Race.

The traveler who regards the Far East as an adventure rather than a necessity of living is either self-conscious in a rickshaw or suddenly aware of his capabilities for extravagant escapade. I am among the latter. I refuse, and have refused from the beginning, to take a rickshaw seriously. Invariably it gives me the feeling of preposterous unreality. Even the fact of a coolie with charging muscles and sweaty skin cannot take away the conviction that I am being borne into adventure at least emotional if not physical.

Having rested, I set out in a rickshaw, with no particular destination or responsibility of purpose.

It was the hour of the promenade. Moths were swooping in the dusk, and the river, seen between the palms, might have been a stream of smoky amber. Stout, ruddy Frenchmen, looking aware of their newly starched clothes, were taking their usual afternoon ride, some in rickshaws or carriages, others in lean little roadsters imported from France; and with them were women, sallow but very alert, evidently determined to support the myth of traditional vivacity among the French even in this sun-scorched colony. Natives moved by on foot, poised and graceful, their curious glances seeming to express surprise that women should try so strenuously to attract the inevitable male, or expressing nothing at all.

On one side of the road were arcades of shops, all bearing signs in French and Cambodian; and on the sidewalk in front of the two hotels were tables filled with chattering Frenchmen. On the other, half-naked brown people passed soundlessly in stealthy flashes of color, all seeming to blend softly in the amber-tinged twilight that floated over moored craft and river.

"Pnom Penh, the town, flows about a gaunt pagoda standing on a hill above it."
Harry's personal photo above compares favorably with the postcard below.

1608. CAMBODGE-PHNOM-PENH
Pont des Nagas (Serpents polycéphales)

"Toward the museum I rode, through a swarm of people that made the late afternoon throb with color."

Pnom Penh, the town, flows about a gaunt pagoda standing on a hill above it. The houses of French and natives, the shops and bazaars, the palaces, all are sunk in foliage, with only the gilded spires of the royal enclosure, the tilting roofs of temples and the cone of the pagoda lifted out of the inundating green. Southward from the residency the main road follows the river-front past the hotels, across a canal into the native town and thence through dust and smells to the flushed walls behind which dwells his Majesty Pra Bat Samdach Pra Sisowath, a king who is a gesture of the autocratic past permitted by the magnanimous present.

Toward the museum I rode, through a swarm of people that made the late afternoon throb with color. Chinese in white suits and helmets, Annamites with bare torsos and full black trousers, and among them surprisingly few Cambodians. They are the Greeks of the Golden Chersonese, these Cambodians; they have a slim classic strength, and their profiles are like the heads on old copper coins. From an esthetic standpoint, the women are less acceptable than the men because they are more addicted to betel-chewing. It is something of a shock when a bronze goddess suddenly smiles and reveals

"Behold this *congai*—a most enchanting remainder of the Khmer civilization."

a mouth betel-stained, like a bloody gash in her smooth brown face. It causes one to reflect that undoubtedly the splendid Khmers, from whom the Cambodians are reputed to have descended, had the same habit and spat red juice all over the temples of Angkor.

But the absence of many Cambodians in the bazaars of Pnom Penh is not surprising when one considers that they are a delightfully lazy people and their competitors are the Chinese and the Annamites, both of whom are mentally lithe and alert. A Cambodian is satisfied with a bowl of rice, a flower over his ear, and a few chansons from some indolent lady.

Now and then in the shops I caught glimpses of small gilded statues that invited me to stop. They were Siamese Buddhas, barbaric little images, winged and splendorously robed, seated on tiered bases and wearing helmets that tapered into spires like those of the dancers. Twice I paused to price them, but each time the shopkeeper, evidently not caring whether I bought or not, refused what I considered a very fair offer. Had they been Chinese instead of Cambodians there would have been fifteen or twenty minutes of bargaining, with the possible result that I should have ridden off with a god under my arm; but these fellows merely smiled negatively, and watched my departure with the passive indifference of a people whose heritage is culture rather than trade.

A third time my fancy challenged me to stop, and this was at a stall near the palace, facing a salmon-pink wall behind which palms and the upturned eaves of a monastery rose. How could I know it was the blind goddess Chance and not an inanimate little Cambodian god that arrested me? Certainly it was a little god of silver that brought me out of the rickshaw, but that was only a snare; for in the shop, in the midst of other silver gods, was that charming companion of Saigon the Tired Cavalier.

And what was I doing in Pnom Penh, he demanded, tipping his helmet in a manner graciously French; he had thought me still at Angkor.

And what was he doing away from Saigon, I questioned; and in the shop of the silver gods?

Did I not recall that I said I desired a Buddha? Well, he lied pleasantly, he was at the point of buying one for me the very moment I entered. Business had brought him to Pnom Penh.

The king's royal barge.

"The next day the Tired Cavalier and I went to the palace."

The boat was starting up the Mé-Kong Saturday, I explained, and as I was to go with it, I had returned from Angkor a little earlier to see a performance of the king's ballet.

"The boat?" he repeated vaguely. Merciful God, I wasn't going up the Mé-Kong, was I? And to Laos?

The climate was terrible in Laos, and there was no good liquor within a thousand kilometers; it was a barbarous place. Why, in Indo-China, one never thought of going to Laos unless he was sent; it was the sort of place one read about after some writer had been foolish enough to go there.

Didn't he remember, I inquired somewhat annoyed, that I was very earnestly searching for ruins up near the Siamese border, and that I was trying to learn something about the Khmer civilization?

Well, yes, he believed he did remember now; but had he thought about it recently he would have assumed that by now I had forgotten those ruins. It was too hot to remember ruins; and it was too hot to seek anything earnestly except the nearest cafe.

"You Americans!" he sighed. "Always looking for dead cities! Now we French know about these places, but we never hunt them—unless there's some profit in the venture or the government sends us. The difference is that you are adventurers and we are colonizers."

And then it became evident why the Tired Cavalier was in the shop. There was a rustle of silk in the rear, and a young woman entered quietly and sat down on the raised portion of the floor where workmen were silvering numerous metal Buddhas. Not the least disconcerted, although he was aware that I looked at him with suspicion, he gestured toward the woman and said:

"Behold this *congai*—a most enchanting remainder of the Khmer civilization."

But she was more than enchanting. There was in her pose a certain proud humility, and she sat there giving us a long, luxurious stare, half insolent and half curious. With the silver Buddhas all about her, she might have been some priestess of the Khmers, perhaps one of the divine *Apsarases*, gazing with outward indifference and inward contemplation at two bleached representatives of a strange and savage race. She looked at me as though I were destined for sacrifice, and indeed I suspected I was, when a moment later she spoke softly in Cambodian to the man with whom I was bargaining for a Buddha. My suspicions were borne out when he proved obstinate. But the Tired Cavalier, exerting some mysterious influence, got it for me for half the original amount.

As we left the shop the divine *Apsaras* followed us with a proprietorial gaze, then snatched the money from the dealer and sat down to count it.

What was I doing that evening, the Tired Cavalier inquired as I got into my rickshaw. He had an engagement until nine o'clock, but if I could meet him at the Cafe Khmer a little later, we could talk, accelerated by a series of rainbow-cocktails....

When I returned to the hotel, the weekly afternoon *dansant* was at its languid height, and the rhythm of a French jazz orchestra stumbled out into the darkness where bewildered natives had paused to listen; while inside, the socially eligible of Pnom Penh were perspiring and simulating what they chose to call *la vie parisienne*.

# 2

Shortly after nine o'clock I found my way to the Cafe Khmer.

He was seated at a table alone, that Tired Cavalier, and before him were two empty glasses. All about him other Frenchmen were unconsciously drinking and consciously being jovial. Among them darted the Annamite serving-boys, silent, barefoot, and in deadly earnest.

Well, was I still determined to visit those ruins, he asked pleasantly. If I was, I should find excellent *épiceries* in Pnom Penh from which to buy caviar, cognac and other things necessary to resist the climate of Laos....

I said, in the course of conversation, that I was to see the Cambodian ballet the next day. A special performance was being given for some visiting Siamese officials.

Ah, fortunate person! he exclaimed. And perhaps he would go with me, if I would invite him. He had never seen the ballet, although he had been through the palace a thousand times, and knew all about the dancing-girls.

"A custom fast dying out," he mourned. "In the time of Norodom there were over two hundred girls in the ballet, but now Sisowath has only about forty. He is a modern, Sisowath; he sacrifices the esthetic for pleasures of the palate.... They say he smokes about seventy pipes of opium a day. And he is over eighty, you know....

With the appearance of a rainbow-cocktail, he became expansive about the ballet.

"From the time of Angkor down to King Norodom it was a religious institution," he said, "but now it is only a pretense of keeping up an old tradition. Another king, and there will be no more Cambodian ballet. Norodom was the very devil on rules. In his time, when a girl was chosen she never left the palace except once a year to visit her parents, and then she had to leave at sunrise and return by dark. On this visit no one dared to speak to her except her family, and old Norodom sent some hag or eunuch along to make sure of it. I believe he did allow the girl's family to come to the palace frequently, but they couldn't talk with her, only look. She stayed there until she died—unless Norodom got tired of her, or she was original enough to form some liaison of her own choosing. Now things are different. Sisowath has extended the yearly leave of the dancers several days; and I suspect those little wenches make up for the opportunities the older ones missed."

I announced I was planning a paper on the Cambodian dancers, and although I knew little about them except that they were strictly segregated, I was determined to call it "The Palace of Stolen Lives"; and so, I informed him, it was up to him to give me some material suited to the title.

"The life of a dancer," he mused. "Saramani...." Then he smiled at me, half reflectively and half in anticipation of what he was about to say. "Of course you remember the *congai* you saw in the shop this afternoon? That's her name, Saramani. God knows where she got it; perhaps some old Khmer ancestor had it, and one of her descendants found it somehow a thousand years later. Saramani, dancer of the Khmers. Enchanting, is it not? Of course, she isn't a dancer. But suppose she were. Suppose when she was a little girl six years old her parents had given her to the king, suppose....

"Listen, I think I have a story. It is the life of the dancer, a life part romance and the rest ugly reality. I shall call this story '*Saramani, Danseuse Cambodgienne*'; you may call it what you like....

"Saramani, she is a child of six—in the village of Kampong Thom, we shall say. As a child she is white, white as the white lilacs that bloom every spring in the town in France where I live. Suddenly a great honor is given her, an

"She has been designated as a gift to the king, she will dance in the royal ballet."

"But there is not dancing every night,
and soon Saramani learns that life in the palace is very dull."

ironic honor. She has been designated as a gift to the king, she will dance in the royal ballet, and thereafter a genie will protect her family. And so on the day set, her hair is scented with jasmine, and she is taken in a bullock-cart to Pnom Penh, and to the palace.

"One of the court chamberlains receives her, appraises her, and finally she is taken into the presence of the king, who sends her family three hundred piasters and many *sampots* and scarfs. Saramani is not old enough to know, but in a few years she will realize she brought a very good price. Sometimes the king pays as low as thirty piasters for a girl, or as high as five hundred. After that she bids her family farewell, and they give her the *sampots* and scarves which the king has given them. Saramani has become another shadow in your 'Palace of Stolen Lives.'

"Very soon she begins her education as a *danseuse*. Every day she must practice from eight to eleven and from two to five under some *baya* who is too old to be in the ballet but still young enough to teach. The technique of the dance in Cambodia is something more than merely learning gestures. To do it a woman must be double-jointed, or better still, have no joints at all. Hyperextension exists naturally among yellow women, you know. But that is not enough. The dancer must have certain joints broken, and she must sit for hours making circular motions to train her muscles. It is also part of her training to crack her fingers daily. Fancy that.

"In the hall where they are taught, these little creatures sit in groups, twisting their arms for each other, so that the bone at the elbow makes a greater cavity than naturally. After a while the articulation of the joints is amazing; wait until you see the performance tomorrow. Also the ligaments and tendons are stretched—greater levity, you know. It is not a matter of months, this training, but of years. When Saramani has mastered the basic technique in one gesture, in other words when she can bend her fingers over her hand, and her hand over her arm, then she may begin to train for an actual part in the ballet.

"She learns the gestures and attitudes. These gestures are always the same, the gift-offering, prayer and worship, and they have been passed on from generation to generation. The dancer herself never knows where these gestures originated or why she does them, she simply says they are done because they are beautiful. Finally, when she has become a finished *danseuse*, Saramani makes her first appearance in the ballet.

Jeune Danseuse Cambodgienne

"She is to be a god, so she wears a *mokot*...a head-dress shaped like the cone of a pagoda."

"She is to be a god, so she wears a *mokot*. A *mokot* is a head-dress shaped like the cone of a pagoda—*prachedee* is the Siamese word for it—and generally made of leather laid over with gold-leaf and ornamented with bits of mirrors so it will shine brilliantly as she dances. Her *sampot*—that is the long silk affair which she binds about her loins with the effect of a sarong drawn up in the center— is of purple and gold; and her jacket is gold-cloth and sewed tight to her arms and body. They never hook or button their costumes on, they are always sewed. In fact she has so much to do, this Saramani, that although the dance does not begin until eight o'clock in the evening, she begins dressing at midday.

"The preparation of her make-up is very elaborate. First she dilutes saffron in coconut oil, and when she has applied this as a base, she mixes some carbonate of lead with water, and makes her face and neck dazzlingly white. After that she melts some black substance on a piece of bamboo soaked in oil—this for the eyebrows. And to color her lips she uses a piece of red Chinese paper. Now Saramani is ready for the dance. She salutes her head-dress, pads it with a scented handkerchief, and after a final look at herself, goes to the *salle de danse*.

"It is a thrilling beginning. But there is not dancing every night, and soon Saramani learns that life in the palace is very dull. She begins to think of her village, of the river where every afternoon the girls bathe; of the market-place where the young men gather to laugh and sing. Her own life, what is it? She is busy much of the time taking care of her costumes—if she doesn't she will be beaten or made to pay part of her little allowance, which is worse—and is that interesting to a woman? True, she has her own apartment in a rather nice pinkish dwelling—but it is in an enclosed court. And what woman likes that?

"Of course she has many things she would not have in her own village—in the cupboard are sandal, perfumes, coconut-oil, and white powder for her face—in the chest, a looking-glass, fans, slippers, scarves and *sampots*. But a woman must have something more than inanimate possessions. And her days—how dreary! The only two events are the meals which are brought at ten and six. Sometimes women come with things to sell, and then she buys such delicacies as bananas dried with vanilla, lotus-seeds or guava-jelly in banana leaves. And she may receive friends—so long as they are of her own sex. The minister of the palace is the only man permitted to go into the dancers' quarters. And the

"Now when she dances in the ballet she wears more than thirty necklaces, each different; her belt is of gold-mesh with a clasp of diamonds."

"Grotesque masks glittered above sheening costumes. One was a boar with red eyebrows; another Garuda, the celestial bird and mount of Vishnu."

minister of the palace happens to be an elderly person.... So Saramani begins to dream of stealing out of the enclosure on dark nights, or simply peeping over the wall to see the young men pass in the road. But she does not dare....

"On certain days it is her duty to attend the king; she fills his opium pipe or sings for him. And suddenly ambition stirs in Saramani. Thereafter when she hands him his pipe she lets her fingers linger caressingly for just a moment, and into her singing creeps a warm, husky softness.... And so a year passes, and Saramani becomes the *lokhon*, that is to say the king's favorite.

"No longer does she live with the other women, but she has a separate house. She wears a *mokot* of pure gold; and she has many jewels. Now when she dances in the ballet she wears more than thirty necklaces, each different; her belt is of gold-mesh with a clasp of diamonds. On each finger she wears a ring, one with an emerald, one with a ruby, another with a sapphire, and one—on the small finger—inset with diamonds. Her earrings are diamonds, too; and she wears two bangles and five kinds of bracelets.

"Yes, it is all very splendid. But soon, as after her first appearance in the ballet, it begins to tarnish.... She looks ahead and sees the end. She will become a *baya*, an old woman, supplanted by some younger girl; there will be the same hot, dull days, without even the prospect of dancing to enliven them, only teaching; and finally, very aged and very wrinkled, she will call for her *mokot* for a last time and burn candles before it, and then everything will be ended...."

As he finished he called for a "boy" and ordered more cocktails.

And that, I said, was the end of Saramani, dancer of the Khmers?

He shook his head. "It would be that way in life. But this, you remember, is a story. ... I said she looked ahead and saw the end. And it frightened her. Again she began to dream of her village, of the young men.... So one night she stole out of the enclosure, out of the palace. She walked the streets, watching the lights and the young men, listening to the sounds, the music from the Chinese restaurants. That was the first time....

"The next time one of the young men spoke to her.... And after that, when she filled the king's pipe and sang to him, he noticed that she was lovelier than ever, that she looked younger. And then, one night soon afterward, another dancer came to him and whispered something into his ear, and then he knew

Harry's personal photos of the royal elephants and, below, the Silver Pagoda.

why Saramani seemed lovelier and younger.... She was beaten and turned out of the palace. It was a great disgrace; she could never return to her people. But what of that? said Saramani. She could live.... And so," he concluded with a smile, "she went to live in a shop where they made silver Buddhas. And that, my friend, is the story of Saramani, *danseuse cambodgienne*."[11]

# 3

The next day the Tired Cavalier and I went to the palace.

Outside the main gate a number of Buddhist monks moved by solemnly in the road, draped in robes of saffron and orange; inside, a guard of his Majesty's soldiers lounged about the sentry-box and spat betel-juice in the dust. The sunlight poured down vertically, with a lucid quality that gave every object and figure the effect of being utterly distinct and separate.

At first glance the palace disclosed itself as a walled enclosure containing several large buildings and pavilions, all with upturned horned eaves, and decorated with gilt and colored tiles. Around the courtyard was a colonnade of stalls, evidently where elephants and horses were kept, a few tall palms drowsed in the heat; there was little else that was green. In the brilliant sunshine the colors seemed done in italics. From the pale dust of the garden rose glaring white and yellow walls supporting roofs of amber color, and all surmounted by irregular tapering cones that seemed to rear up from behind crenellated ramparts. It was theatrical and a bit worn—like some flamboyant and middle-aged actress determined to impersonate royalty.

Of all the buildings in sight there was but one that was gracious and stately, the Throne Hall. Before it a broad stone terrace rose between balustrades formed by the bodies of *Naga*, the seven-headed cobra; and slender columns, framing doors with tiara-shaped carvings above them, ascended to a first roof, which after the Cambodian fashion slanted upward and then broke, to rise steeply to the horned ridge. At the angles of the roof were upturned points, and gold fretting gleamed beneath the eaves. Two spired pinnacles, rising from behind the hall itself, gave height and poise to the building.

---

11 In fact, Hervey based this entire chapter on *Saramani, Danseuse Khmère*, an epic French novel by Roland Théodore Emile Meyer (see photo p. 44), published in Saigon in 1919. Meyer's 185,000 word work offers a sweeping view of Cambodian history, geography, flora, fauna and culture revolving around the royal dancer Saramani and her family. While Meyer presented his book as fiction most of its content is historically accurate. DatAsia Press is finalizing the first English translation of the unabridged book. Read more about *Saramani* and Cambodian dance at www.Devata.org.

The Throne Hall.

The *Salle de danse*.

At the gate a young Cambodian official joined us—one of the princes, the Tired Cavalier informed me, adding that the king had so many sons, each with a claim upon the throne, that when the matter of succession came up before the resident superior, who very definitely influenced such affairs, he would have a devil of a task.

Accompanied by the young prince we made an elaborate gesture of seeing the palace. It was a gesture because, like all visits to all palaces, there was something futile and annoying about the fact of being guided around without the privilege to wander or linger at will. In the first place, a palace, while a species of architecture, is not regarded as that by all, and has no business to be thrust under the vulgar and professional scrutiny that a Tour of Inspection requires. In the second place, it makes Tourists out of People; individuals who come with the perfectly sane purpose of seeing nothing definite and much that is indefinite, and suddenly find themselves being paraded gaudily about an Interesting Edifice. And, anyway, the regulated inspection of any place sufficiently distinctive to warrant a visit is a vain display of that form of human frailty called curiosity.

And so... I saw the relics of a dead king and the throne room of a living one; I saw the sword which a god gave to a man; I saw the *salle de danse* and the *salle des fetes*. I walked through dim, musty rooms where golden things kindled softly; I stood in front of jeweled gods and marveled audibly. And then a liveried "janissary" called the Cambodian prince away, and the Tired Cavalier and I, left alone, passed from the court of the Throne Hall into the court of the Silver Pagoda, and ceased to be tourists.

All around a paved enclosure were cloistered galleries, vivid with mural decorations depicting parts of the Hindu epic, and in the center, flanked by golden tombs that aspired to reach the sun, stood a dazzlingly pure temple. It was the Silver Pagoda. A roof of burnt orange, tipped with those twisted golden horns, seemed to tongue the sky.

It was amazing, set there against the cobalt zenith; and we walked about, the Tired Cavalier and I, gazing at it from all sides. The tombs were bewildering piles, gilded and inset with particles of broken glass that glittered violently. They were more fascinating because we were not told whose bodies occupied them, but could believe, if we wished, they were entirely empty, or that in one lay the spiced body of a young king and in the other his consort, her cold limbs kissed by rotting silks.

The tomb of King Norodom in the Royal Palace.

An old guardian unlocked the iron gates of the pagoda for us, and we moved up the glaring steps into dusk that was confusing after the sunlight. Gradually I became aware of a floor of metal, of lead I thought until I grasped the incredible fact that it was silver. But that was the least spectacular of the pagoda's treasures. On the altar, surrounded by a wilderness of things gold and silver, was a god of clear green jade; and beneath it were numerous other images of all sizes, many of pure gold and smoldering with diamonds; all seeming to leap into one savage flare that left me dizzy and intemperate.

I stood there dumbly until the young prince returned to tell us the dance was about to start.

Back to the court of the Throne Hall we went. The guests were arriving, all in motorcars, and a line of native soldiers drawn up beside the gate flashed their rifles impressively. Already a crowd had gathered in the *salle de danse*— court officials and attendants of the palace. The guests were Siamese, some uniformed and some wearing European clothes, accompanied by a number of French officers immaculate in khaki.

The party was met by royal functionaries, who escorted it to a place of honor in one end of the pavilion. At the other end a thin partition stretched across the entire breadth. It was from behind this partition that the dancers would appear. All around the hall rose tiers of brown faces, their features made dim by the bright sunlight which shone behind them. I looked for the king, but he was not there; the Tired Cavalier explained that he was ill.

A place was assigned to us near the Siamese Mission; and I waited, feeling the anticipation that ran through the many watchers.

The music, rising from primitive xylophones, drums and gongs, commenced a low, rhythmic throbbing, which seemed to swell stealthily until without warning it filled the pavilion with a delirium of sound.

It was an episode from the Ramayana we should see, the young prince announced. We could distinguish between those who represented women and those who were impersonating men, for the former wore head-dresses that came down about their faces in the shape of an inverted crescent. The *mokot* was the helmet of a god, a king or a prince; the *panntiereth*, shaped like a crown, was that of an officer; and the head-dresses of favorite servants were truncated cones surmounted by tiny wings. The young girls wore tiaras....

"The *première danseuse* became a fiery vortex around which they swirled."

Suddenly the music became heraldic, and from the doorway of the partition appeared a tiny ballerina, who darted into the center of the pavilion with the sure, glittering swiftness of a mailed dragonfly. She paused a moment, posturing, her iridescent flanks quivering, then spun about on naked feet that twinkled and flashed. Her face and hands were white with a passionate chastity, and as she danced there was something votive in her detached intensity, as if she offered herself as a living sacrifice. On her shoulders were curling epaulets like spread fins. Her *mokot* was atremble with bits of mirrors and tiny flowers on springs. Limbs and breasts were sheathed in gold cloth, and her *sampot* had a sheen of yellow on it, like pollen on a fuchsia.

Her dance was a thing of twilight and flame, a pantomiming of vague impulses which suddenly twisted into one shivering emotion that was desire unleashed and purified.

A crashing dissonance of music unleashed demons from behind the partition. Grotesque masks glittered above sheening costumes. One was a boar with red eyebrows; another Garuda, the celestial bird and mount of Vishnu. There were other birds less fearsome—dancers mailed in scaly gold and with gilded papier-mâché feathers that curled up flamewise from their loins. Some held lotus-flowers; others carried swords or scepters.

This brilliant army surrounded the premiere danseuse, falling into attitudes that slipped easily into gestures more incredible as joints moved without articulation and trained muscles drew the limbs into amazing postures.

The music was a brazen epic. It clamored for blood; and the dancers seemed to answer with savage abandon. The *première danseuse* became a fiery vortex around which they swirled.

And then into the center of the floor sprang Hanuman, the monkey god, white-faced and terrible. Behind him loomed the green mask of Brahma, the black head of Ngos, both standing out in dreadful relief against the faces of the simian host that surged in the wake of Hanuman.

It was the moment of rescue: Sita, the heavenly princess, was about to be saved from the Asuras.

Whirl of masks and white faces; whirl of crowns and helmets; whirl of limbs and spinning toes; all rising in a greater whirl that was the genius of a people; rising, rising higher into sexless madness, an offering divine and super-civilized, beyond the limitations of cold intellect, beyond the restrictions of reasoned formulae.

And then, suddenly, the center of the floor was empty of figures. But the air still shook and seemed animated, like a body newly dead.... "Another king, and there will be no more Cambodian ballet...."

For some reason I remembered then a great mass-meeting I had seen in China not long before. Yellow faces upturned in the rain, raised to a voice that poured out syllables unintelligible to me; but something in the compact welding of hot, soaked bodies that touched me terrifically. And I remembered also a book I had read long before that, a book by an Anglo-Saxon who so far forgot himself as to find a fleeting and illusive quality—an emotional superiority—in darker men.... This Cambodian ballet, I felt, was more than a vain gesture of the past. Undoubtedly, its beginning was a tribute of a king to himself. But, paradoxically, it had become a tribute to the people. It was their soul. Curiously, that soul now was in the hands of the ruler—who might take it into history with himself. But surely France, the Protectress, could "influence" the new monarch, who would be a monarch only at her sanction, to keep that soul alive....

The Siamese Mission had left the pavilion, and its members were getting into the motorcars. I wondered what they thought, these quiet yellow people who belong to a nation that once was the mistress of Cambodia. Ahead of them, a car filled with French officers had started. As it shot through the gate the soldiers lifted their rifles in salute.... Behind the car a whirl of dust rose giddily.

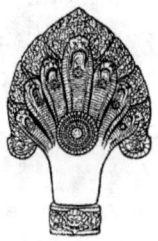

## Chapter IV
# Green Serenade
### *Tells of Profane Beauty*

PNOM-PENH — *Vapeur des Messageries Fluviales; embarquement des bœufs*

"The boat?' he repeated vaguely. Merciful God, I wasn't going up the Mé-Kong, was I? And to Laos?"

1681. CAMBODGE — Kompong-Cham - Résidence    P. Dieulefils, - Hanoi

"Toward dusk we reached Kampong-Cham."

# Mé-Kong

## 1

IT IS a primitive interlude set to the wild serenade of an Asian river....

Out of mysterious Tibet it flows, the Mé-Kong; down through Indo-China, dividing Siam and Laos, spreading across Cambodia, and soiling the blue sea off Cochin-China. Mé-Kong, Mother of Waters.

Once a year, when the rains swell her stream, her mood is fury. Often men wonder at the irony of a God who exchanges death for birth; and the brown people living along the banks of the Mé-Kong must wonder at this Mother who destroys. ... It was during the rains that I set out from Pnom Penh for Bassac.

That mysterious force which orders events far from mysterious set me off earlier than expected. One of Indo-China's drowsy and disconcerting charms is its abundance of misinformation. I had settled down to the prospect of three days longer in Pnom Penh, having been told the boat left on Saturday, when I was suddenly informed that it departed early Wednesday morning. That was Tuesday afternoon. And with no supplies bought and a quarter of an hour before the bank closed!

But for the help of that charming friend the Tired Cavalier I should not have been standing on the deck of the *Bassac*, in the midst of luggage, tinned goods, crates of bottles and other supplies, when she moved off the next morning.... On the bank, a sudden flame as pagoda spires caught the sunlight;

a glimpse of flushed palace walls; masts rising from a shambles of sampans; and then Pnom Penh astern, folded in green.

There was something epic in the breadth of the stream. It flowed out of the blue-hot sky, settling down into a thick, flat current. Even where the wild swamp-grass grew down to the water, mingling its green with the shadows close to shore, the river did not entirely lose its copperish sheen.

Several craft drifted by, manned by Cambodians who stared at the passing river boat. Their naked bodies seemed bas-relief figures upon the tawny background of the river. Brown river, brown banks, brown people: it was a heroic song exalting the color of a country.

Crowded together aft and separated from the cabin passengers by a railing were many natives. Some wore jackets of brilliant pink, of yellow and other raw colors; and some wore long, full trousers that flopped around their ankles. The less sophisticated among the men were content with only wide drawers, while the women satisfied their sense of propriety with a draped skirt and a scarf.

Their meals had just been served by a deck-boy. The poorer could not afford ship's fare, but had to wait until the boat made a stop, there to buy from the venders who would crowd the landing. Among those eating were a few Chinese, and they used chop-sticks, as did the Annamites; but the Cambodians ate with wooden spoons. The food was rice cooked with red peppers and bits of meat or fish. Most of them were talking, and their strident voices blended into a lazy monotone consistent with the heat. By the aft rail a little boy was playing on a long reed instrument that made quavering music.

Forward, the Scandinavian-looking captain stared at the river. I moved up beside him. There were more cabin passengers than usual, he said. The director of the Messageries Fluviales was among them; and the commandant of aviation and his aide; a priest; a merchant; an engineer of navigation; a mining-engineer; the administrator of the district of Ta-Keo; and a fat woman from Pakse. She was the only one going beyond Khone....

In a sprawling chair under the canvas I drowsed and watched the river. The noonday seemed to linger, as though succumbing to its own heat; on the stream, still the lazy pirogues. Once a lonely junk drifted by with swooning canvas. Palms and banana-plants sprang up with amazing luxuriance from the mud banks, and among them were a few native huts, pole-raised and inhabited by brown people, who watched our passing without visible emotion.

Toward dusk we reached Kampong-Cham. In the west was a glow of flawless tangerine, and its reflection gave a rich flush to this little outpost. It was larger than the usual Mé-Kong village, built beside an indenture in the stream; across the river were great rubber plantations.

A gangplank was flung between steamer and landing stage. Immediately coolies in cone-shaped straw hats began to unload cargo. There were sluicing, squelchy murmurs as the current whirled past, set to a stealthy obbligato as mooring lines lapped and grew taut in the stream. Cries in the soft Cambodian tongue mingled with a torrent of heated French. In the air the smells of ripe fruit, of grain and salted fish.

Worn steps rose from the floating wharf to an embankment fronting the river. Beyond was an arcade of shops. Blue blinds shuttered their windows, and the facades were barbaric with Chinese writing. The light of a few lamps revealed the whitewash peeling from the plaster arches; and mold gave them a soiled, tired look. They had an air of tragic resignation to rain and staring sunlight.

Numbers of native soldiers swung along the road, lean-muscled, indolent fellows, whose natural grace could never be disciplined by military training. With them moved classically built Cambodians; lithe Annamites bare to the waist; and laughing girls, wearing huge turbans or flowers in their hair, and carrying baskets of food against their hips. A group of Frenchmen stood on the landing, jovial and red-faced, all talking excitedly. Not two yards away, natives strode down to the stream, solemnly loosened their sarongs, held them on until the water reached their waists, then removed them and enjoyed an evening plunge.

I became aware of a quality warm and startlingly intimate in the scene. Those figures so alive against the dead whitewash of the shops. Flexing motion of shoulders and hips, the suave play of biceps, the pliant mold of thighs and legs, bare feet caressing the soft earth. This rhythmic movement animated the colors of their garments; colors that grew fluid, as sweat sealed them to heated bodies.

Hot orange, startling purple, lewd magenta. Primitive as the forms that wore them.

People, colors, sounds, smells, all blending into a harmonious whole that possessed a secret which the friendly dusk was trying to translate.

For a moment, as I watched, I experienced a desire that disconcerted and alarmed me.

I wanted to go down from the deck, into the torrid swarm of that roadway, and mingle with them, bare and unashamed.

It was an emotion stark, utterly naked. There could be, I realized, no mistaking its implication. For what could I, one of a race sophisticated and civilized intellectually, have in common with this people, simple and civilized emotionally, except the same basic sensuality?

It was as though a furnace door had been opened.... Suddenly the heat of the night flowed through my veins into the veins of those men and women in the road. All of myself I emptied into them, and they in turn transfused my being into the soil, the river, the very air; into the heart of Indo-China itself.

I wanted to analyze; I could only feel. Indo-China rubbing flanks with me. Indo-China purring in my ear. Whispering something. Something lost to my mind, to all minds consciously concerned with psychology and ethics. Something so very old and uninvolved. Something I wanted desperately to understand.

The boat's whistle screamed savagely. It was like an angry reminder that I belonged to a race which does not tolerate miscegenation of the intelligence. One may be permitted to sleep with a dark lady, that whistle shouted, but it is treason to your blood to try to comprehend her viewpoint. It seemed to accuse me of having been seduced, and not normally. And it made very clear certain of my deficiencies.

In the past I had been much in the East, wandering through city and jungle, across desert and mountain, but always the East itself had been a background. I was the self-conscious writer surveying his scene. Now, on a sudden, this little village by the Mé-Kong had reached out and drawn me to it. Through it I had felt the warm body of the East. My fingers had strayed amorously in the hair of the East. The East was inviting me to bed with it.

I was definitely disturbed by this suggestion of assignation.

## 2

That night I met Gilbert Filleau de Saint-Hilaire.[12]

He appeared at dinner resplendent in a newly starched suit, and wearing a broad scarf unchallengeably Parisian. He was rather stout and short; his mustache well trimmed. He had what might be called an air. Those who have this "air" may possess no other distinction, mental or physical, but theirs is the exquisite path in life.

Undoubtedly Gilbert Filleau de Saint-Hilaire had something more than an air. That was evident. The cabin where we ate was directly forward, and numerous huge insects swarmed in, circling around the oil-lamp and planing perilously near the food. But they might not have existed so far as Gilbert Filleau de Saint-Hilaire was concerned. His manner was that of one determined not to be disturbed by the intrusion of insects, even such creatures as these flying mammals. He drank his wine with just the faintest sound of appreciation, as all good Frenchmen do, pausing only to remove straying night-beetles from his glass, and then finished off with cognac, after which he excused himself and passed from my admiring gaze.

Later, I encountered him on deck. He had the cabin next to mine and was attended by a Tonkinese "boy," whose air of sharing the superior confidence of his master made my own Chinese servant seem a low form of menial life.

"Yes, I know all about you," was his first remark, in excellent English. "You are an American, you write books, and you are trying to find some ruins up in Laos."

It was rather annoying to have such a magnificent person as Gilbert Filleau de Saint-Hilaire tell you all about yourself before you had a chance even hurriedly to assemble your own estimate in spoken words.

"Well," he said in the next breath, "so long as you don't come over in my district and find any ruins; I have enough to do without writing more reports to be laid away in the archives at Hanoi."

---

[12] Hervey's original text spells the name with two extra letters: Filleau de Saint[e] Hil[l]aire. In fact, the 1904 *Annuaire illustré du Cambodge* (p. 306) lists Gilbert Filleau de Saint-Hilaire with a 3rd class rank as *gérant de caisse* (credit manager) in Thpong Province (just west of Phnom Penh). In 1920, St. Hilaire published a paper about sapphire mining in Pailin Province from 1915-1918. Another record lists one Jean Marcel Filleau de Saint-Hilaire, born in Pondicherry, India on May 6, 1888, who died in Phnom Penh on August 8, 1925 at the age of 37. Which man Hervey met is a mystery.

Then we talked about the commerce of the country. I was not interested, nor was he. But Frenchmen have an idea that strangers want to know all about the industrial development of Indo-China.

"I suppose you write books on economics?" he demanded suddenly.

I hastily defended myself by saying he was very complimentary but I wrote novels.

"Ah, novels!" And by his tone I understood I had won the confidence of Gilbert Filleau de Saint-Hilaire. "And I like poetry, too," he added, very wistfully; then murmured, "Lamartine and Daudet, Gautier, Loti, Baudelaire and Anatole France. Their names are like poetry, eh? Yes, I read a lot where I live. I'm going back there now. The coast for two months—it made me sick. Saigon, its cafes and bad music: it is nothing. I had to leave my village—I am the Administrator of Ta-Keo. *Fièvre de bois.* I was very ill. But now I return. From Stung Treng I ride three days on an elephant—or in a bullock-cart. It depends on how I feel."

Then I asked him about the natives. One always asks about the natives in a Far Eastern country. And the French usually present an interesting viewpoint, quite unlike the stereotyped opinion of the British in India.

"Likable people," he replied with the air of one who knew. Indeed, the very positiveness of this gentleman of the jungle was one of his charms; he believed what he was saying whether you did or not. "'*Les petits frères*', the government calls them; and on the piaster note we have a delicately colored engraving of France, the Mother, with her arms protectively about two natives. But that is too—gauche. We reach the natives not by stupid sentimentality or lying but by two things—the men through the military; they love uniforms—and the women through—well, shall we say affection? ... In Saigon—all along the coast—the natives are spoiled. But I suppose it is not their fault.

"Now in the interior it is different. Particularly along the Mé-Kong. You will like the Laotians—they are more like your Hawaiians; I have been in Honolulu once. They have not yet been rewarded with the white man's uplifting altruism. Singing, dancing, music of the *khène*; a gay, simple people. Sometimes I think it is the influence of the river. A great river, *la Mère Mé-Kong*. Gentle and with no complexities—yet capable of terrible things. Elemental, that is the word. And the natives are like that. Consider their history, the wars, the disasters —yet always an underlying simplicity.

They are born simply, they die simply. Things are inevitable. Strange how it gets into everything here, the river—something inevitable about it too. At one time of the year there are floods, in another season the stream is almost dry in places; these things are inevitable. And these ruins you are hunting. Someone told you about them; perhaps he spoke truly, perhaps he lied; whichever he did it was inevitable. Because here you are, whether a lie brought you or the truth. Perhaps many people have seen these ruins—I myself have heard of them vaguely though I know no one who has seen them—perhaps no one has. And if you do not see them, someone will sometime. It is inevitable. You, the individual who is seeking them, and I, the individual who cares not a *sou* whether they exist or not so long as they are not in my district—we do not count in the inevitable scheme of things."

And then he said abruptly: "You are going to Bassac. Good. I shall give you a letter to the governor; he is a Siamese."

For a few minutes we were content to sit in silence, staring at the river. From out of the shadowy mass of natives aft came the mournful treble of a woman's voice.

*"Amelia seek kdey*
*ti somienh nhoeuy*
*pum luo pras chenh*
*oeu oeuy pi o oeuy ra...."*

"A Cambodian *chanson*," the Frenchman volunteered. "Haunting music. Like the river. The name of that song is 'Si Nuon.' It says, 'Forget this affair, O my friend. It is but a little flutter of my heart.' Or something like that. It is typical of the Cambodians. Nothing very profound or lasting with them. Not even their religion."

Did he mean, I probed, that they were not extremely superstitious about occult things?

"Oh yes! But they don't take it too seriously—like the East Indian for instance."

And, I continued with design, if a white man stole a ruby out of an idol's eye—or, say, the idol itself—they wouldn't track him over the world and when they caught him murder him in some exquisitely torturous manner— as in books?

He chuckled—reminiscently. "You are not considering any such rash thing, are you?"

Then I confessed I had a desire, suppressed so far, to steal a Buddha for my collection of gods. The adventure, the excitement . . ,

"I stole a Buddha once," he interrupted. "Up in Laos —near Nong Khai."

I settled more comfortably in my chair to listen.

"I must have read a book about someone who did that," he said; "anyway, I had the inspiration. I used to spend a month up there every year. I like the country. Once walking through the forest I found a pagoda I had not seen before, and a monastery. The Buddha was in that pagoda. It was a very fine one, too, very rare—Buddha preaching. I wanted it badly—I too collect gods—and I knew it was useless to try to buy it. Sometimes you can do it, if you have a native go about it for you; never yourself. But that would have been too tedious. And I wanted to steal it—as you said, the adventure, the excitement....

"The plan was very simple. I would go back the next night after dark and take it. They never lock the pagodas. The only difficulty was the possibility that they might be praying at the shrine.

"Well, the next night I went back. It was a night for the devil; it had been raining. The mud was up to my ankles. I could not use my flash-light all the time, and there were no stars, so I ran into trees and tore my clothes and bruised myself. Finally I got near the place. The monastery—very close to the pagoda—was dark. I crept up, just as they do in books. Of course the pagoda was open. It was easy. I felt my way in, then, for an instant, used the light. I made one mistake, a grave one. As I started to leave I had—well, I suppose I might call it an Anglo-Saxon pricking of the conscience. So, fool that I was, I crept back and put a ten-piaster note on the altar.

"Yes, it was a great mistake. The next morning I left the village where I had been staying. I had a devilish time keeping the natives from seeing the thing; it was about two feet high. My Tonkinese boy—the same one I have now—wrapped it in my soiled clothes and packed it in my bag. The coolie who carried it did not like the weight, but finally it was deposited in the pirogue, and we started off.

"I suppose I should have felt frightened all day; instead I forgot about it. The river always enchants me. That night we were moored near a village, and perhaps I did feel nervous when some bonzes came down and examined me with customary curiosity.

"The next day it happened. ... I had stopped for an hour or two of shooting, and as usual I took Nguyen, the Tonkinese boy, to carry my gun. When we returned there was great excitement in the pirogue. The head boatman was talking with a young bonze, who seemed determined to go under the thatch where I kept my baggage. I must say I felt not—*comfortable*. But I intended to have no foolishness. That is the way to deal with natives when they are unpleasant—a bold front, the grand manner.

"And so I walked up, looking very angry, and demanded to know what the devil he was doing in my pirogue. He was a sullen-faced fellow, that bonze. I remember him very well; one of the veins had broken in his right eye. I could not speak Laotian then, so Nguyen was my interpreter. I told him to ask the bonze what he wanted. Nguyen replied with a scared look that the priest said I had stolen a Buddha from his pagoda and left a ten-piaster note on the altar. As proof he produced a ten-piaster note from his belt."

Gilbert Filleau de Saint-Hilaire paused, and I wished it were light that I might see if there were any scars visible on his person.

"That eye with the broken vein," he said, "seemed bloodier than ever as he talked. At least I thought so. He delivered himself at length, and angrily. Nguyen said the fellow claimed I had violated the sanctity of his pagoda, and a lot of other nonsense. Yes, I answered, I had taken the Buddha, violated the sanctity of his shrine, and all that. But I had paid for the image—and what was he going to do about it anyway? Nguyen looked uneasier than ever as he translated my speech. Then, after the bonze had spoken, he turned to me with a queer expression and said—Well, what do you think he said, you *romancer*?"

I replied that I could think of a lot of things he might have said; but the only thing I was certain about was that Monsieur de Saint-Hilaire at least had an eloquent trophy on his person in the form of a scar or even the ghost of a scar.

He chuckled, that reminiscent chuckle.

"You, monsieur, are a *romancer*; life is a *farceur*.... He said, 'Master, he wants twenty piasters more. ...'"

Then Gilbert Filleau de Saint-Hilaire stretched and yawned; and it was just the proper effect.

"Well, finally," he finished, "I gave him ten piasters, half of what he asked, and he went off with his right eye looking redder than ever because he had not received the whole amount...."

After that we sat in silence for a while, I disturbed by a feeling that adventure was more realistic than life, and he quiet about it all. Overhead the sparks from the smoke-stack made a trail of vanishing stars among the other stars. Suddenly the Frenchman sat up and shouted, "Nguyen!" A moment later there came an answer of *"Oui, monsieur!"* followed by the appearance of the boy himself.

"Well, I go to sleep," announced Gilbert Filleau de Saint-Hilaire. "And before I forget, if you have a copy of one of your novels, I should appreciate it to read on the elephant from Stung Treng to my village.... Good night."

# 3

The next morning the sky was gray, rain-sogged. Beneath it the Mé-Kong was a sickly chocolate hue, stirred to dirty foam where the current rushed past half-submerged trees. The scenery had taken on a wilder look. On the banks were a few ramshackle native huts, like discarded kindling in the torrent of vines and bushes. Narrow streams crept inland, some so shallow one could see the black roots of trees writhing in their mud beds. These dark waterways groped into high grass and pendulous foliage. Soon it commenced to rain.

Growing in the water were trees bound together by naked, roping vines and long clusters of leaves like feather boas. Beyond them, fragile green valences touched the current, plumed by bushes that seemed to rear up and burst in gossamer tatters. Over all, the hazy fountains of the bamboo.... What splendor, a tropical forest! And how much more splendorous seen in the rain! The moist, soft sheen of the trees seems to dissolve in the fume of the shower with an effect of tremulous green, strange and lovely as the haunting twilights that are reputed to drown the moon.... In our wake, the muddy, rain-pitted undulations separated rhythmically and went slithering in among glistening roots and verdure.

And the towns. Names that are savage little poems. Kratie, Sambor, Stung Treng. The people who crowded down to the landing at each place were like troupes of gay, moist butterflies as they brushed against the side of the boat, laughing and talking with the natives on board. The bodies of the half-naked coolies in their midst gleamed like larvae.

Among them were always a few colonial officers; one or two sallow Frenchwomen, who came down to chatter with the fat lady from Pakse; and the local representative of the Messageries Fluviales, bowing and gesticulating to the director of his company; all talking at once and contributing to the general clamor.

At midday we reached the Moyen Mé-Kong, or the Middle River. Here the stream frothed in evanescent contours above rocks close to the surface, eddying madly toward the shore, there to break and seethe about ledges barely immersed. The jungle had become the original Mystery, anterior to Man. Rising out of the flood were trees of new green, whose torn planes made designs upon the darker green of the forest. In this cliff were gaps of foliage like the open mouths of caves. Creepers seemed to spurt from the dark reaches in almost obscene convulsions, jetting upward on the ascending branches and reaching a final triumph of verdant disorder among the highest boughs.

It was a stretch of unrestrained life, wild and awesome. It was not lascivious, as terrible growths of swamp seem. There was something godlike in its very escape from limitations. Here life broke from the soil with natural prolificacy; and I wondered why the rich soil of men's minds could not yield such unrestricted freedom without disaster. Was the soil of earth finer than the soil of men's minds? Or had centuries of increasing evasion and dissembling of truth made anything but restraint seem gross and abnormal? Was there a secret of living that white men, the civilized, did not know? Surely the natives must know something; a difference in color could not account for the fact that they lived in freedom without degeneration. Had they taken something from the forest, from the river?... In the shaggy rampart of green, birds made strange, wild calls, and flowering trees gave out a sweetness like the ghosts of orange-blossoms.

Toward evening the tiers of green tumbled down. There were still many submerged trees, and the water rushed over and about them in foamy maps, whirling by the ship with a lisping croon.

"And the towns. Names that are savage little poems. Kratie, Sambor, Stung Treng."

BAS-LAOS. — Caïman des Rapides de Sambor.

"A great river, *la Mère Mé-Kong*. Gentle and with no complexities —yet capable of terrible things."

We stopped at a confluence under a brazen sunset. There we would remain for the night, as travel through the dark would be dangerous. When the ship had put in beside a little point, the boat-boys plunged shoulder-deep into the river and waded ashore with the mooring lines. The current seemed doubly swift at this confluence, and piles of debris spun past, scattering into fragments as they struck some half-inundated tree or remaining lodged in the sodden boughs.

This point of land boasted trees with flushed blossoms and rose-tinged leaves, beyond which the jungle towered dank and gloomy. We were so close to the bank that a board could be placed between the lower deck and the shore. Some of the natives slipped overside and modestly prepared for the evening bath, but the majority contented themselves with lowering cans into the river and drawing up water with which to cleanse only their insides.

A few moments after we were moored, the gangplank sagged treacherously under the person of Gilbert Filleau de Saint-Hilaire. He was attired in khaki, with boots and one of those abominable broad-brimmed hats which seem to delight Frenchmen. Behind him walked that dark shadow of himself, the Tonkinese boy, carrying a high-power Mauser rifle. *"Attendre le tigre!"* the fat lady from Pakse called out jocularly; and with a flourishing wave of his hat Gilbert Filleau de Saint-Hilaire disappeared into the jungle.

The sun was a blood-clot in a sling of flame. The river spread away ominously still but for that fuming rush among the drowned trees. And then, swiftly, as though flung from its burning socket, the sun disappeared, and in the east a purple bruise crept upward, darkening the sky until it obliterated even the rim of red that was the west.

Shortly afterward there was a hollow shattering in the forest, followed by an instant of accentuated stillness, then the excited chatter of the natives. A few clambered ashore, then reconsidered and hung about the dank thicket where Gilbert Filleau de Saint-Hilaire had vanished.

After a long while he came, waving his hat in that magnificent manner, and followed by the inevitable Nguyen, who triumphantly bore the Mauser and a nearly shattered male peacock.

A gong announced *diner. Crème de laitue, poisson, poulet rôti, omelette an cognac*; and a bottle of *Cordon Rouge*. Strange fare for the jungle. Then the deck, cigarettes. And the moon, behind a film of clouds, making a ghost-light

"Card mailed from Stung Treng, close to the Laos and Annam border where tribal peoples—like these Mois merchants—crossed easily to trade for cotton and salt."
Source: *Picture Postcards of Cambodia*, Joel Montague.

on the river; while on the point, not three yards away, the drooping silhouette of trees darkened the tarnished silver of the stream. Murmuring natives ; a few words in French; and the sound of water.

# 4

In the morning we stopped at Stung Treng.

Before we reached the town the banks were a tumble of bamboo and banana-plants, in which numerous pile-raised native huts were visible only by their roofs; the water was gray-green and blotched with mud, for here, at Stung Treng, the Se-Kong empties its clearer water into the soiled flood of the Mé-Kong.

There was no wharf, only a plank thrown between boat and shore. Two slippery paths led up a high embankment to a road. Stung Treng, like the other outposts on the Mé-Kong, was built along one main road. Unusually tall palms bordered that thoroughfare, and beyond them, in the midst of bougainvillea and spiny yellow blossoms, the houses of French officials looked out at the river. The air was rich with sunlight, with warm earth-smells.

I walked along the embankment from one end of the town to the other. To the north were the Chinese shops, their whitewashed walls plastered with ideographed red posters. That is one scene stenciled deep in my mind, white walls, ideographs and a few palms; a part of every town and village. And always many Chinese shop-keepers animating the picture. They are wherever commerce has begun, the Chinese, and even in spots where they are the beginning of commerce. Quiet, clever, usually orderly—a stolid people. In the bazaar at Stung Treng they were many, forming a somber background for the natives.

It was there I first saw a Laotian woman. Wrapped in a rose-colored scarf woven with silver, her loins bound in a sarong-like garment of raw green silk, she moved along to the accompaniment of clashing anklets. And very gracefully she moved, with the freedom of limb and pride of a people who cannot be cowed although politically subjected. Her black hair was done in a flippant knot on one side and circled with flowers; and she sang softly as she walked, a soft, wild thing, warm as her golden skin.

When I returned to the ship I found Gilbert Filleau de Saint-Hilaire waiting to tell me good-by. With him was a whiskered, mushroom-helmeted official, whom he introduced as the *Administrateur* of Stung Treng. He gave me the promised letter to the Governor of Bassac, then tapped my novel, which was under his arm, assuring me it would prove great diversion on the journey to his village. Then he and the whiskered official disappeared into a shack marked "*Douanes et Régies*"; and thus passed Gilbert Filleau de Saint-Hilaire, gentleman of the jungle, exquisite in exile, whom I shall always picture plunging through the forest on an elephant, reading a tale of adventure less probable than his own experiences but no more thrilling.

# 5

That afternoon the music of the river reached a mad height.... We had entered the Drowned Forests of Prepetang.

Rain, gentle scherzo of the rain; purring like steam as it descended on the river; tapping and rustling in the leaves; running down the banks with a gurgle and hissing lightly at the current. And in the downpour the jungle, a magnificent depth of green that seemed to diffuse its color in soft rays between the rain-lacquered trees. Wind in the tall grass, shaking the spears of new bamboo shoots and taunting the drenched foliage.

Those wet, drooping trees that mourn beside the Mé-Kong! Silent, green, dark and weeping they stand; the forsaken daughters of the river.

We were moving in the midst of what seemed a dull sheen of copper splotched with the tops of nearly inundated trees. The river had become a great lake; its borders invisible in the rain. Leafy branches scratched the sides of the boat, their sounds dissipating in the purling rush of water.

The stream glided into what appeared to be an impassable forest, but as we continued the branches drifted apart as if by magic, leaving a tortuous channel between islands of forest. Suddenly there was a solid bank of foliage on one side, festooned with creepers. It slipped by weirdly, rapidly, as on oiled rollers. Its topmost boughs shot up high in the rain. There was something unreal about that vine-encumbered forest sweeping past in such lush splendor. It was again the original Mystery, this time terrifying.

On the deck beside me the engineer of navigation was talking. In that mighty drowned jungle his voice sounded impotent; he, we all were impotent in the presence of such majesty. He was saying that the trees had great roots slanting about them like tripods which made it possible for them to resist the current. This spot for six months— during the dry season—was little more than a sandbed, and ships had to take a sinuous course far to the west of the present channel. Then his voice ceased. Only the even, rhythmic gurgle of the river, seeming to sheathe the silence in gossamer.

Still that narrow channel between lithe, delicately tangled tree tops. A nameless and haunting fragrance stole out through the rain. And now the channel grew even narrower, becoming far ahead a vanishing point in. that forest which glided by so spectrally. The tawny undulations astern were like breathing flanks. As I watched them they seemed to duplicate their rhythm in my mind.

Flanks....

Poignant and shining it went through me again, that feeling I had known at Kampong-Cham. Husky and wild, like music from a bronze throat. From a brown man's throat. From a brown river's throat. Young soldiers and gay women. Natives squatting in the bazaar; natives laughing in a theater. Natives squatting and laughing at life. Something calling in their laughter, something far off and lost to the civilized....

Look at those fellows aft, you white man. You pursue beauty through a studio, in a lecture-hall.... Look at those bodies, at the flexing of their muscles as they move; the dark, tragic mystery of their eyes.... Make that live, you writer; and can you bring that into a lecture-hall?... Something lost, something trying to speak through those bodies. Bodies without lust. Find it, white man! Damn the creed of your blood. Here is the East offering her lips to you, offering to translate the sorrow in her heart; and you stand hesitant and afraid.... Until you understand her, how do you expect to know the secret of living without the evasion that is the code of your race? Find that secret, read it there on the river. Flat surface stirred to writing by the current; a copper frieze full of cryptic meaning. And the trees; exquisite bas-reliefs supporting the sky. A temple. Drink the incense, white man. Musk of a wild beauty.

# 6

The dusk was simply a deepening of the twilight tone that already submerged the forest.

I did not realize it was night until I found it difficult to see a flight of birds moving in tremulous pattern across the sky. The trees had acquired a brilliant gloss in the darkness; they glistened like lacquer. The air was gently astir, as though breathing freely after a great strain.

The cliff of jungle had crumbled; as I watched, it had seemed to separate and go floating off in small pieces. We had entered what the French call the Region of Four Thousand Isles.

The wind, blowing across the bow, was like damp gauze. Very soon, said the captain, we should see the lights of Khone.

# Chapter V
# Laos
### *Tells of the Land of Tattooed Men*

"...her black hair was done in a flippant knot...circled with flowers; and she sang softly as she walked, a soft, wild thing, warm as her golden skin."

# Mé-Kong

### 1

N THE moist night thickening out of that day fuming with showers, the boat slipped between countless shadowy isles and into a dark indenture on the southern end of the largest island, where a single light thrust its ray across an ominous depth of shadow to announce an intermission in the long journey.

The ship's engine subsided to a husky, broken discharge. We drifted toward an immense shape that became a two-story open warehouse built partly over the water. Natives appeared mysteriously with flares. Where there had been only a dark sheet of jungle, pierced by a single light, now was a luminous aperture, like a tear in black tissue paper, filled with ruddy torches and drifts of smoke, all serving to limn the gleaming bodies of running men. Below the upper platform of this strange wharf the bank sloped down past wooden trestles and beams into the water, now seeming splashed with flame and platinum in the torchlight. There were squelchy, heavy sounds as coolies plunged waist-deep into the stream to make the ropes fast. A ramp, obviously for cargo, rose through an opening in the floor into the main part of the warehouse, and several bluntly built natives raced down this incline into the water, laughing and crying out as they helped with the mooring lines.

The deck where I stood was lower than the second story of the shed, and visible between the flooring of the wharf and the ship's awning was a pair of muscular white legs that rose from patent-leather dancing-pumps into the

"Cambodia was behind; here at Khone was the beginning of Laos."

folds of a sarong. I leaned over the rail, staring up at the owner. There stood a Frenchman, flushed and helmeted, and carrying an ivory-tipped cane, which he used on the coolies when his sharp orders were not instantly effective. His only other garment was a white jacket, open and revealing a hairy chest. As I peered out he touched his hat politely, then turned about to meet the captain, who was already on the wharf.

Across the island, separated by some few kilometers of jungle, was the town, Khone Nord. But as the little narrow-gage railway that carried freight did not operate until morning, and there was no other means of transportation, I was forced to remain overnight on the boat. From the other side, where the swollen Mé-Kong moved furiously over and through the Region of Four Thousand Isles—the Khong Archipelago, to be exact—I would go in a smaller boat to Bassac.

As I moved down the gangplank, two naked fellows were climbing up on the beams between the piling to put on their trousers, and their bodies were tattooed with intricate patterns stretching from thighs to navel like gauzy tights. The sight of these two brown men so elaborately tattooed and crouching on the beams startled me with the realization that I was among another race.

Cambodia was behind; here at Khone was the beginning of Laos.

Up in the warehouse were more natives. All wore *patois*—strips of colored cloth bound about the waist, the loose ends drawn up under the groin and tucked in at the rear—and above and below these scanty garments tattooing was visible. Their strength was evident in knotty thews and biceps, unlike the sinewy muscularity of the Cambodians, and they were short and very solid. Some were tawny, but the majority were a deeper brown. Hair black and straight was brushed back from the forehead. There was a touch of barbarity about these men seen in the flush of torches; and they conjured up a picture of that early race which the ancient Chinese called Ngu, or the Great Bowmen, and which inhabited northern Laos.

There is something vital and challenging about a locality where a race was born; and this section of territory, undulating down from Luang Prabang, was the forested cradle of not only one but several races. When I think of the rise of a Far Eastern people it separates into three parts, the Epic of Soil, the Epic of Art and the Epic of Blood; and not infrequently the last two are mingled. These epics in Laos are a series of flashes in the haze of mythology and misinformation.

History, when elevated above cold, naked fact, is a matter of emotion instead of dates; and the history of Laos is the story of simplicity that grew into fury and then rose to the brutal beauty of conquest and empire. The Epic of Soil began against a cool background of virgin mountains, amidst the stinging blue scent of wood fires built by naked tattooed men, who hunted with great bows and arrows and were called the Mon. Into their midst came another people, migrating from the Kin-Lung mountains in China, merging with them and producing the Shan race —another naked people who moved against the background of unspoiled wilderness.

And then the Epic of Soil ended. For the Thai came, building their temples that spired heavenward; and this was the beginning of the Epic of Art. Slowly emerging from these peoples appeared the Thai-Shan, a race part Mon, part Negrito and part Chinese. And then there began a brazen clamor in the spired temples, and the scent of wood smoke was thick with the smell of burnt flesh; for the third epic was insinuating itself upon the second.

The Karens surged down. All through these blending periods moved the Annamites, who had dwelt along the eastern coast from a time forgotten.... The drama of growth had become the drama of life through death, of that ironic principle of destruction of the people to perpetuate what their rulers call the race. There were wars with the Siamese and the people of Fou-Nan. Mighty-kingdoms rose and fell; the Kingdom of Vien-Tiane, of Luang Prabang; and there were times when Laos was a vassal colony of other countries of the Golden Chersonese.

The Epic of Blood ended in anticlimax. No more did war-pirogues sail on the Mé-Kong, and the elephants that once carried kings now worked with the timber and bore strange, anemic men of another race on their odysseys of colonization. The Epilogue had come. A Frenchman named Pavie was made consul of Luang Prabang. Two years after that Laos became a "protectorate."

The Mé-Kong was a vein that carried this new blood into the country. Little villages of plaster-walled houses sprang up on its banks, and signs startlingly foreign marked the warehouses and dwellings of this spreading race. *Douanes et Régies, Service Forestier, Garde Indigène*. At intervals tiny boats, equipped with powerful engines to war with the rapids of Prepetang and Kemmerat, went as far as Vien-Tiane carrying crates of champagne and cognac, and tinned goods from Marseilles and other French ports. The thread of civilization, following the Mé-Kong, wove its way stealthily into Laos. But on either side of the great river, beyond this thread, the cycle had swung. Again naked tattooed men moved against the background of inexorable mountains, amidst the stinging blue scent of wood fires; only now they did not carry great bows and arrows, they were forbidden to carry any weapon. For a race must always lose the symbols of its virility in the process of becoming civilized.

Yellow-robed monks chanted in the ruins of those spired temples. Men and women in scarves and *sampots* that were shadows of former splendor made sad music which told of the Epic of Art and the Epic of Blood. They laughed and danced, because these things were their heritage, and because with the Epilogue they at least had peace.

These men tattooed on flank and belly, working there in the warehouse, belonged to that rugged people, and as I paused a moment to watch them, they made personal for me the heroic vitality of their race.

A wind strayed in the surrounding forest, cool after the humidity of Cambodia and Cochin-China, and it distilled moist, green smells that mingled with the smells of hides, of opium and supplies under the shed.

I wandered outside. The clouds had cleared, and the stars were very bright. Somewhere in the jungle the sudden anguished tremolo of a night bird bruised the silence. That silence was very strange; I seemed to hear it, as though the faint roar of distant, swollen waters crept into the quiet and intensified it.

At one side of the warehouse a path ran into a density of gloom that invited. I had started to follow it, perceiving a bridge, when a voice halted my adventuring; a very annoyed voice that asked me in French if I didn't realize I might fall over an embankment or be eaten by a panther if I continued. I paused and, involuntarily using English, replied that he, whoever he might be, was very kind but I rather liked the uncertainty. Whereupon the voice exploded: "My God, an American! ... I have been to Gulfport!"

From previous experiences I had learned that often it is fatal to leap into the fraternity born of a sudden mutual knowledge discovered in some far place; so I made my way back to the warehouse in a leisurely fashion, curious but determined upon a course of discretion.

And there he stood, the man of the patent-leather dancing-pumps and the sarong. With characteristic French politeness, he removed his helmet and introduced himself, all the while standing with the ivory-tipped cane thrust under his arm as though he had paused in a stroll along the Seine instead of along the Mé-Kong.

"I was on a ship once that stopped at Gulfport and Nouvelle Orleans," he explained.

In the light of the torches I could see he was very blond and sunburnt, and he was heavily set, with that Slow-moving muscularity characteristic of Scandinavian men. His name was quite French, but eyes intensely blue looked out from a face guilelessly Swedish.

"We will go on the boat and talk about Gulfport and *Nouvelle Orléans*," he announced.

And so to the boat we went, into the little cabin forward where insects hurtled about the oil-lamp or poised momentarily on the soiled table-cloth. "*Boi-ee!*" he called loudly.

"*Oui, monsieur!*"

"*Deux Martel-Perrier!*... And now," he said, "we will talk about Gulfport...."

I quickly exhausted the subject by saying I hadn't been there since I was six years old, and then disarmed him by asking what he was doing at Khone.

"Oh, I travel on the boat that makes the trip to Na Phong and back," he said. Then he inquired what I was doing there.... "So you are a writer," he mused. "You will write a romance of Laos?"

No, I was going from Khone to Bassac, and then to a pile of ruins called Wat Phu, presumably built by the Khmers, and afterward I would do a book about the journey.

"I know nothing about the Khmers," he remarked.

Perhaps he knew something about Laos, I suggested.

Well, he knew a little about the natives. And then he asked: "I suppose, at Pnom Penh or Sa'igon, you heard the story of de Lagree's mission about fifty years ago?... Wait a minute and I will tell you. *Boi-ee!*"

"*Oui, monsieur!*"

"*Deux Martel-Perrier—tout de suite* . . . Then he turned a very Scandinavian look upon me, this Frenchman. "Once I read a book about colonization in the tropics—it was by an Englishman, or maybe he was an American—anyway, he said that whenever France annexed colonies it was for love of glory, because there was nothing in our national character that was appealed to by the difficult, unromantic work of colonization. That made me laugh; I still laugh when I think of it. It is difficult, this colonization, but as for being unromantic— well, what about the story of de Lagree and Gamier?

"Of course you know who Francis Gamier was; you couldn't escape that in Indo-China—there is a street named after him in every town, and all the colonial records and memorials are filled with his name. De Lagree isn't so prominent, although he paid the price for that mission. They set out from Saigon in 1866—or maybe it was 1867, I don't know—however, the important thing is that they set out Dates are so confining to the imagination—and who gives a damn about them, except scholars? The purpose of the mission was to see if it were possible to open a trade route from

Yunnan to the Mé-Kong and down the river to the coast; then the trade of southern China would flow out through Saigon.

"They started in two shallow-draught gunboats—a damfool thing to do, but how could they know the Me-Kong then?—and two days after leaving Pnom-Penh they were forced to change to pirogues. De Lagree was head of the mission, and Gamier was second in command. A fellow named de Carne was political officer. Gamier left the party at different times and made explorations of his own. He went to Angkor and had a lot to say about the Khmers, but I don't remember what it was. Oh, he was a dreamer, this Gamier! And he loved Indo-China—and the Mé-Kong.

"The mission stopped for some time at Stung Treng, which was in Siamese territory at that time. I believe they found some Khmer ruins near there—one temple, I think, which some Dutchman traveling on his own had discovered about a hundred years before. Oh, this exploration business is amusing. Some Frenchman, or an American, or anybody finds a big pile of stone and some rotten carvings and gets all excited because he thinks he's the first white man that ever saw this glorious ruin of the What-not Empire; and then he suddenly discovers that an Englishman or a German has been there two hundred years before—although usually it's a Jesuit or some other missionary looking for converts. That's the way things go. When you get to Wat Phu you will probably find that instead of only a few people having been there before, the whole French Annamite army camped there at one time and cooked food in the old incense-burners... *Boi-ee!*"

"*Oui, monsieur!*"

"*Deux Martel-Perrier—et la glace....* But about this de Lagree mission. They came through Khone, and I think it was here, in the midst of all these rapids and islands, they realized the Mé-Kong would never be navigable like the big rivers of America and Europe. But they went on. They stayed at Bassac for some time, and there de Lagree had his first attack of fever. Trouble came all at once. The brandy and wines were ruined by insects, and the flour was spoiled too. Then the men began to get sick, and those who weren't sick seemed filled with the devil. At Ubone they sent back some of the soldiers of the escort because of their bad conduct; and later at Siam-Leap they had to leave two officers and three men who were ill with fever.

"…the *Garcerie*, a river boat some forty feet long…jerked through a low jungle of bamboo that tumbled down to the very edge of the track."

"It was at Ubone, too, that they left the river and marched overland to Kemmerat with bullock-carts and Laotian porters. Later they returned to the river and went on to Nong Khai. This is just across the stream from Vien-Tiane. They did some exploring around there. Vien-Tiane hadn't got over the rebellion against Siam about forty years before; it was in ruins and overgrown with jungle....

"Beyond Vien-Tiane the rapids forced them to take to the shore again, but finally they reached Luang Prabang. That must have been a great day. The king received them and gave them passports to go farther. So they went on ... to Chieng-Hsien, and then... well, there isn't much more to tell except that, as you know, they got to Yunnan—they arrived in the midst of the Mohammedan rebellion—and went even beyond. Of course it is stupid to dismiss a journey like that with a few words, but a man can't put sweat and smells, hunger, fever, pain and loneliness into sentences—at least, I cannot.

"It was after leaving Yunnan that de Lagree was stricken with fever again, and at Tong-Chuon, while Garnier was rushing over to Tali-Fu, he died.... In one respect the mission had failed—this fellow de Carne wrote in his book that since the Mé-Kong was impossible as a trade route, France would have to turn her attention to Tonkin, then under Chinese suzerainty. But the mission had succeeded magnificently in completing a terrible journey through country that was mostly unexplored. Later, de Lagree's body was removed and stuck under a tombstone, and it received what the government called a Glorious Tribute, while Garnier went back and had flowers and mud thrown at him in turn, because some thought he was a great explorer and others thought he was stealing his dead friend's triumph. And that's the way things go.... So let's have a drink....

# 2

In the morning I was awakened by the coolies unloading cargo. The warehouse was filled with piles of hides, tinned supplies and cases of opium and of *nuc-mam*, the latter a salty liquid used by the natives to season their food. This cargo was being packed in the cars of a narrow-gage train which stood under the shed and which would transport it from Khone Sud to Khone Nord.

The journey was less than half an hour, and I was jerked through a low jungle of bamboo that tumbled down to the very edge of the track.

Khone Nord was more pretentious than the southern harbor. At the wharf, parallel with a small warehouse, was the *Garcerie*, a river boat some forty feet long that made regular trips between Khone and Naphong; and near the warehouse stood the *magasin* maintained by the Messageries Fluviales. Not far to the left, gleaming with startling pallor in the sunlight, was a modern stone causeway, under whose several arches a branch of the Me-Kong flowed swiftly into numerous waterways hidden in the jungle and on to the Khone Falls. The dim roar of those falls filled the air.

In the other direction, beyond the *magasin* and the warehouse, a road tapered into trees and dwellings. Here, as in all the outposts along the Mé-Kong, the houses faced the main road, beginning with the few fenced structures of the French inhabitants and ending with the whitewashed shops of Chinese and natives.

The train had stopped near the wharf, and convicts were transferring the cargo. These fellows, all stocky Laotians, were fettered, and between the iron ankle-bands were two linked rods connecting at the joint with a chain fastened to their waists, thus permitting them to work without chance of escape. A native soldier was in charge, uniformed and barefoot; and many men in *patois* lingered about watching the work with the uncertain air of those expecting to be drawn into it but too interested to preclude the possibility by removing themselves.

A number were tattooed like the men I had seen at Khone Sud. These, I realized, were the "black-bellied" Laos, so called because of the elaborate designs needled into the skin of their abdomens.

Tattooing has long been a custom in this country—it is known of as early as 130 B.C.—and it gives the men a curiously barbaric appearance which their usually gentle manner belies. Many of the Burmese believe that tattooing keeps away the *nats*, or evil spirits, and some Laotians think likewise, but that is not the principal reason for this widespread custom among them. Like the Dyak women of Borneo who tattoo themselves to attract lovers, these men cover their bodies between ribs and knees with intricate designs to make themselves more alluring in the eyes of the women. It is the sign of virility, the visible proof of the thoroughly masculine male. The pigment is made from the soot of burning lard and the bile of wild bulls, mixed with water, and it is generally put on by the bonzes, although some women are proficient in this art.

One fellow on the wharf, a Laotian tall for his race, was decorated with a particularly fascinating pattern. It began at the waist and extended well below his knees in delicate gauzy tracery. At the top was a scalloped border of *nok jung*, or peacocks, with a number of fierce-looking *rachsees*, mythological animals, below that, while his thighs were a bewildering tapestry of clouds, pigeons, bats, vultures and serpents, ending below the knees in a band of lions. I was entranced, and I very rudely asked if I might inspect the tattooing closely.

Curiosity, in the white race, is exterior to the Legend of Chivalry, which is one of the first delusions they are taught to chant; it is a privilege that comes of being civilized. If a Laotian, finding himself in America by some strange circumstance, were to walk up to a lady and ask to examine the rouge on her face, he would be properly chastened. Yet here I was asking this Laotian if I might inspect his femoral epidermis, and to myself excusing this display of bad manners with the explanation that it was done in the interest of a public eagerly waiting to be instructed.

Just above the *Garcerie* was another and smaller craft, the *Ibis*, which I surmised was the boat that had been placed at my disposal to finish the journey to Bassac. At first glance she was a slovenly, rusty little craft, with a certain tawdry flippancy about her uptilted bows.

As I approached, a dark fellow, who looked neither Laotian, Cambodian nor Annamite, emerged from the cabin. He was, I discovered a moment later, an East Indian; and he was the patron of the *Ibis*. Lean and gaunt, he gazed out at the world through eyes that expressed a melancholy resignation to the fact of his being. His very glance was eloquent of the agonizing truth that life, and his life particularly, was a series of lamentable circumstances that must be borne gravely. I, the latest lamentable circumstance, was accepted with the same fatalism, and he solemnly offered to show me over the boat.

After this tour of inspection I had my luggage put on board, and then the *patron* produced a bottle of cognac. While I enjoyed his hospitality he informed me, with somber pride, that his name was Monsieur Tambia and he was a Frenchman born at Pondicherry. This coming from a full-blooded East Indian was a bewildering expression of loyalty. ... It was arranged that I should sleep on board that night; the *Ibis* would leave some time before dawn.

59. - Chutes de Trians (près de Bienhoa)

The waterfalls of Khone. "The current, milky copper in color, was lathered with foam, and yellow mist hung in soiled rainbows where the spray was flung."

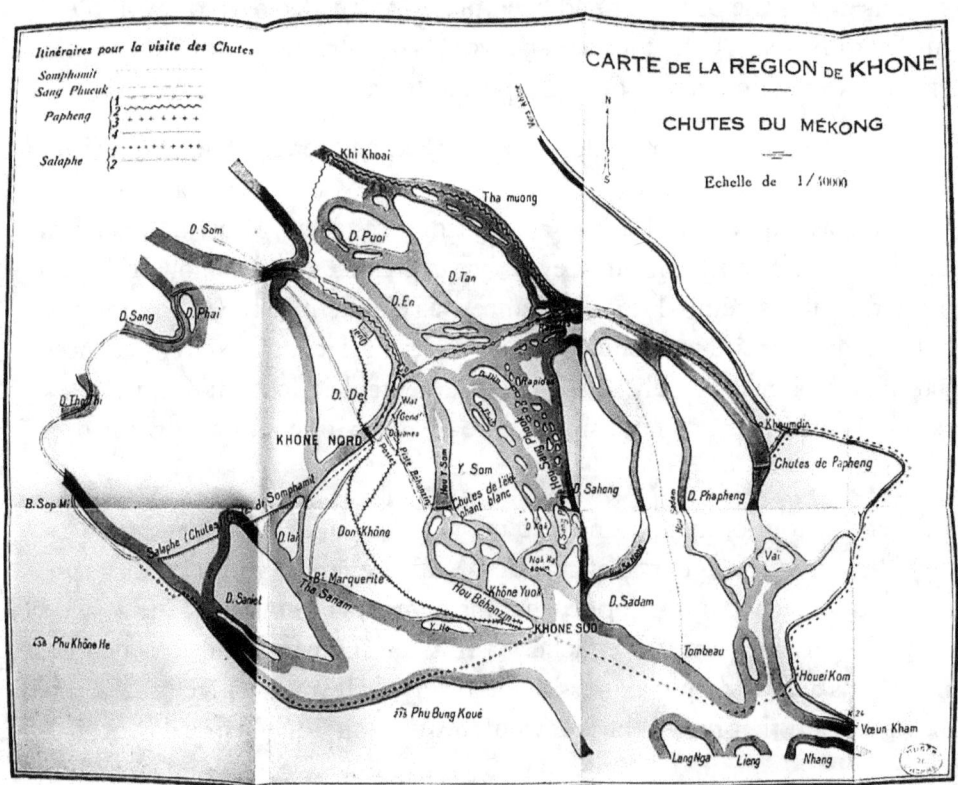

A hot, drizzling day swooned on Khone, and in the late afternoon I met the Swedish-looking Frenchman who the night before had offered to show me the Khone Falls. This afternoon he was not wearing the amazing costume I had first seen him in, but ordinary khaki.

We walked past the causeway over ground that made succulent sounds beneath our feet. It was one of those afternoons when the sun sets invisibly, and an unreal yellowish light tinges the gray air. It was made more unreal by the distant roar of the falls. That echo was a gossamer net that trapped the silence, and in it Khone was a throb of green enmeshed like a damp living thing.

Most of the ground was under water, and in places the footpath was submerged ankle-deep. The trees that thickened about us dripped moisture, and the deepening gloom seemed to enter the atmosphere with an effect of dank green twilight in which we moved like creatures walking in blurred sea-bottoms.

We passed through an inundated open space, drenched to the knees, and as we entered a rift in the jungle, lithe, swinging shapes in the branches overhead sent a shower upon us from the moisture-laden leaves. The monkeys scampered away, chattering, and then the rumbling silence shut down again.

I had the feeling I was walking through a tunnel of gauze. Great stalks of bamboo hurled high their fume of green, melting into the boughs which met over the path. A few orchids stained the dusk of the forest, and splashes of tiny purple flowers, heavy with rain-pearls, seemed to run fluid about the roots of trees.

Now the roar had swollen, and the calls of crickets were like veins from which the sound poured. A rise of ground ahead was covered with a foamy mane of pallid roan. It was the first waterfall. Or so my friend informed me. It was little more than a rapid pouring over a rocky ledge. A narrow bridge spanned it, and then the path crept deeper into the jungle.

The second waterfall was no larger than the first. Here a small stream rushed out of twilight, and tall bamboo arched over it like a green causeway. It seemed incredible that rapids of such size could make so much noise, and when I yelled this thought to my companion he shrieked back that the sound was not from one or even two streams, but from many surging madly through the flooded region.

The third waterfall, called Som-pha-mit, was a great basin in the forest where the stream plunged over a low, jagged ridge to swirl furiously across a wide stretch and around boulders shaggy with plants that had sprung up in soil-filled rifts. The current, milky copper in color, was lathered with foam, and yellow mist hung in soiled rainbows where the spray was flung. On the other side vines were tangled in trees; there was no bridge.

The Frenchman lifted his voice to tell me that we could not get to the great falls from this point because of the floods. And he added that once an engineer had proposed to dynamite the Khone Falls and thus make a navigable waterway, but a Laotian bonze had said it was written in a sacred Pali manuscript that if this were ever done, there would never be another drop of water to drink in Laos, and so the government abandoned the project....

When we went back, my friend pointed out a log-raised house surrounded by palms where he said he stayed while at Khone. He suggested we stop a moment, and then, with no further explanation, splashed along a watery path toward the hut.

It proved to be the dwelling of none other than Monsieur Tambia. That melancholy gentleman himself was seated at a table reading when we entered, and I was startled; for over his shoulder I saw a china figure of Our Lady of Sorrows, and the gentle image, vague in the candle-glow, and seeming to rise behind this gaunt, dark Indian like an incongruous vision from his own mind, was both dramatic and grotesque.

"We have come to clean off the leeches," the man who knew Gulfport announced to Monsieur Tambia. Then he said to me, "Undress and regard yourself."

But I did not need to undress to see. I was wearing shorts, and between the breeches and the tops of my stockings many tiny black creatures clung to the skin like horrid swollen growths. The Frenchman had quickly discarded his clothing, and I forgot the leeches in my surprise at seeing him tattooed about the waist after the fashion of a native. An elaborate procession of *rachsees*, with heads of dragons and bodies of lions, stood out vividly against his white skin. He noticed my glance and laughed.

"I did that to please a lady," he volunteered. "I intended to have it done all the way down to my knees, but it was too painful. It required five sittings to put those beasts on—and the lady was satisfied, so I stopped."

Then as an afterthought he inquired: "Would you like to meet the lady?... Wait a moment."

He called loudly, and after a few seconds a brown boy entered silently and he spoke in Laotian. "I've sent for her," the Frenchman announced as the boy went out.

In the next few minutes I removed nearly thirty leeches from my body; my limbs and torso were marked with little spots of blood where I had pulled the creatures off. The Frenchman was still busy when I finished, and Monsieur Tambia sat by in melancholy silence, watching with the air of one pleased to find a new verification of his belief that life is a succession of torments.

My white friend had wrapped himself about with a sarong obtained from the Indian, and I had just retreated into the folds of another while waiting for my clothes to dry, when there was a sound of bare feet on the veranda, and a woman entered so soundlessly that she seemed to advance into the light like a figure thrown on a screen.

Her hair was blue-black in the candle's rays, and done in a knot on one side of her head after the mode fashionable in Laos. A little jacket of some gauzy material clung tightly to her body; from her hips the loose folds of a silver-woven *sinh*, or skirt, flowed down to her very toes. Her skin was smoothly tawny, her eyes dark with a certain slumbering mystery that might have been only dullness but seemed an expression of secret and endless repose.

Monsieur Tambia and I might not have been in the room for all the attention we received; her half-smiling gaze never left the Frenchman. The hem of her sink was wet, muddy; there were drops of water on her face, as though flung there by foliage brushed aside hastily—I , remember that well. It gave me a feeling of something tireless and devoted; and these emotions had to do with more than the woman herself....

The Frenchman spoke a few words to her, I was surprised that his voice was flexible enough to blur his usual harsh tones. Then she turned to me and held out her hand with a simplicity that seemed to say she accepted me without question or surprise. And her touch was very soft, very gentle. It explained much that I wanted to know; for it was more than a mere pressure of the hand; it was the subtle yielding of the uninvolved savage to the technically civilized intelligence of a people it believed superior.

"I would never have a European wife," said the Frenchman, "not after having a native one. The Lao woman, she is quiet, tender and she makes no claim except upon the affection—but the French woman... No, no, I have seen too many. They are too much trouble— and love is a matter of moods with them. And when they get out here, they turn yellow and develop a bad temper...."

The Laotian woman sat down cross-legged at his feet, and something in the manner in which she did it gave me the feeling she was not subject to him, but like the other women of her race her natural inclination was to blend with the will of the male.

Monsieur Tambia gloomily called for a boy to bring cognac.

"You said last night you were on your way to some Khmer ruins near Bassac," the Frenchman remarked. "Since then I've been talking with Tambia here, and he tells me that the old Laotians used to call the Khmer empire *Tevada Nagkon*, which means the Kingdom of the Angels."

Monsieur Tambia assented solemnly.

"They were my ancestors," announced this Indian who earlier in the afternoon had claimed to be a Frenchman. "The Khmers came from the Ganges valley," he added. "They became so great, and their empire was so large, that the natives here believed them gods. At one time they conquered Laos," And he looked down at the woman mournfully as if to ask what one could expect from anything so somber as life.

"How far into Laos did they go?" I queried.

Monsieur Tambia did not know, but he had heard they went as far as Luang Prabang. However, the priests at Bassac would probably have some old Pali manuscripts that might contain records of the Khmers.

The boy came in silently with a bottle of cognac. ... I remember that scene as one incredibly fantastic. The Scandinavian-looking Frenchman, tattooed about the waist, with his native mistress seated at his feet; and across a table gleaming with glasses, the lean, dark Indian over whose shoulder the gentle figure of Mary gazed benignantly; all unreal yet sharply significant. For I realized then that whether I learned anything about *Tevada Nagkon* or not, at least the journey would have unfolded the secret of another nation's Conquest and Glory.

# 3

The *Ibis* slipped away from Khone the next morning while dawn was still a promise in the east.

As to the aspects of that dawn I cannot testify intelligently, for it happened I was thrown into the midst of it with bewildering violence. Flung suddenly from the bunk, I jumped up, trapped in crackling thunder that rent all sleep from me and left me staring at stalks of bamboo pouring over the bow in green flood.

Gradually it came upon me that we had rammed the shore, and the loud angry voice of Monsieur Tambia, the *patron*, verified the fact as he cried out orders that seemed punctured by the continued popping of bamboo branches.

For a moment I felt acutely uncertain. Then Leung, my Chinese boy, came lunging in, exclaiming, "Migaw!" —which was his interpretation of an ejaculation he had heard his model of conduct use on occasions—"Coolie smoke opium at wheel—run into bank!"

There was no danger. But my equilibrium had been sufficiently upset to dismiss the possibility of further rest, and I established myself on the railing forward, wrapped about with a blanket, while the coolies struggled with the boat and a shower fumed down out of sagging clouds.

For nearly two hours the crew, throat-deep in the water, worked with the *Ibis*, their muscled bodies appearing and reappearing in the muddy flood like fish gleaming and darting close to the surface. Stalks of bamboo broke and fell over the boat as though to strew a funeral barge. Then the rain slackened, and a motorboat crept out from Khone, sinking her hooks into the *Ibis* and dragging her into midstream with a trail of broken bamboo floating behind like storm-wrack.

As we nosed out between the tiny islands a film of rain blurred the shores. The trees seemed out of focus and furry, the sky a soiled haze that reflected the copperish, rushing stream. In the humid atmosphere I felt reduced to a fleck of mold on a spoiled world; and at that moment I did not care what had become of the Khmers or who caused their downfall; my interest in them, if any, was only a vague, jeering satisfaction that they also had been forced to endure this climate, together with a certain sarcastic surprise that they had survived so long in it.

When Leung brought coffee my mood improved; and the appearance of Monsieur Tambia, disheveled and greasy but carrying a bottle of cognac, drew my hope out of the quicksands entirely. Behind the somewhat bewildering Latin flavor of his name was an altogether different Monsieur Tambia. In the first place, although born in French possessions in India, which he seemed to think gave him a claim upon French nationality, he was a Tamil. I suspect that in his youth he tried to look at life with the eyes of a Parisian, and his Indian heart would not let him; and the result was a lean, ascetic-looking person, very dark and very melancholy. Had he entered the cabin without the cognac, undoubtedly he would have depressed me considerably....

At Khone the Mé-Kong widens to a breadth of more than three miles, separated into narrow channels and waterways by the numerous islands; and beyond Khone it becomes even broader, in places spreading until it covers a stretch of seven or eight miles. We were in that region now, and the shores seemed wrapped in green fog as the bamboo blended, diffusing feathery reflections that rode off on the racing current

Near noon we passed Khong. In the wake of the rain had come a still humidity that rose from the river like steam, hot with the smells of jungle water and damp aromatic roots.... From Khong we followed a reach of the Mé-Kong toward Ban Wounthong, there to take on wood for the engines.

Noon had descended, and with it the swooning indolence of midday on an Asian river. Plunge and charge of pistons, a clamor of oily, metallic things that sounded obscene in the hot silence; the frequent jangling of the boat's bell; steam rising from the exhaust, mingling with the heat on the stream and seeming to ascend visibly as the clear sunlight became a white haze in the incandescent sky. Even the tall palms rising scornfully above the other verdure seemed stricken by the glare.

At such a time there is a deadly precision about the details of life and even the inanimate things surrounding life. And the *Ibis* was not a craft designed to comfort one bound in this heat-spell. Her small cabin, outfitted for two and planned with no thought for beauty, was built almost in the bows, opening out upon a small triangular space forward. The engines were thrust directly behind the cabin, with the narrow decks moving past them to the galley and a semi-rotund canvased-in space aft, where the cook and the coolies stayed. Overhead was an awning-covered deck for the crew.

The only inviting spot was the little space forward, and from there I watched the sunlit monotony of the Me-Kong.

As evening came on, blue mountains rose out of the long reaches of forest. At dusk they were taller, like a growing mirage, and the aftermath of a pale sunset shone luminously behind them. The wide river was as still as faintly grooved steel. On the shore, the palms were like many-winged bats that clung to the jungle and folded with day.

We moored by the bank for the night. Over *foie-gras naturel* and an omelet with burning cognac—some of the privileges of a French protectorate—Monsieur Tambia discoursed in a melancholy voice upon subjects I cannot remember except that I am sure they were gloomy.... Trees lisped softly, and there was a fragile ripple beneath the decks; breaths of sound that mated and trembled in the darkness like sighs rising from bruised harpstrings.

## 4

When I awoke in the morning, we were close to the western shore, following that endless slanting wall of bamboo.

Soft, misty shoots were flung up like spray from a green waterfall, and high above it, isolated in the air on their tall trunks, were long-fronded palms. Many huts and sheds of thatch peeped out from the green; natives busied themselves with mysterious tasks, looking up solemnly as we passed.

Even the stream seemed stealthily alive. Floes of teak-wood logs, bound to rafts of lashed timber, floated soundlessly by, carrying naked brown men who squatted on mats or stood alert with poised oars. At one place we passed a whole fleet of great covered pirogues—long canoes made of dug-out tree-trunks with arched rattan shelters—filled with people in colored *sampots* or sarongs, the men tattooed elaborately from belly to knees.

I noticed many monasteries on the banks, some of them merely log-raised platforms under a palm-leaf roof, and in most of them were huge drums, to be beaten during prayer or some ceremony. The monks perched about these shelters like flocks of strange yellow parrots. Frequently I saw saffron robes hung in the

"Bassac—*finis!*" he said with an eloquent wave of his hand."
The Catholic mission of Bassac seen above.

trees, while not far away their owners squatted or lay in the water, wrapped in whatever contemplation Laotian monks find engrossing on a hot morning.

In the afternoon the engines suddenly died out in a husky whisper, and we were moored for several hours while Monsieur Tambia sweated gloomily with the coolies in an effort to bring the *Ibis* to life. Mountains had appeared over the bow, and through the afternoon they smoldered and quivered like some vapor emanating from the heat. When we finally started the sun was a smoky red pistil in furling rays.

We should have reached Bassac in mid-afternoon, but now Monsieur Tambia said it would probably be well on to midnight before we arrived. We were near the shore and moving cautiously, for after dusk the Mé-Kong is dangerous. Someone on the upper deck was smoking opium; the pungent odor drifted down into the cabin with the smells of oil and garlic....

It was a cool night, and over the breadth of the river dwelt an epic silence that the charging engines only measured. Now and then a stroke of lightning throbbed down a vein of the sky. Something in the night made me think of a fine, dark animal with quivering flanks. I felt excited. For ahead was Bassac, and not many kilometers beyond it, Wat Phu, those Khmer ruins that had dreamed through centuries.

About ten o'clock the *Ibis* increased her speed. Monsieur Tambia entered the cabin and surprised me by smiling.

"Bassac—*finis!*" he said with an eloquent wave of his hand.

Just two seconds later I was lying full length on the floor and above me the oil-lamp pitched about like an orange rag flung in a pit, and then vanished, I had a last glimpse of Monsieur Tambia following me like a comic picture suddenly dropped from the wall, then he was lost in the same black crash that had swallowed me.

For a moment it seemed silly and unreal, and I lay there giggling, all the while feeling that the darkness was going to fall on top of me. I remember the ring of shattered glass, a grinding thud which sent me rolling against something that felt like the upturned leg of a table; and then all motion ceased with stunning abruptness, and I was on my feet in the midst of dark silence that pounced on me like a black cat.

Monsieur Tambia, lurching against me, swore a dreadful Hindustani oath; and another figure darting in through the grayish blur of the companionway yelled, "Migaw!" A moment later Leung was dragging me out on the deck.

The Mé-Kong was incongruously calm, and little ripples danced up as the current sucked past the *Ibis*. But there was something fearsome in the gloomy expanse of the river.

"Coolie smoke opium again," whispered Leung, and then he swore half in Chinese and half in the language he had heard his model of conduct use.

I suddenly remembered my money-belt and the letters of introduction to the Governor of Bassac which were under my bunk, and as I rushed back to get them I saw, through the forward companionway, a looming mass that could be nothing but trees. All visions of swimming the brutal current of the Mé-Kong collapsed.

Monsieur Tambia lighted a candle and stood glaring at the wreckage of crockery, glassware and overturned furniture like a destroying archangel.

First I found my money-belt and the letters, then a look outside showed me that the *Ibis* was not five yards from shore, evidently astride a shoal. The forest was dark and still but for the rustling of leaves.

For more than an hour naked shapes labored with the little steamboat, then Monsieur Tambia, emerging from the water in a pair of drenched breeches, suggested that I let some of the crew put me ashore and guide me to Bassac. The town was less than a kilometer away, and there was a *sala*, or guest-house, where I could stay. It might be many hours before the *Ibis* could stir....

I got together a few possessions, leaving the rest on the boat, and with Leung following, was lifted from the railing of the *Ibis* on muscular shoulders and carried to the bank, where I was deposited on what appeared to be dry ground but which accepted my weight with a sucking noise and let me sink almost to the knees.

Crawling out of the mud, I climbed the embankment into a thicket of bamboo that brushed my face with moisture. One of the natives moved ahead and crashed into the bamboo, holding the branches aside. Rustling noises traversed the silence, and I could picture gliding things that fled before the warning crack of the bamboo.

Having ripped my shirt and scratched myself over the face and hands, I was not in an entirely pleasant mood when we emerged into a clearing. At one side a path ran like fluid into the gloom. I could see the black outline of what appeared to be an elevated native hut, and as we approached several voices rose inquisitively. One of the Laotians called out something, A moment later a gleaming figure darted from the house, and there followed a brief conversation, after which the figure hurried off along the path. Leung informed me that one of our coolies had instructed the man to prepare the *sala*.

A sudden pulse of lightning brought a number of thatched houses into livid relief against the trees, and then the gloom closed about us as we followed the footpath.

Abruptly we came out into a road, and ahead were pallid, crouching arcades. I recognized the familiar facades of shops. There were no lights, and the tall palms shot up over the houses like guttered candles. Dogs barked; once a door swung open inquisitively.

We came to the end of our journey in a little fenced-in compound where a hut rose on poles, obviously the *sala*. There were no evidences of life, not even when I mounted the sagging boards that were steps. The interior smelled of mold. I had brought a candle and matches, and the light wavered upon a room bare of furniture. There was no sign of the fellow who had been sent ahead, and I was too tired to care.

Leung disgustedly exclaimed that it was no place for a gentleman, and although I agreed with him, I undressed, wrapped myself in a blanket, and lay down on the floor with my coat for a pillow. I heard the coolies murmuring on the veranda as I fell asleep.

## 5

The next morning I awoke to the green life of Bassac.

In the compound a peacock was stretching lazily, and the trees whispered with the passage of many birds. A young Laotian or Siamese was squatting on the veranda, and beyond him, at the gate, a group of children had gathered to stare curiously.

At my appearance he rose and saluted. He was a very splendid person in a lime-yellow jacket and a dark *sampot*; and in clearly enunciated French he informed me that he was one of the secretaries of the governor, and his Excellency, who had been apprised of my presence, would be glad to receive me at the Tribunal Indigene. I gave him my letters of introduction, instructing him to tell the governor I would see him in an hour.

Leung, with Chinese resourcefulness, had managed to get a frying-pan from somewhere, and the result was a breakfast of eggs and salt meat, prefaced by bananas and coconut-milk.

I sent one of the Laotians to see if the *Ibis* had arrived, but evidently she was still struggling on the shoal; and so I set out for the governor's, followed by Leung, the coolies and a trail of curious children.

My appearance in the one street of Bassac caused something of a stir. Natives stared with frank interest, and then called to those inside to come and look. They seemed friendly, for many smiled, and some of the men touched their foreheads with a ghost of cowed servility in their manner. They were a light brown color, and had a Siamese cast to their features; indeed, I knew that many of them were full-blooded Siamese, for Bassac belonged to Siam before France insinuated it into the territory of Laos.

The road ran near the river, and on one side the stream gleamed in ruddy gold beyond the palm trunks, while on the other, houses crouched among the arrogant green plumes of the jungle. White dust powdered the road, and farther on it seemed to blend with the soiled pallor of lime-washed shops. In the clear sunlight, the town had an aspect of color undiluted by anemic civilized restraint. The people wore garments of Prussian blue, of purple, of orange and lime-yellow. Very few were tattooed, like the "black-bellied" Laos I had seen at Khone and along the river, and their nostrils and lips had that delicate fineness which white men call animal sensitiveness.

The Tribunal Indigene was a big open building with solid walls only half-way up the sides and wooden bars continuing to the roof. Several native soldiers lounged in the enclosure. The coolies and the children halted at the gate, but Leung followed me inside with a guardian air.

His Excellency was a very gentle-looking Siamese, who went barefoot and wore a blue *sampot* and a white starched jacket like those of French officials. He smiled over gold-rimmed spectacles and led the way to chairs in the gloomy, barred-in house. Then the secretary in the lime-yellow jacket brought cigarettes; and his Excellency began to talk.

There was one difficulty at the start. Although I had the governor's word for it that he spoke French fluently, and I thought I knew the language fairly well, we could not understand each other. He seemed very disturbed by this. Finally, in order to facilitate conversation and yet not offend him, I told his secretary to explain to his Excellency that there were many ways of speaking French, and that evidently he spoke one way and I spoke another; therefore would he permit his assistant, who knew the French that I knew, to translate for him?... This arrangement had its effect.

The letters said I desired to go to Wat Phu, the governor began.

Yes, I replied, I wished to study the ruins. A man who had been there had described them to me as resembling Angkor. It was not generally known that the Khmers built cities so far north in Siam as Laos, and if Wat Phu was the work of the Khmers, then it might yield further information about this people who rose and fell so spectacularly.

Very good; he hoped I would be successful. He himself knew little about Wat Phu, although it was not far away; in fact, he had never seen it. However, as the letters had requested him to extend every courtesy, he would assign his secretary to me, and undoubtedly he could help. Also he would be delighted to procure horses for me to use on the journey.

I told the secretary to thank his Excellency, and say, however, that instead of horses I preferred elephants.

Both the secretary and the governor stared.

Monsieur wished elephants? the young Laotian inquired incredulously. Why, the journey would require nearly two days by elephant, whereas a horse could make it in half a day!

Nevertheless, I replied, monsieur did desire elephants. As it happened monsieur was a very whimsical person, and as he had planned to go to Wat Phu on an elephant, he did not intend to be switched onto a horse at the last moment.

The secretary translated my speech.

Very well, agreed the Governor. But how many elephants did monsieur desire?

Three, I said. That would be sufficient to carry *monsieur*, his servant, his Excellency's secretary and the supplies.

He was sorry, he apologized, but he could not get the elephants today; it would require a little longer, perhaps he could have them by tomorrow—or the day after that....

Monsieur would find several days in Bassac very pleasant, I returned, inasmuch as he wished to learn something about the bonzes, and he understood there were many monasteries thereabout.

His secretary would be glad to render any service I required, said the governor.... And that was the end of the interview.

As I left the compound I observed a number of curious Laotian ladies peeping out of the governor's house, next to the Tribunal Indigene, and to judge by their whispered comments and giggles, they must have found his Excellency's visitor a most amusing sight.

In the afternoon the governor sent a rusty, sagging cot to the *sala*. Indeed, he was most prodigal with attention; for with the cot came a young Laotian girl who seated herself on the veranda with an air of permanence, and whose purpose, inasmuch as she did not state it, was vaguely disconcerting.' Leung regarded her with high disfavor, and asked me if I didn't think the presence of a Laotian lady would make me "lose face" with the community. I replied that it was not his privilege to question the hospitality of the Governor of Bassac, and that personally I thought the lady looked very ornamental on the veranda, and as long as she remained in that capacity, I was quite content to have her....

The day went by—a drowsy butterfly beating with heavy wings. Insects strummed in the hot, earth-scented air, darting drunkenly over the shadows that lay like spilled wine beneath the trees. Bare feet beat up the dust in the road.... Just before noon Monsieur Tambia appeared to say that the *Ibis* was safely moored by the embankment. His gloomy eyes disapproved the slim brown creature who sat listlessly chewing betel on the veranda.... The sun descended toward the blue mountains behind Bassac, and the Laotian girl called to a passing youth who came with a *khène*—a long reed instrument whose music sounds like the echo of a wild organ—and his tune brought a number of people, who squatted in the compound and laughed and clapped their hands as another youth danced.... White walls gleaming between the palms, and the blur of many moths.... Night on Bassac.

# 6

"*Ukasa: Vanthami Phantay sap Phong A:Pa:Rathang Kha:ma:tha:may Phanta ma:gna Ka:tang Poungnang Maihang Tha tap phong Sathou a:noumathame....*"

"I acclaim, pray the Saint to have pity on my faults and be patient. ... I offer Thee all merit I have acquired. Please share with me Thine own...."

It is the prayer of a bonze in one of the monasteries of Bassac.

They had an air of wisdom sleeping under a honeycomb of mold, those monasteries of Bassac. The two with which I became most familiar were at the southern edge of the town. One was lime-washed and had maps of damp green about the base of its walls; and in the little enclosure were two *stupas*— conical Buddhist memorials— also furry with decay. The other was a great thatched pavilion, with a drum under a roofed platform nearby. Both were in the dark green shadow of trees in obedience to the command of the Master that all monasteries should be built in the shade.

I went to them not as one visiting the dilapidated museums of a religion also decadent, which is the usual approach of the white man; nor did I go in search of esoteric truths, as do the theosophically inclined. I went as one individual who desired to know how certain other individuals lived. Also to enter into a mood through which I hoped to learn something of a mood of the past wherein the religion they represented had played a supreme part.

They were quiet places, these monasteries. There was no suggestion of cloisters or ascetics' cells about them, for these native structures never give the feeling of being "inside." They seem a part of the forest. Nor was there that sense of organization and worldliness characteristic of modern theological seminaries. They were simply retreats into which those desiring meditation and wisdom according to the Buddhist scriptures could retire.

I found the monks neither very friendly nor very unfriendly. They answered my questions according to their teachings. Their replies were clothed in formulas. If their intelligence went further they discreetly kept the fact a secret, as do most who follow religion as a vocation. And I found myself against a wall. I read Buddhist passages and then questioned the people in an attempt to connect the two; and they were utterly different. I felt myself failing miserably.

And then, one afternoon, the secretary in the lime-yellow jacket asked me why, when the principles of Christianity taught unity, the Christian religion was divided into sects, each separated by mere theological clauses. Suddenly I began to understand the faith of the Yellow Robe.

It is simply this: a religion can never be explained to an outsider through the historic documents upon which it is based, for they are the archaic expositions of an elemental truth which cannot be applied literally to the same truth a thousand years later. Between birth and death are the years

# 178 KING COBRA

1669. CAMBODGE – Phnom-Penh
Chef suprême des Bonzes

of growth, of splendor and corruption. And, regarded calmly, a revealed religion is the application through human lives of the principles of one enlightened mind desiring to hold together the multitude with a code of physical and spiritual conduct.

Buddhist bonzes are neither recluses nor priests, because they do not shut themselves off from the world nor, on the other hand, go about the world proselytizing their creed. Theoretically, they are men seeking self-culture through a healthy body and a clean mentality. In practice, they are everything from scoundrels to saints.

On the surface it would seem that Buddhism is a selfish religion. But it appears to me to be selfish only in that it promises salvation to the individual as an individual and not as one of a congregation, and that it was founded by a great teacher who did not proselyte but interpreted, and then left his principles to be followed, not through any intercessor such as a priest or a clergyman, but personally; in other words, he commanded that all who believed should themselves become monks. That this injunction has been obeyed to a certain extent is evidenced by the fact that in Laos, Siam and Burma it is customary for every young boy to spend some time in a monastery. In the past they stayed for two or three years, as it required that long to master Pali, the script in which the books were written; but now the boys generally remain only six months or a year unless they intend to stay permanently. When they leave the monastery they know something of their religion, and they either put it into practice or forget it, according to their individual temperaments. If they remain permanently, it is because they desire to wear the yellow robe as a symbol and adhere strictly to the precepts. Or, in some cases, because their psychology requires a gaudy manifestation of what their minds dimly perceive and their imaginations devour.

At Bassac I saw numbers of little boys in the monasteries. It was their school. When they entered they took a vow not to kill any living thing, to satisfy the requirements of the body without yielding to the senses, and to study the teachings of the Master. Their heads were shorn so that they would not be guilty of vanity or attractive to the other sex; and there were certain rules of conduct which they must obey, among them the injunction to eat but twice a day and never after noon.

Their robes were simple and in five parts: the *pha-sabonz*, a strip to gird about the loins; the *pha-dai-dsong*, a belt; the *pha-tse-vone*, a robe to bind about their bodies under the armpits; the *pha-sang-kha*, a sort of toga to be carried on the left arm; and the *pha-khap-pha*, a small piece to go over the shoulder.

Each morning they set out with one of the monks and stood outside the houses of the laity until given an offering of food, then, without thanks, they continued on their rounds.

A bonze must never give thanks for food or a gift. Nor is he allowed to accept money, although there are some monks who are not above yielding to temptation. An expression of gratitude is superfluous; for is not one taught that the good receive all that is necessary for their wants and the givers themselves need no reward other than the merit of their act?

His life in the monastery is made up of reading the sacred books and meditating upon them. At times he interprets the holy laws to the people, and always he is a schoolmaster; but otherwise he has none of the responsibilities of a parish or a flock, those burdens of the Christian minister or priest. He is by the example of himself a sermon unto the people.

And although a celibate he is not an ascetic; for did not the Lord Buddha himself, after years of self-inflicted privation in the forests of Nepal, condemn this as a sinful and ugly practice?

The most popular myth about Buddhism is the belief that Buddhists worship idols. Go to any of the numerous pagodas scattered through Laos and watch some woman or man kneel before an image of Gautama and pray or burn a candle for someone who is ill. It is simply the dim yearning of the heart for a godhead that it cannot understand except in human shape, together with the veneration of a simple mind for a great intelligence; and no matter what words are used to interpret it, it is that and nothing more or less.

One of the edicts of Buddhism commands that no supernatural powers shall be attributed to a monk or an image. If superstition—which exists in the civilized mind as well as in the so-called savage brain—lends mystical authority to an image or a man it is no fault of the religion. It is a curious fact that there are no saints in Buddhism, only the supreme saint himself.

Strangely, Buddhism is a religion that condemns mysticism. Now, twenty-three centuries after it was founded, mysticism often is practiced by the monkhood and the people.

Frequently, in Laos, a bonze visits the sick, burns candles and prays in front of flowers and a bowl of alcohol, then ties a fillet of cotton around the wrist of the patient, after which the afflicted one is supposed to be cured. This and many other superstitions are current, but they are violations of the pure faith. As it so often happens, the design is a beautiful and finely wrought creation, but the stencil becomes a formula that slips occasionally.

Consider the influence of the Yellow Robe upon the Khmer empire.

From two hundred years before Christ, up to the ninth century, Brahminism was the national religion in Cambodia. It was then that the cities of Angkor, Lolei, Banteai Chma, Prah Vihar and others sprang up. The Brahmin gods, who were the puppets of lustful priests, demanded empire. And so Angkor the Great, capital of the Khmers, became a fabulous city. Smoke of battle mingled with the smoke of altars. A litany of steel praised Siva the Destroyer. Carried upward on a barbaric surge, the Khmers became so powerful their empire received the name *Tevada Nagkon*, the Kingdom of the Angels. These "angels" were the angels of fury, speaking from the lips of caste-marked priests.

And then Buddhism flowed in quietly, a religion that was the antithesis of this cruel Brahmin creed.

Golden lotus-flowers unfurled on the towers of Angkor Wat, and where the lingam of Siva had exalted, was a simple figure of the Master of Kapilavastu.

From fury to the lotus is a sweep of worlds. Many became lost in the abyss; and the lingam of Siva was re-carved to represent Buddha, and Buddha was often pictured seated on a phallic-stone. A people bewildered spiritually was suddenly attacked by the enemies it had subjected in the past.

In the thirteenth century came the great invasion of the Thai, then two hundred years later the onslaught of the Karens, and a century after that the attack of the Laotians.

Buddhism had supplanted Brahminism; the voice of the Destroyer had become dim. The result was that in 1570 those Portuguese and Spanish explorers traveling in the interior reported Angkor the Great deserted—and the paradoxical truth was borne out that a religion of peace cannot save a nation at war. If a nation is to remain united and physically dominant, it requires more than a religion that offers salvation to the individual. Mohammedanism might have held the Khmers together; Christianity could not have done it.

The Khmers, first debauched by the Brahmin priests, then emasculated by the Buddhist monks, had entirely lost their virility.

Now, five hundred years after they have dissolved into the many races of Indo-China, an explanation of their decline lies under the mold and rot of the monasteries.

Once again, as so often in history, the priesthood had transcended sex and accomplished an exquisite seduction.

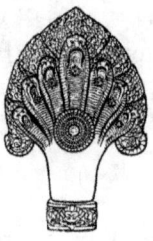

## Chapter VI
# The Twilight of the Khmers
*Tells of a Dead City*

Nhahœuns (Bassac)     LAOS - *Série E,*

"There was a touch of barbarity about these men seen in the flush of torches."

# Wat Phu

## 1

THE LATE afternoon was celebrating high mass when we came out of the jungle, and over the broad Laotian plain the tips of the trees seemed to take fire from the sun and glow like votive candles.

Somewhere a drum was beating, far off and at long intervals. It seemed a melancholy fulfillment; it was the voice of that dead people whose ruins I had traveled here to see, beating, beating the years to dust.... And it was only fitting, I thought, that a drum should announce the arrival of a stranger, no matter how unimportant that stranger.

As I heard it and looked across the plain, I was conscious that I should feel very emotional; for this was a great moment. Instead, I was inexpressibly tired and aware only of something tragic in the beauty of the sunset.

That morning we had left Bassac while the leaves were yet heavy with the night's showers: Leung, my Chinese boy; Souk, the young Laotian assigned to me by the governor; and several native porters.

A wet trail led us out of sunshine info a haze that seemed to fray apart and release the rain. For the next two hours I swayed in a howdah that looked like a halved drum, while water trickled over the brim of my helmet and ran through my clothes, and greater streams went coursing down the pachydermal skin that wrinkled beneath my feet. At first, flung back and forth with the roll and plunge of the elephant's gait, I felt nauseated; then this sensation became attenuated in a chill that ran up and down my backbone. The *mahout*, a young Laotian with a *patoi* bound about his middle, sat on the monster head with his feet crossed between the elephant's eyes, and the rain dripped from the glistening point of his hair and ran down his back in films. At one side of him was a raw sore on the beast's head made by the ankus[13].... The porters sloshed through the mud beside us; behind, Leung and Souk rocked along on two other elephants.

The houses we passed seemed drenched in ragged green fountains as palms drooped over them; houses typical of Laos, gaunt structures raised high on logs, most of them consisting of a veranda and a single room, and all with hooked points at the corners of the eaves tilting toward roofs that slanted up at a gradual incline, then broke and continued at a more acute angle. The people seated cross-legged in these houses or on the verandas stared at us, and some came out and touched their foreheads in salute, half awed and half friendly. This was indeed unspoiled wilderness, this part of Laos where white men were so rare the tradition of their superiority still existed. When natives passed they stopped and removed whatever head-covering they wore, whether a rag or a battered helmet, and some knelt in the mud and rain and, with bowed heads, joined the tips of their fingers together in a point against their foreheads.

Sometime after we started, while the rain was beating down furiously, I looked behind and saw Leung vomiting over the side of his howdah, and his glazed eyes stared at me accusingly for having made him ride an elephant when he could just as well have ridden a horse. Souk, looking very gay in spite of the weather, gave me an amused glance that seemed to ask what better you could expect of a Chinaman. I smiled back with equal good-humored contempt, although I felt that my face was the color of his lime-yellow jacket....

The rain stopped at noon. A hot breath seemed to steam from the drenched ground. We halted for an hour, and as my forehead felt flushed and my temples danced, I took some quinine. Then we moved on, rolling across a low jungle where the white sunlight lay motionless and tense.

Mountains ascended vaporously behind the bamboo, their crests absorbed by the sagging clouds. In the fields were pools, mottled with slime, where lotus-flowers exhaled a stealthy odor. Toward late afternoon we came into open country; and at sunset I heard the drum....

---

[13] A stick used, especially in India, for goading elephants.

Out of the plain rose a long, lonely mountain, its ridges, silhouetted against the west, smoldering with a rim of fire like the last glow on the edge of charred wood. At the foot of the mountain the trees became blue ashes, and nearby, set against a tumble of miniature huts, were several naked figures gleaming in the rosy dusk like tiny bronze images. It was from the mountain that the throbbing sounds came.

Souk, sitting on the elephant behind mine, spoke.

"It is the drum in the monastery."

Then he pointed to a white spot trembling in the ruddy twilight like a throb at the very heart of the mountain.

"Wat Phu," he said; and something quick and poignant stung my nostrils like the smell of burning pine.

# 2

The trail curved past a thatched shed where several natives sat in a silent group gazing at us. Souk called to them, and they came in a body, kneeling and saluting in that supplicating manner. After a few words with them, he said we would find a better camping site farther on but we could dismount here.

My muscles ached and there seemed a flame in my bones; a sour smell rose from my damply clinging clothes. I cannot remember when I have been so tired and sore. But I was not too exhausted to want to see the ruins. Instructing Leung to look after the details of the camp, I took Souk to lead the way to the temple.

Some few yards from where we started, the foliage thinned and disclosed a ruined terrace overgrown with weeds and bushes, beyond which a lake lay as though dusted with the settling night. Upon climbing the terrace I saw it was not a natural body of water but the remains of an ancient tank. It stretched away in a smooth oblong surface between banks showing traces of a stone coping that once had enclosed it.

From the other side of the terrace, across from the tank, the remnants of a stone causeway furrowed the green, losing itself in a welter of low trees from which piles of ruins rose blurred and indistinct in the dusk. There the mountain ascended, its flank seeming tattooed, as irregularly placed stones marked the course of a stairway scarcely visible in the profusion of growths. At the top of the stairway, on a broad shelf between summit and base, was the temple itself, shrouded in forest.

As a result of fatigue, the retina of my eyes had caught and held the fire of the now vanished sun, and wherever I looked the landscape seemed touched with illusive burning designs. In the breathless stillness, which checked every sound except the mournful beats of the drum, and with these ghosts of flame dancing before me, the entire scene had an aspect of hushed unreality, as though enclosed in the breath-stained glass of a museum-case.

With Souk behind, I followed the ruined approach, passing stone balustrades of *nagas*, which seemed to creep along close to the ground like smoke. Indeed, a thin purplish vapor was assembling, as if the hot soil gave a visible sigh of gratitude to the evening. I felt chilled myself, and a giddy spiral of fireflies whirling about my head made me faintly dizzy.

As we reached the two great ruins at the end of the causeway, I discovered that these luminous spots were not fireflies. I had a shuddery sensation, as though something cold had run down my back. My teeth chattered, although my temples felt hot. I was suddenly terrified by the conviction that the mountain was toppling down upon me, and the ground seemed to rise like an awful catapult to fling me into it....

I came out of this cataclysm to find myself sitting on the edge of the causeway vomiting. Souk raised me to my feet and started toward the encampment. I was aware that he was saying something about "*fièvre de bois*," and I found an absurd satisfaction in the discovery that an elephant hadn't done it....

# 3

That night while I lay on a cot in front of my shelter, a yellow panther moon crept into the sky, and clawed the vaporous exhalations of the earth, leaving the mountain and the plain to stand out clearly in its shadow. , . . Souk and Leung had wrapped me in a blanket and built a fire close by. The fever was passing out of my body through pores that seemed to release an endless flow of perspiration.

I was awake at dawn the next day. I had no temperature, but I felt weak, and my mouth had a feverish taste. Souk and Leung promised a long illness, even worse, if I got up. But I would not listen. The morning was warm with crystal-pure sunlight; and a few hundred yards away, on the forested slope, was Wat Phu.

The mountain, called Lingaparvata, faced the east, and its worn approach followed the course of the sun; a fact immediately significant when I reflected that the great buildings of Angkor, with the exception of Angkor Wat, looked toward the sunrise.

In the early morning the sacred lake (itself another significant fact, for did not most Hindu temples have a tank nearby?) was like blurred pewter. To the east the mountains of Boloven were becoming bluer as the day opened sleepy eyes.

I walked along the causeway, followed by Souk and Leung and a porter carrying my camera. The balustrade, smoky-dark in places, was indisputably of Khmer design. The half-obliterated *nagas* that once had formed the railing, were smaller than those at Angkor and had five heads instead of seven. At intervals between the *nagas* were blunt stones resembling phallic symbols; indeed, they were almost identical with the lingams I had found in some of the ruins at Angkor.

On either side of the approach were stretches of low ground that evidently had been sunken gardens; perhaps filled with jasmine-flowers and tiny lotus-pools in whose green-padded mirrors strolling monks were caricatured in blurred mimicry. Now the jungle had sucked up the lotus-pools and strangled the jasmine; and where the monks had walked blue dragonflies made veins of fire in the sunlight.

At the end of the causeway, on the first level of the terraced rise, were two ruins, one on either side. In the merciless sunlight, they were tragic, broken pyramids with gray piles of tumbled stone along their upper terraces to hint at towers that once mocked the blue. Vines sprayed them like green fluid shot into the veins of dead things.

The entrance to the building on the northern side was choked with creepers, but the main doorway of the other stood out sharply against the rays of sunlight descending behind it.

As I entered, a swarm of insects droned up from the weeds and floated off like singing sparks. Over the entrance was a crumbled tower. The gate itself was well preserved, and on either side were slabs exquisitely carved. Inside,

I had the feeling I had entered a fortress, for I found myself in a narrow space between walls, like a moat surrounding an embattlement. The outer wall was about six yards high and three feet thick. No cement had been used in its construction, the blocks of stone having been fitted together with such cunning that they had held through centuries. The inner wall was tufted on its farther edge with foliage, giving the impression that the space behind was filled in with soil or with high trees.

I followed the moat-like enclosure to its northwestern corner, into a small roofless chamber. Through a breach in one side I could see behind the inner wall into a wildly overgrown courtyard lying stricken in an agony of silence. A lone dragonfly, creature of lacy flame, rode the deathly hush; otherwise there was no breath of life in that strangled enclosure where the devouring growths had even fastened upon the tops of the walls and hung down in satiated tendrils.

I turned away from the courtyard to its walls, which at least were carved with a semblance of human life. In places the stone slabs became filigreed panels, and over the door was a mass of fretwork with a seated image in its midst. The figure was not Buddhistic but Brahmin. It made me think of the seated Sivas carved in the cloisters of Angkor Wat. In the past this evidently had been one of the dwelling-places of the priests and attendants attached to Wat Phu. I could picture this building in its former grandeur, surrounded by a town of wood and thatch houses that soon had rotted in the tropical climate.

Returning to the stone approach, I passed between several sculptured lions to a slightly higher level. The first flight of the mighty stairway loomed ahead. Its stones were worn and vine-grown, mounting to a terrace from which another stairway, set back some distance from the edge, climbed gradually up the mountain to the last grandiose flight. On either side were heaps of broken stone lying in a symmetrical formation indicating that here two buildings had flanked the approach as on the lower level, but structures much less pretentious.

From this terrace I could look between the grayish, creeper-bound masses of the twin edifices below and down the long avenue to the tank.

After a rest I went on. A number of low steps finally flattened out into an incline before the greater stairway. On a dwarf terrace *nagas* lifted their plume-like heads, and between them the staircase began, seeming flung up almost perpendicularly. My imagination crumbled under the magnificence of this stairway—grander than any at Angkor. As I climbed, my vision seemed to mount ahead of me and then fall back giddily. The stones were worn and grass grew between them; most of the time I had to move sidewise; often I rested. Breathless, I reached the top, flinging myself down between two stone Buddhas and staring below at a landscape that danced behind yellowish flecks.

This last level was a natural one, a broad plateau on the side of the mountain, and behind it a cliff rose sheer to the sky, draped with pendulous vines and trees emerging miraculously from crevices and ledges. The plateau itself was rank with jungle, sunk in dismal shade.

A short approach led from the tremendous staircase to the temple. The building itself seemed packed away in foliage, like some precious thing preserved in evergreen herbs. The stones were so grayed that in places an entire wall took on shadow, merging into a formless background for the few pilasters and slabs that caught rays of sunlight and stood out in panels of aureate filigree. The tall slender trunks of palms vanished in overhanging green. Creepers flowed down the walls and over the roots of trees. All around the temple banana-plants spread themselves luxuriously, their broad leaves glowing in veined fans of jade as the sunlight burned behind them. It was as intensely tropical as the jungles created in the dreams of the very young.

I moved toward the entrance, thrilled by this fulfillment. The front was a carved facade of triple doors, the middle one lower than the other two and with the torso of a giant image visible in its frame. This middle door was set back between sculptured pilasters and two slender pillars of turned stone close to the frame, with a few weed-grown steps leading up to it and over the lintel a carved panel with a god seated on a three-headed elephant in the center of it. Above this frieze a series of ledges graduated inward and up to a crumbled mass that once had been a tower. From the front I could see that the three doorways led into three parallel passages continuing to the rear.

I passed through the middle door into what had been the penetralia[14] but now was a roofless courtyard enclosed in moss-stained walls. The giant image,

---

[14] The innermost parts of a building, especially the sanctuary of a temple.

"I passed through the middle door into what had been the penetralia."

whose torso I had seen from without, sat cross-legged on an altar between two pairs of columns, and was fully ten feet high. In front of this enormous figure sat three other Buddhas of lesser size. All were covered with gold-leaf and wore spiked head-dresses that mounted in bristling array to a crowning point. A large fiber mat was stretched over them; mats were on the ground below them; and the altar was strewn with fruit, rice and other offerings. On the right-hand side was a tablet inscribed in what I imagined was Sanskrit, preserved in a frame built like a spired pagoda. These curling characters gave me a sensation half fear and half joy; for surely they explained something about Wat Phu.

But more commanding than the tablet was the great image dominating the three lesser ones. It was a figure of Buddha, but its face expressed nothing of the benign character of the Master of Kapilavastu. There was something tormenting about its placid, smiling immobility. It sat there as though enjoying a cruel joke on humanity. It was Nature ridiculing idiotic Man.

Doors led out from each wing of the penetralia, and on either side of the shrine was a passage connecting with the roofless remains of a little chamber behind the sanctuary. There, on a shelf in the vines, were at least half a hundred miniature images of wood and stone. Opposite to this shelf of gods, a single white lily was framed in a doorway opening into a thicket. A few yards behind the temple the cliff rose through the jungle into bewildering heights of green.

Returning to the sanctum, from which the tank, far below, could be seen, I noticed the light seemed grayer, and I gazed up out of the enclosure at a sky swollen with clouds. A stealthy wind was running its fingers through the trees.

"*La pluie,*" Souk warned.

When I paid no heed, he said if I did not care about myself, at least I should consider the camera. I told him to wrap it in his coat if it rained, and went on with my inspection.

Viewed from without, the building was a torn wraith of a temple haunting the green dusk. The walls were inset with numerous panels that crawled with carving. On the outside of the two projecting flanks that formed the sides of the main entranceway was a mass of sculpture crowding about a shrine where

"...a carved panel with a god seated on a three-headed elephant..."

"These *Apsarases* were different from those at Angkor Wat."

an *Apsaras* stood in deep relief. These *Apsarases* were different from those at Angkor Wat. They were about three feet tall, and instead of the conventional tiara-shaped head-dresses, they wore strange caps tufted with either leaves or feathers. Each held a lotus-flower in her right hand, and the stem curved behind her neck and showed the blossom over her left shoulder.

On the outer sides of the two doors set back slightly from the main entrance, were panels bearing mailed warriors holding swords and enshrined in the midst of elaborate scrollwork. The windows were very curious. Part of the way down they were closed with blocks of stone, and then three ornamented ridged bars appeared in relief against slabs of rock, giving the effect of curtains partly lowered over segmented windows.

At intervals on the walls were figures of warriors,

*Apsarases* and gods; and between them vine-gripped pillars supported ridges that once had borne the weight of towers. The entire structure, set there in dank twilight, achieved an effect of splendid desolation.

The rain fell suddenly, rattling the leaves and obscuring the far-away tank. Souk dutifully wrapped the camera in his coat, saying that we could take refuge in the monastery.

This retreat of the bonzes was a short distance to the north of the temple, a rambling pile-raised structure, thrice dismal in the rain, with trees brooding drearily over it. Several yellow-robed monks were leaning out of the windows, and at our approach they vanished like a flock of frightened canaries.

To get inside we had to climb a crude stair that was nothing more than a ladder. I found myself in an immense bare room with stalls around it where the monks sat to pray and meditate and a shrine against one wall. When we entered there were only two bonzes in the room, but immediately others appeared and hung about the doorway to another apartment, staring with mingled curiosity and hostility. Souk spoke to one of them, and he shook his head sullenly; whereupon my young Laotian guide let forth a stream of angry words that showed me all natives were not awed by the yellow robe. One of the monks in the room spoke to those in the doorway and they disappeared. Souk looked at me apologetically.

"They are stupid, monsieur. I told them you were a friend of the governor, and to send the head bonze immediately."

After a few minutes he came, moving with a simple dignity that distinguished him from the other monks. He offered his hand and we sat down on the floor.

He listened attentively while Souk explained what I wanted to know, then nodded and spoke at length.

"He says that the tablet in the temple is written in Pali," Souk translated, "and that it tells what offerings are proper to make at the shrine."

This was disappointing but not entirely surprising; for many of the inscriptions found at Angkor gave, instead of history, the same sort of information.

I then explained that I wished to learn something about the past of Wat Phu. It was my belief, after seeing the carvings and type of architecture, that it had been built by the Khmers, that Cambodian race whose kingdom was called *Tevada Nagkon* by the ancient Laotians. But I would like to hear something of its history, of the century and circumstances in which it was built.

Souk replied: "He says that Wat Phu was built by the Brotherhood many hundreds of years ago."

A cold draught floated across my hopes. That was quite plausible, I returned; naturally I had assumed it was built under the direction of the monks, but I wished to know what people had carried on the actual construction, whether Laotians, Cambodians or another race.

All races were one in the Brotherhood, the head bonze replied through Souk.

Then, I continued skeptically, it was built by *Buddhist* monks?

Yes....

This was ridiculous, for one even faintly familiar with Oriental religions would know that the monks of the yellow robe would never erect a temple bearing Brahminic figures, even if there were images of Buddha on the altar several hundred years after its construction. He was evading my queries, either for a reason known only to himself or because of a false pride in his faith, which forbade him to admit that the temple in which he worshiped had been constructed by the priests of another religion.

What had caused its ruin and abandonment? I pursued, feeling that I was against an immovable wall.

Everything must go to ruin except the souls of the enlightened, he said; and how could I even suggest it was abandoned when anyone could see that daily it was used as a place of worship?

I knew it was hopeless, but I went on.

If it was built by Buddhists, I inquired, then why were Brahmin temple-dancers carved on the walls?

Oh, those were not temple-dancers; could I not see that they represented Yasodhara, the Master's wife whom he forsook, and Queen Maya, his mother?

It was so stupid I couldn't help smiling, and he smiled back at me serenely.

For more than half an hour I questioned him, and in that benign and placid manner he gave contradictory answers that accumulated misinformation in my mind. It was more annoying than amusing, and I returned to the encampment wet and discouraged, and with a slight temperature. I knew without a doubt that Wat Phu was a Khmer ruin, but I was no nearer any knowledge of its history than when I arrived, and there was little hope of learning anything from the monks.

That night while I lay on my cot watching for the moon, the head man of the near-by village came bringing a young Laotian of a type quite different from the majority I had seen. His skin was a pale tawny color that seemed to glow in the firelight like the dull pallor reflected from the shade of a paraffin-lamp; nostrils narrow and sensitive, cheek-bones high, given a certain breadth by large wide-set eyes. His sensual lips suggested those of some of the sculptured Khmer heads I had seen at Angkor. Instead of the usual native costume, he wore a sort of Norfolk jacket of salmon-pink and wide white trousers that drooped full about his bare feet.

Souk explained his presence.

"The head man of the village brought him, monsieur, because he says he knows something about the people who built Wat Phu. He is from Luang Prabang."

The fellow did not kneel, as did the head man of the village, but touched his hand to his forehead and smiled.

"I went to school at Vien-Tiane, monsieur," he announced in fairly good French. "Also I have been to Hanoi; I was the 'boy' of Monsieur—who belongs to *l'École Française d'Extrême Orient.*"

This was unusual, for Laotians generally are too proud for the occupation known as "boy," which means a personal servant or valet. I told him to sit down, and he carefully chose a grassy spot and squatted after the manner of his people.

First he showed me his identification card, which is required of each native by the French government, and it bore the name Pheng; then he proudly asserted that he knew something about the Khmers. His master in Hanoi had told him a little, and had given him some French books on the subject. Also he had learned much of the history of Laos at Vien-Tiane and Luang Prabang; only he called the latter "*Muang Luang*," meaning affectionately "my town." And there were traditions and songs among his people which told of the time when Laos was attacked by the dark people of Cambodia. The country of the Khmers had at one time extended well beyond Bassac, and they had built temples there. Wat Phu was one of them. The Khmers had even penetrated as far as Luang Prabang. Proof of this was the fact that one of the sons of the present king of Luang Prabang had found some pieces of Khmer sculpture there. He did not know when the Khmers had been at Luang Prabang, nor had he any idea when Wat Phu was built except that it dated back "many, many hundreds of years."

This was the first information of any substance I had had, if it could be depended upon. I asked the Laotian if this son of the king was still in Luang Prabang.

He replied that he was living in Vien-Tiane, and his name was Tiao Phetsarath.

Could he, the young Laotian, read Pali? I asked hopefully.

No. Of course he had spent some time in one of the monasteries when he was younger, as it was required of all boys in Laos, but he had not remained long enough to learn the language of the bonzes.

I told him of the tablet in the temple, which I believed might disclose something of the history of Wat Phu if it could be read. However, I added, the monks seemed reluctant to give any information, but perhaps if he would try he might be more successful with them. I would be glad to....

Yes. He would try tomorrow.

We talked for some time, and then he gave that careless salute and went off with the head man of the village.

I felt elated. One thing I had decided: from Wat Phu I would return to Bassac and go on up the Mé-Kong to Vien-Tiane, perhaps to Luang Prabang; for I knew then that I had been waiting for even the slightest excuse to lengthen this adventure.

# 4

The next morning I went to the Wat again. That the exertion of the climb might excite a temperature, I knew, but I could not endure to lie inactive at the very foot of the temple.

Wat Phu, calmly reviewed after the first visit, disclosed itself as a symmetrically planned and exquisitely executed series of buildings, arranged to inspire the worshipers who climbed to its temple. At the time of its occupancy, and perhaps a while afterward, a town must have spread about the base of the mountain; but this town, built of perishable materials as were all the lesser structures of the Khmers, had soon succumbed to desuetude, leaving the Wat alone to rise above it like a mighty skeleton.

The tank had been laid out as a foreground, then the causeway of the *nagas*, crossing the sunken gardens to those twin buildings that had housed the monks, or perhaps the princes and governors who ruled there; although the latter seems illogical in view of the holy figures carved on the walls. Between these had commenced the series of levels upon which the grand staircase paused; then two more structures, perhaps for the *Tevadas*, or sacred dancers, and the secular attendants; and finally the great stairway itself, mounting sculptured terraces to the holiest of all levels where the temple, towered with crouching spired masses, proclaimed the majesty of the gods.

That morning I wandered behind the temple, and slightly to the south and rear of it found the remains of a wall of terrace. Crossing these weathered

260. - RUINES D'ANGKOR
Cambodgien faisant ses dévotions à une Divinité des Ruines

"Each held a lotus-flower in her right hand..."

stones was a little stream trickling beneath moist growths that almost concealed it. A short distance beyond, approached over slippery rocks and through high plants, was a small cavern-like space beneath a ledge where a tiny pool swelled out of the ground. This, Souk announced, was the sacred spring.

Returning to the temple, I made a few rough sketches of the figures on the walls, to compare with some photographs I had made at Angkor. Also I took some pictures, and lingered indolently under the sculptured lintels and in the roofless chambers until mid-morning.

With noon I had a slight temperature. I felt enervated and faintly nauseated. The thought of returning to Bassac on an elephant made me positively ill. I asked Souk if he thought he could get horses in the village, and he said I would have to send to Bassac for them; if I desired, he would dispatch the porters with the elephants and they could return with ponies.

After a rest I looked over my photographs of Angkor.

Wat Phu, compared with Angkor Wat in all its prodigal detail of carving and sculpture, seemed simple and restrained. Upon first consideration it appeared that here, in this temple in Laos, the Khmers had achieved the same grandeur but with a certain delicate repression, as though their first passionate and excessive expression of power had become more clearly modulated and refined. This hinted that Angkor Wat was slightly anterior to Wat Phu —which seemed impossible when I regarded the meager historical facts that influenced and had a direct bearing upon Khmer architecture.

Angkor Wat obviously was the last building erected at Angkor. Yet such a building as Wat Phu would have had to be built by people with unlimited resources and time at their command; and this could not have been after the thirteenth century, when the Khmers were plunged into successive wars and civil troubles. For between the time of the Chinese Ambassador's visit in 1295 and 1570, when Cristoval de Jacque, the Portuguese explorer, found Angkor Thom deserted, the empire had collapsed and disintegrated—all in little more than two centuries.

These historical events, as I reviewed them, seemed to place the erection of Wat Phu before the thirteenth century, during the Khmers' ascendancy, which commenced about 800 A.D. This was the beginning of the period of building and expansion. After that the Khmers conquered what is now known as Cochin-China, and parts of Siam, Annam and Laos. They had

"...when I came to the pictures of Prah Khan...I found myself staring at a wall carved with *Apsarases* identical with some of those on the walls of Wat Phu."

enormous wealth and thousands of slaves to work. It was then the magnificent edifice of Prah Khan rose at Angkor; also the city of Angkor Thom; the temple of Bayon, the palace of Phimeanakas , the Baphuon, and other equally splendid structures.

As I considered these events, with their influence upon the people and their activities, it seemed logical that the construction of Wat Phu occurred sometime between the ninth and thirteenth centuries.

In theorizing, I realized, I had to give supreme importance to the religious element. Quite evidently Wat Phu was built a Brahmin temple. And

Brahminism was introduced into Cambodia in 68 A.D. Almost four hundred years later, in 422, came Buddhism. Sometime later, about 581, the pure Indian dynasty ended. That Buddhism was not immediately all-powerful is evident by the Chinese envoy's memoirs, written in 1295, wherein he sets forth various Brahmin practices that were widespread among the people at that time. Thus it became apparent that Wat Phu, although dedicated to one of the Brahmin deities, eventually, at some date impossible to determine, had become a Buddhist temple, perhaps toward the decline of the Khmer empire as it was then that Buddhism advanced.

That afternoon of conjecture and theory, lying under my tent in the midst of photographs, notes and sketches, had an exciting climax. For when I came to the pictures of Prah Khan, one of the temples in the Angkor group, I found myself staring at a wall carved with *Apsarases* identical with some of those on the walls of Wat Phu. This was a fact worthy of consideration, inasmuch as the *Apsarases* of both temples differed from the sacred courtesans carved on other Khmer ruins. These two were the same, I observed, except for two slight discrepancies: the head-dresses differed somewhat in their shape, and the feet of the Prah Khan *Apsarases* were turned toward the right while those of the Wat Phu *Apsarases* were turned to the left. Otherwise they were alike in pose, in dress, in ornamentation and in the fact that both held lotuses in their right hands and the stems of the flowers curved around their necks, with the buds visible above the left shoulders.

I was so excited I set out for the temple immediately. The climb in the heat of the afternoon drained me of strength, and when I reached the top I was nauseated and burning. But my elation was stronger than the fever —particularly when I compared the sculptured figures with those in the photographs and saw they were the same with the exception of the slight differences I had already noticed.

Then I found other analogous details. Some of the windows of Prah Khan were closed with blocks of stone like those of Wat Phu although not entirely in the same manner. Also there was a strong similarity between the buildings in the stone fretwork that paneled both, and among a few of the lesser images. Prah Khan was built about 800 A.D. Therefore, the two structures being contemporary, as suggested by the identical workmanship, I realized that Wat Phu must have been erected sometime between the eighth and tenth centuries. The fact that Prah Khan was a more tragic victim of the jungle, could be attributed to its natural surroundings or the possibility that it was abandoned earlier than Wat Phu. As to the time of Wat Phu's surrender to the forest, so far I had found no means of determining it. But Vien-Tiane and Luang Prabang were ahead, full of the history of Laos and its various conquerors, and surely there I should discover some facts that would at least hint at the time and cause of the ruin of this magnificent temple and its attendant buildings.

Having reached those conclusions, I sat down in a brassy dusk of vertigo, and later, when I was able to walk, returned to the encampment with a rising temperature.

# 5

That night Pheng, the Laotian from Luang Prabang, came to report that the information on the tablet would be of no use to me, for according to the bonzes it concerned secular matters. But I was not discouraged or even disappointed. It was sufficient to have established at least the century, if not the actual years, during which Wat Phu had been built.

For the two days following my temperature varied, and then my pulse subsided to the tolling that quinine always celebrates in my ears; and on the third day I returned to Bassac, not on horseback as I had planned, but in a bullock-cart.

A week later on the Mé-Kong, just before reaching Vien-Tiane, I awoke out of restless sleep to find myself shaking with a chill. The fever had tracked me from Wat Phu.

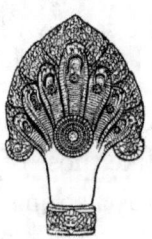

## Chapter VII
# Sun-Weary Town
*Tells of a Prince and the Fortress of Santal-Trees*

281. - LAOS. - Une Pirogue de Passagers sur le Mekong

"It was disconcerting to be met with a motorcar after voyaging more than seven hundred miles up a jungle river, traveling at times in pirogues—small native canoes—and exploring the forests on elephants and in bullock-carts."

Collection Raquez  LAOS - Série F, n° 11
Comment on voyage au Laos - e) Déchargement des éléphants pour la traversée d'une rivière (Hin Lat)

# Vien-Tiane

## 1

N THE French maps of Indo-China it is called *Kilomètre Dix-neuf.* Instantly one pictures an outpost where sunburnt *légionnaires* impose khaki-clad law on the jungle. In reality, it is a mud bank where a road glides out of the forest to drop into the copper-flushed current of the Mé-Kong. There is not even a native dwelling in sight to make the familiar bas-relief upon the monotony of the sky. Only white-hot clouds, trees whose branches seem limp in the heat, and the muddy, shimmering expanse of the stream. *Kilomètre Dix-neuf* is one of France's little jokes on the jungle. The significance of it is that nineteen kilometers away is Vien-Tiane, the so-called French capital of the Protectorate of Laos.

I arrived there one mid-morning when the air lay in a sensual swoon, having come by an interchange of tiny river boats from Bassac. That journey, in retrospect, seemed colored with the unreal hues of a dream.

On one side of the river was Siam, on the other Laos, but the bamboo-crested banks were so similar it was like traveling between a mirror and the original.

Below Kemmerat were many waterfalls whose sifted fire singed the dark ledges of gorges that had drunk almost to their brim of the swollen stream. In the rapids of Ma-Chien, the water spun beneath the boat like a fluid relief-map; and although the engines were running at full speed, there were times when the small craft jerked and shuddered without moving. In places the banks were uneven terraces of stone. Behind them rose those immense, silent forests of bamboo, those endless tangles of peacock-haunted green.

I remember a dawn at Na-Phong when, in the soft blue-violet light, with the misty sprays of color ahead where the sun was rising, it seemed as if we were plunging into a rainbow.

At night, the reflected stars were like cryptic Sanskrit writing on the river. There came a last memorable sunset when a fragile yellow haunted the curve ahead, vanished quickly and left the black trees standing stiff against a lilac sky.

The next day we reached *Kilomètre Dix-neuf.*

It was a very auspicious occasion, that brief landing, there in the fainting midday. His Excellency the Governor of Laos would be there. "I shall meet you at *Kilomètre Dix-neuf* and take you to Vien-Tiane in my car." That telegram had been delivered to me the previous day at Pakhinboun. It meant, the captain of the little boat explained, that his Excellency would make it possible for me to reach Vien-Tiane some three or four hours earlier than the Pavie, thus avoiding unnecessary travel in the middle of the day. It was disconcerting to be met with a motorcar after voyaging more than seven hundred miles up a jungle river, traveling at times in pirogues—small native canoes—and exploring the forests on elephants and in bullock-carts.

But I was the only one thus disturbed. The other four passengers of the Pavie gathered on the deck to watch the landing, interested not in the fact of an automobile so far in the interior but in the event created by the appearance of a governor who exerted himself to meet an inconspicuous American traveler. The schoolmaster from Vien-Tiane was there, telling me I should find the Laotian *phu-saos* most diverting; his Italian-looking friend who knew ten words of English, silent as usual but smiling a dark, infinitely wise smile; and the peasant-like post-office official with his red-haired mistress....

As the ship glided up to the mud bank, I saw a shining new car and a motor-truck; a moment later, I was in the car, my luggage in the truck, and beside me sat an immaculately clad Frenchman who spoke English with enviable perfection.

The red-haired mistress of the post-office official waved from the deck, then the Pavie was receding. I felt a little sorry to leave the Mé-Kong....

## 2

It was a day bewilderingly out of focus with the panorama of wild life the last two months had led me to expect.

I entered Vien-Tiane by an excellent French road, whirling past towered ruins blurred in the sunlight, native houses and rows of yellowish plaster dwellings, and shot through a gate where' a brown soldier stood at attention outside a sentry-box, into the grounds of the *Résidence du Laos*.

The governor's palace faced the Mé-Kong through a line of palms and low trees. Within, blinds created an ashen dusk, and numerous Buddhas, collected by his Excellency, startled the conventional atmosphere. Barefoot servants moved soundlessly in the midst of French furniture.

Dejeuner was an elaborate rite celebrated by a strange male company present in my honor. A missionary priest, very gay in spite of his cassock; two officials with starched collars buttoned close about sunburnt throats; his Excellency and myself. It began with cocktails, followed by wine which flowed through nine courses, and ended with chartreuse.

When the perennially excited French conversation had subsided in the wake of the guests, there descended upon the residence that ghastly afternoon hush that swoops upon every household in the tropics at this hour. I was left alone in a high-poster bed, ostensibly to rest, which is the solemn duty of every white man at this time of day, but really to lie there thinking if it were not possible to effect a revolutionary measure whereby life could be sustained through the deadly hours of the siesta, thus preserving the sanity of those unaccustomed to such somnolent indulgence.

At four o'clock faint stirrings animated the residence, and at five a charmingly Parisian aide of the governor's called to take me to the "*cercle de Vien-Tiane*" where, he explained, the French inhabitants gathered to "resist the climate."

The shining motorcar that had brought me from *Kilomètre Dix-neuf* whirled us along a road close to the Mé-Kong, and past the ruins of a pagoda where some Laotian boys were kicking a ball in an absurd imitation of cricket. In the roadway were several yellow-robed bonzes; an empty rickshaw rattled past drawn by a native in a breech-clout. It was bizarre. I felt as though this scene half French and half Laotian should suddenly shift, like the colored glass

*Precious prize, Close your eyes,*
*Now we're goin' to visit love's paradise,*

First published in 1911, the ragtime love song, "Oh, You Beautiful Doll," with lyrics by Seymour Brown and music by Nat D. Ayer was apparently still popular 14 years later and half-a-world away.

of a kaleidoscope, and fall into another extravagant picture. "You are in the jungle," I told myself solemnly.

The *cercle* was a small buff-colored building facing the river, and in the rear was a tennis-court where flanneled Frenchmen and women in sports skirts darted at balls which, when truant, were recovered by little brown boys there for that purpose. Tennis stopped as I was presented to the socially select.... One delicately lovely creature with tawny-ivory skin and hair blue-black—she came from Martinique—proudly exclaimed "Good-by!" as she gave me her hand; and then added, with a soft, disarming accent, that she knew English very well....

...Did monsieur dance? Ah, then they would have a *soirée!*.... And that last book of Andre Gide.... shocking.... Had I heard there would be no opera in Saigon this year? No; well, there would be none. *Ça ne fait rien!* It was terrible anyhow.... Did I know Paris well? And France?.... There was a rumor that the tango was coming in again.... America must be very dull now that the regime sec was in effect.... Had I heard that the Princess Murat had come up the Mé-Kong in a pirogue?.... Very few visitors came to Vien-Tiane; it was the signal for celebration.... Would monsieur come to tea tomorrow?.... And then dinner afterward, at *Monsieur Le Maire's?*.... Thirty love!... It was terrible, this exile.... Did *monsieur* like the *phu-saos*? A *phu-sao* was a Laotian girl.... There were not enough Frenchwomen in Vien-Tiane; that was why some Frenchmen took *phu-saos*.... It was shameful. *Monsieur So-and-so*, who had a high position in the *Service Civil de l'Indochine*, had not only one *phu-sao* but two... Ah, well, this exile!.... *Tres chaud*....

Bats were careening across the court when I retreated from the *cercle*. Instead of riding to the residence, we walked along the Mé-Kong, the charmingly Parisian aide and I. He said he knew an American song, and commenced to hum "Oh, You Beautiful Doll!" ... A pirogue stole soundlessly on the river, leaving a streaming reflection.

Tomorrow, said my escort, abruptly breaking his song, we would visit the *ville indigène* and the pagodas.

Somewhere in the dusk a native was playing on a *khène*, and the notes danced a stately saraband.

Ah, Laos! sighed the Frenchman; I would love it, he predicted. The music, the cool nights, the river, the *phu-saos* with flowers in their hair....

"Early the next morning the Parisian aide came in the shining car to take me to meet Prince Phetsarath and see the ruined pagodas of Vien-Tiane."
The town's eponymous pagoda is seen here, with Harry's personal photo below.

Was there a native prince living in Vien-Tiane, I asked —one of the sons of the King of Luang Prabang?

Yes, Phetsarath lived there. He held a position in the Civil Service.... A prince in the Civil Service! It hinted at grotesquerie, I thought. I said: I should like to meet this Phetsarath.[15]

Tomorrow....

While at Wat Phu I had learned that the Khmers had penetrated Laos as far as Luang Prabang; Prince Phetsarath had found some Khmer sculpture there. And so I wanted to talk with this Phetsarath.

Was I going to Luang Prabang? asked the aide.

Perhaps.

It would require about twenty-five days in a pirogue; the season was bad. But Luang Prabang was *charmant*. The mountains, the pagodas, the music of the *khène*, the gay *phu-saos*....

When we reached the residence it was quite dark.

That evening his Excellency and I dined on the terrace under a sky heavy with stars. Not more than a hundred yards away, the Mé-Kong flowed past silently, the dark shadows of pirogues pinned to its surface with reflected stars.

## 3

Early the next morning the Parisian aide came in the shining car to take me to meet Prince Phetsarath and see the ruined pagodas of Vien-Tiane.

As we rode about the town preparatory to going to the offices where, incongruously, the Laotian prince carried on his duties with the French Protectorate, I tried to adjust myself to the incredible reality of Vien-Tiane.

---

15 Prince Phetsarath Rattanavongsa was born January 19, 1890 so he was 35 years old when Hervey met this educated and historically significant man. Just six years earlier he had received the title Somdeth Chao Ratsaphakhinay, one of the highest ranks in the country previously held by his father. He was also Somdej Chao Maha Oupahat ("His Highness the Vice-King") making him the first and last vice-king of the Kingdom of Laos. From 1942-1945 he served as Prime Minister of Laos and played a large role in politics until his death on October 14, 1959.

It is uncertain if this was one of the "Chinese-owned *épiceries*, which stock champagne, cognac, truffles, anchovies and other such requirements of the French digestive systems."

"At night the bugle calls of the *Garde Indigène* have a shuddering echo in the tremolo of wild things in the surrounding jungle."

Such a town could not be in British colonial possessions, nor in American. When a traveler ascends the frontier of India he finds isolated outposts with a few white men in charge of hundreds of natives, an atmosphere military and very somber. It is the same in the hill regions of Burma. In the interior of the Philippines, Haiti and the other few island possessions of America there are garrisons. But that feeling of gaunt isolation exists.

And here was Vien-Tiane... a little town on the upper reaches of the Mé-Kong, a journey of nearly a thousand miles from the Cochin-China coast, separated from Tonkin by forests and mountains almost impassable, isolated on the other side by the upper wildernesses of Siam, and very close to the range of mountains that rises into Tibet; yet a town startlingly unlike a jungle outpost.

From Saigon it requires at least fourteen days of the swiftest travel possible to reach Vien-Tiane; travel through forests, over rapids, among mountains and river islands, and by sundry means of transportation. My journey had been longer, a matter of two months instead of weeks, because of the vicissitudes of my particular mission; and after this long period spent in jungles and on the river, transported by motorcar, horse, bullock-cart, elephant, steamboat and pirogue, I found Vien-Tiane disconcerting.

In spite of the contention of the French inhabitants that they are in exile, the fact remains that Vien-Tiane has its club and various social strata; its government offices, including those of the telegraph and the telephone; its remarkable clinic and industrial school; its well-planned roads for motor traffic, and its Chinese-owned *épiceries*, which stock champagne, cognac, truffles, anchovies and other such requirements of the French digestive systems.

And yet those excellent roads taper off into jungle; not three kilometers from that industrial school natives harvest in the drenched rice-fields as they have done for more than a thousand years; nearly naked women move languidly by the club where French ladies sit in gauzy frocks from the Grand Magasin Charnier in Saigon; the ruins of ancient temples clutter the back yards of the plaster houses of the French; and frequently at night the bugle calls of the *Garde Indigène* have a shuddering echo in the tremolo of wild things in the surrounding jungle.

"Near the rue du Marche I noticed a Laotian theater..."

Thus Vien-Tiane lies beleaguered by undulations of forest and mountain, connected with the outside world only by the Mé-Kong and the telegraph lines. In trying to grasp and explain the incongruous facts of its being, the only logical answer I could summon was the peculiar faculty of the French to civilize the natives by themselves accepting something of the native viewpoint. For I had learned by then that a Frenchman can live among brown people, even as one of them in habits, without deteriorating, whereas the average Englishman or American cannot do it without being a superior tyrant or a degenerate.

Therefore, the French give a semblance of France to Vien-Tiane, and it does not matter how isolated it may be, or how many accessible approaches it has, so long as it is in touch with some source of supplies.

That morning Vien-Tiane lay in a smother of green, its blanched, sun-weary houses meshed in hedges of crimson hibiscus, in bougainvillea and yellow-flowering teak-wood trees, and its tiled roofs stamped with the shadows of tall palms. The names of its streets suggested burlesque: Quai Francis-Garnier, Quai Pavie, Boulevard Circulaire, rue Marechal Joffre, rue Marechal Foch....

On these streets listless coolies wandered with rickshaws or carrying pole-swung burdens. Soldiers from the *Caserne de la Garde Indigène* moved by in a burlesque of military precision. Women sat in the market beside their baskets of vegetables and exotic fruits; and in long rows of whitewashed shops Chinese and Annamites stirred languidly among their wares. Near the rue du Marche I noticed a Laotian theater; and from there the roads ran straight into a parallel avenue flanking the river where bazaars, pagodas, dwellings and the Residence looked out upon the Mé-Kong.

It was mid-morning when we called for the prince. A khaki-clad, barefoot orderly went after him, and presently he came, apologizing in exquisite French for having kept us waiting. At first I thought he was very young, then I realized he was one of those people who do not show their age. He was very small and slim, and his wrists had that fine slenderness which goes with well-wrought fencing foils. His sensitive features, crowned with a high, thin forehead, were given a certain distinction by a carefully clipped mustache. He seemed curiously suited to his costume of black shoes, black silk stockings, a *sampot* of changeable blue shot through with greenish lights, white shirt and jacket, black tie and sun-helmet. On another that combination of native and French dress would have looked ridiculous; his manner dignified whatever he chose to wear.

As the motorcar purred off in the hot sunlight he announced that he had spent some time in England about four years ago. Also he had been in Paris for quite a while. He had been informed, he added, that I was interested in the Khmer civilization. Perhaps he could help me a little. He himself was preparing some manuscripts on Laos and Cambodia, recorded from the ancient annals of the court of Luang Prabang. He would get his notes together and we could look over them. Would I dine with him the following evening? We would find time then to talk. He would have Laotian food....

We went first to a Wat near the market-place. This Wat, the Prince announced, was called Sisaket, and was built in the reign of King Anou, inaugurated on Thursday the Ninth-Moon-Growing-Day of the Sixth Month; that is to say, in 1814. It was one of the more recent temples, for some of the pagodas of Vien-Tiane date back before the eleventh century.

It was surrounded by a high wall. In front of the gate sat a large bronze Buddha with a spired head-dress similar to those of the Cambodian and Siamese Buddhas, and flanking it were two great stone *prachedees*, or sacred memorials. Prince Phetsarath called to a young yellow-robed neophyte lingering nearby and sent him for the head bonze. Meanwhile, we inspected the worn buildings that stood outside the wall. One was the old library. The steps were broken and rotted, and inside were frescoes, once gaudy pictures of mythological events but now faded panels from which even the pigments seemed sapped.

Across from the library were the houses of the monks, raised on piling in the midst of palms. Here we were met by the head bonze, a gentle-mannered middle-aged man draped in the customary saffron vestments. He took us into the monastery and unlocked cases where images of pure gold and silver were kept with cheap Japanese flowers in glass caskets; then he led the way to the temple enclosure and admitted us to a quadrangle surrounded by a continuous roofed gallery.

These galleries were amazing. In tiers of peaked niches sat several thousand tiny Buddhas of golden terracotta, bronze, wood, and stone. Below these shrined images other Buddhas, some broken and many crumbling, sat on shelves and ledges. Prince Phetsarath said there were 6,820 Buddhas in golden terra-cotta alone....

From that maze of gods we wandered into the temple. The balustrades of its stairways were formed by elaborately carved ascending dragons, and the corners of the eaves were tilted and gilded in the manner characteristic of Laotian pagodas. Inside, in gloom cellar-damp and cool, was an altar overburdened with images of silver, bronze and gilded wood, seated or lying in the midst of tiny sacred umbrellas, votive chalices, burnt-out candles and joss-sticks, and cheap imitation flowers. Here, as in the galleries, were the arched niches for diminutive Buddhas, and the walls looked aged with faded frescoes.... The entire number of Buddhas in this Wat was about 9,500.

From the Sisaket temple we went through other Wats whose names were barbaric puzzles. All were similar: whitewashed walls staring between palms, tall-ridged horned roof, and an immense Buddha, sometimes twenty feet high, seated in the interior dusk and surrounded by silent, curious monks.

The morning ended, incongruously, over Picon-grenadines at the club; which is the inevitable climax or anticlimax of every morning in the Far East, varied only in the brand of liquor and the amount consumed. Then the shining car took me to the residence, where I was left to face a cocktail, wine, nine courses and a liqueur; after which the siesta hour descended, and Sun-Weary Town curled up like a great cat and lay sprawled in the glare with insects buzzing above it as over the dead.

## 4

That afternoon, just before the heartbreak of the day, I went to Tat Luong.

A road wanders out of Vien-Tiane toward this ruin, past thatched huts and cultivated soil, into the wild green where it mourns. Water-buffaloes lie nostril-deep in the pools along the way; butterflies wheel drunkenly over the piles of dung. If it is late—as it was that afternoon— tawny men will be coming in from the rice-fields, their legs and thighs sheathed in mud.

I approached Tat Luong in a whirl of dust that subsided as the motorcar slowed up in the midst of palmettos. A few extremely tall palms tilted up out of a tumult of foliage and leaned their bushy crests against the sky. On my left a double row of pilasters escaped from entwining creepers; evidently the supports of a pagoda roof in the past, but now ending in rugged summits from which little bushes took life mysteriously. At the far end of this stark colonnade an immense Buddha humped out of the piled leaves, like a sleepy fat vagabond suddenly aroused from a haystack.

A path emerged from the palmettos and crawled around a clump of jungle. The great tapering central tower of Tat Luong, surrounded by its smaller but identical towers, pressed into the bluish-white sky ahead. I paused under the arch of a gate resembling a shattered antechamber. The low walls surrounding the enclosure were almost entirely overgrown with vines.

The courtyard, sunk like a moat, surrounded the pagoda, and its outer edges were defined by low pillars that in the past must have formed the colonnade of the monks' cells. The center of this enclosure seemed inflated

"The morning ended, incongruously, over Picon-grenadines at the club; which is the inevitable climax or anticlimax of every morning in the Far East, varied only in the brand of liquor and the amount consumed."

as this immense stone mound swelled out of the earth, grooved with terraces and thrusting its obelisk up to a tapering point of gold. This one rich glimmer, set against the sky, was startling on that pallid, monkish pile.

At certain seasons, I am told, festivals are held here, and the music of *khènes* profanes the solitary terraces and colonnades, and over the great courtyard lanterns swoop and tremble like a harlequinade of sparks. This late afternoon the stillness was like stiff plush, and a few butterflies embroidered it with tiny throbs of pale blue, of black and yellow.

From the courtyard—which had been brick-paved but now was softened with grass—I could see the plan of Tat Luong: four entranceways into the enclosure and four stairways up the terraces to the pinnacled mound, there lost in masses of weathered iron-dark stone, whitened in places as though scabbed with bleached rust. It was much simpler than the architectural extravaganzas of the Khmers. Nor was the stone covered with carving, like the temples at Angkor and Wat Phu. Chiseled dragons made undulating balustrades, their tongues forking out in a blanched mimicry of flame. Otherwise there was no attempt at sculptural decoration.

After circling the "*tat*" I found that I had entered from the rear. The roofless main gateway stood gaunt in the clutch of tall bushes growing from its sides, and locked muscled tentacles about the crumbling brick and mortar. A few yards from it was the front stair of the "*tat*," mounting to a small building with a series of four roofs graduating inward to a point. This shrined an elaborately carved *prachedee* of white and gold surrounded by tiny gilded Buddhas.

On another side of the mound, set against the enclosing wall, was an entrance-chamber obviously new. Here again were the graduated roofs, with carved dragons lifting their heads from the projections of the eaves, and the addition of two curved prongs jutting from the top roof.

On the opposite side, built into the crenelated terrace, were stairs ascending to the ruins of a covered portico. This second terrace was coped with stones shaped to represent the petals of lotus-flowers, while the insides of the crenelations of the lower wall, those of the first terrace, were set with little shrines each containing a miniature Buddha. Between these two copings ran a narrow space, which continued entirely around the base of the "*tat*."

I wandered to the rear of the first terrace where a broken stair led to the second. Above this level, where the stone mound rose from its graduated base, was a row of small *prachedee*-like towers—originally there were nine on each side—crouching beneath the mighty central spire.

Seated between the lotus-like projections of the coping, I gazed over the terraces and courts and the enclosing wall into the palm-spumed rollers of verdure that melted into the surrounding green turf. The day was just ending and a sorrowful hush lingered over Tat Luong. For a moment this jungle-ruin ached with a tender mood, then the pity of the dusk came down, accompanied by ironic stars.

# 5

Although I went early to Prince Phetsarath's, hoping to arrive before the other guests, I found three already there: the tawny-ivory lady from Martinique, who again graciously greeted me with "Good-by"; her husband; and a young Annamite, a pallid fellow with a French name and a trace of Parisian smartness in his manner.

The prince wore a dinner-jacket with every detail correct; his *sampot*, drawn up from black silk stockings, was a vibrant imperial blue with changeable lights of gold in it.

The house was built after the native fashion, raised on logs; and a huge roof hooded it, its shingles seeming alive when restless branches scratched them. The great living-room was a sort of closed-in veranda, and between the rattan blinds were gaur horns and other trophies of the hunt. Insects rasped about a yellow-shaded lamp; outside, the night seemed to rest on furry paws.

Soon the other guests arrived. The *commissaire* and his wife came in a motorcar attended by a native chauffeur and native footman; and following them, the Parisian aide, also, with his wife in a victoria.

While we were drinking *apéritifs* the prince's wife entered, a frail, shadowy woman, who looked older than he and who smilingly shook hands with all the guests and then retired, leaving with me the curious illusion that she had not really been in the room but only a ghost of the prince which appeared momentarily to complete his hospitality.

The dinner, although Laotian, was served in the French manner. A little basket containing warm rice cooked to a glutinous consistency was placed at each plate, to be eaten with the courses that followed. First came *khao-poun*, a sort of macaroni in broth, then *pha-fok*, a fish custard; *som-cai*, red caviar; *mou-nein*, shredded pork; and *cai-phat-king*, chicken cooked with ginger. The food would have been most acceptable had it not been flavored with *nuc-mam*, a salty fish-water which the natives use to season every dish. With the dinner *lao*, or rice wine, was served along with French wine. This native liquor is like transparent white fire; and it is customary, after drinking it, to turn the cup down and say "*khouam touei*," meaning "return the glass," which is a polite expression of satisfaction.

Liqueurs in the living-room.... French conversation mounted in a flushed heat. Musicians unseen in the darkness outside made music on *khène*s, those wind-instruments of perforated bamboo reeds bound together like the pipes of an organ. The *commissaire's* wife essayed a Laotian dance, and the pallid young Annamite sang the words in French. The *khène*s marched through the rhythm of "*Votre est Village*," a fantastic thing that seemed to chant the war-hymn of trees before the advance of the wind. Then came "*Se Bo Key*," a trembling *chanson*.... "*Le Chant de Piroguier de Nam-Khouan*"... Prince Phetsarath sat quietly in the midst of the gaiety, a smiling part of it yet exhibiting that friendly aloofness which is the heritage of royal blood....

Soon the guests departed for the club, where the *soirée* had already begun, but I remained to follow later with the prince. When we were alone I began by saying I had heard he had found some Khmer sculpture at Luang-Prabang.

Yes. Among the pieces he had found was a particularly interesting head—in sandstone. The lips were very full and sensual, the nose broad, the eyes with a hint of laughter at the corners, suggesting that it belonged to the period after Shan blood began to flow into the pure Indian strain of the Khmers. The hair was done into a knot on the top of the head, with an ornamented band about it.

"The Khmers were at Luang Prabang in about 1366," he added.

Then I told him something of my journey. I had spent a while at Angkor, among the ruined temples and palaces; and then I had traveled up the river to Bassac, and visited Wat Phu, which I believed to be the ruins of a Khmer town built sometime between the ninth and twelfth centuries; probably about 800, because of the resemblance of the sculpture of Wat Phu to that of Prah Khan at Angkor, which was erected in the ninth century.

He nodded. "Wat Phu was built by the Khmers... Then, after listening interestedly to some of my observations on those ruins, he said: "I like to find foreigners studying this country. As for myself, I love to study it.... The history of Laos is similar to that of Cambodia in that both countries were born out of terrific wars...."

As he talked he smoked; and he was one of those few who know how to use a cigarette-holder. His lean fingers seemed to caress the carved ivory and mold into it as though they were a part of the design.

"We Laos come of the so-called non-tattooing branch of the Shans," he explained in his delicate French, "although the majority of the people do tattoo themselves. And Vien-Tiane is very old. Its correct name is Vien-Chan, 'the Fortress of Santal Trees.' The kingdom existed as far back as 574 a.d., and it grew after the Annamites conquered the Karen kingdom Lin-y, which was more powerful than Laos at the time and had dominated it.

"The first religion was like the Shamanism of the Tartars, the worship of spirits. Many of our people still believe in *phis*, or evil ghosts. Buddhism came in sometime during the tenth century from Cambodia, where it had been disseminated since 422.... We got more than a religion from Cambodia. The thirty-sixth king of Laos —the ruler of Vien-Tiane, or Vien-Chan, a man named Phaya Fa Ngum—married a Cambodian princess. That was in 1316. It was during his reign that the Khmers were at Luang Prabang—in 1366.... Undoubtedly Wat Phu existed at that time, but then it was in Cambodian territory. You see, it could not have been abandoned at that period....

"By 1373 Laos had become a great power. Phaya Fa Ngum had been victorious over the Karens, and Cambodia was friendly. But about two centuries later Laos joined in the civil wars of Annam, and although she conquered Zimme, the Shan capital, it spent her strength, so that half a century later when the King of Pegu—in Burma—attacked Vien-Chan, the kingdom was almost destroyed. The then capital of Laos, Lane Sang, was so shaken by the incursions of the Burmans that the court moved to Vien-Chan and commenced rebuilding. At that time Tat Luong—you visited the place, you remember?—was restored. It had been erected originally in the eleventh century.

"Then we began to have trouble with Cambodia. The Khmer empire was almost at its end. The Khmers were fighting Siam, their old enemy, and in a last desperate effort to conquer more territory and perhaps a people to help them, they attacked Laos. There was a big river battle near Stung Treng, and many of our war-canoes were destroyed. A year later Laos unsuccessfully attacked Cambodia. Perhaps it was in that period that Wat Phu was sacked, for it was in Cambodian territory and very close to the Laotian border.... Does not that seem logical? ... So you can construct the active life of Wat Phu, from its erection sometime in the ninth century, to 1571, when we warred—unsuccessfully!—upon Cambodia....

"In the same year the Pegu Burmans started war with us again. In 1592 Laos was conquered by Burma. A hundred years of vassalage and fighting followed, and by 1628 the kingdom of Vien-Chan had asserted itself again. But only for a short time. Civil war started;

Luang Prabang declared her independence. Laos began to fray out. Many of the people migrated. In 1712 a great number settled at Bassac, near Wat Phu, and that territory became a part of Laos—until about fifty years later when the Siamese attacked Laos again. Vien-Tiane and Bassac were left in ruins; and if Wat Phu had not been abandoned before that time, it surely was then....

"Vien-Tiane ... it has had so many wars. The Tonkinese attacked it toward the end of the eighteenth century; and then came the awful invasion of the Siamese in 1827. Previous to that there were sixty-two Buddhist temples here; after that not one was left intact.... The Siamese pressed on to Luang Prabang. For more than fifty years Laos was the serf of Siam. Then in 1893 Pavie, the Frenchman, became consul at Luang Prabang, and two years later Laos accepted a French protectorate...."

He did not sigh as he finished his story; he sat there with quiet dignity, smiling a smile that was reflective instead of bitter, and clasping the cigarette-holder with lithe fingers that seemed a part of the carving.

Before we left for the club he took me under the house and by the light of a lantern showed me a pet tiger he kept there. It was a young female, and with the rattle of her chain and a low purring growl, she slunk forward out of fetid gloom, her eyes opaque in the light. She rubbed against the prince's legs like a great amorous cat. He said he got her when she was a cub; instead of caging her, he kept her on a leash, and he did not allow her to eat meat or see blood. As a consequence she was quite gentle.

...And I wanted to say I imagined it was just such care exerted by France that preserved a mood of peace in Laos.

We took a roundabout way to reach the club. A bugle sounded from the *Caserne de la Garde Indigène*, and its echo seemed to take refuge among the stars and set them to trembling. A great mass of ruins crouched in the darkness on our right, given an illusion of unsteadiness by the vines and trees surrounding it, which answered the breeze with shadowy sighs.

"It was the Wat Phra Keo," volunteered Prince Phetsarath. As we walked on he amplified. "It was built in 1612 as a temple for the famous Emerald Buddha that now is at Bangkok. The Buddha was brought from Ceylon to Xieng-Mai, and then here. But the Siamese took it when they destroyed Vien-Tiane."

A few minutes later, as we neared the club, he added as an afterthought: "Some of my people believe this Buddha came out of a rift in the ground during an earthquake...."

From the lighted windows of the club reeled a dizzy blare of music, made wilder by the sharp obbligato of laughter. They were playing "Madelon." Suddenly a boisterous French voice took up the words....

"But long ago," said the prince very quietly, and I think with a smile, "I was taught to accept everything with— how do you say it?—with a grain of salt?"

## Chapter VIII
# River and Drum
*Tells of the Gentle Moods of Mother Mé-Kong*

"The crew numbered seven; Leung, my Chinese boy, Deng, the head man; and five coolies, all blunt Laotians…"

"Presently one of the coolies got a *khène* and commenced to play…. There were about twenty Laotians, men and women, gathered on the edge of the clearing."

# Mé-Kong

## 1

FOR some months I had been tampering with the dead passions of an empire. Now my work was finished. I had intended to continue up the Mé-Kong to Luang Prabang, but the trip was no longer necessary. From Prince Phetsarath, at Vien-Tiane, I had gained enough information to establish the approximate date of the erection of Wat Phu, and also the time of its desertion, as well as other historical details that explained the disappearance of the Khmer race.

In addition to being unnecessary, the journey to Luang Prabang would have been inadvisable. I was filled with malaria, and six or seven weeks in an open boat (the time required to make the trip up from Vien-Tiane and back) would undoubtedly have aggravated my condition.

Consequently, after three weeks in Vien-Tiane, I began the descent of the Mé-Kong. I would go as far as Savannakhet on the river, then plunge through the forest to the coast of Annam, thus obviating a repetition of travel. This time my craft would be the most primitive sort—a raft.

It was in no sense an ordinary raft, but more like a house-boat. It was built on a long, broad pirogue upon which shafts of bamboo were laid lengthwise, bent and lashed to the shape of bow and stern. In the middle was a house of bamboo, walled with woven rattan. The roof was made of strips of thatch laid on bamboo beams. The doorway at the front opened upon a roofed deck where the coolies stayed, and in the rear another doorway gave access to a small space, also sheltered, which served as a galley. Beyond this was a raised bamboo platform where the steersman crouched with his oar thrust between two wooden pins. On either side ran a narrow platform which made it possible for the coolies to go back and forth without coming inside.

Slightly forward in the side walls of this house were two openings with sliding doors worked on rattan cords; and between these two doors a wide runnel in the floor with a bamboo covering. Underneath, baggage was kept in the belly of the pirogue.

The room thus created was not more than six feet high at the beam, eight feet broad, and thirty in length. The entire raft measured about fifty feet. No nails were used in the construction.

The crew numbered seven: Leung, my Chinese boy, Deng, the head man; and five coolies, all blunt Laotians, tattooed from waist to thighs and naked but for the customary *patoi* bound about their loins.

The runnel between the two doors served as a social dividing line; I lived aft of it, on many rattan mats and in the midst of books, bags and a typewriter; forward, Deng sat or reclined according to his mood, and beyond him, on the fore-deck, the coolies crouched at their oars: primitive oars made of long poles with boards lashed to the ends, and worked in grooves like the nock of a sling. Leung, who did the cooking, was the only one permitted the freedom of my part of the shelter; but most of the time he was in the little space that was the galley. Behind his quarters, the steersman squatted on the raised stern, a solitary brown figure motionless as a piece of sculpture.

It seemed perfectly natural in this setting that I should discard boots and garments that fit too closely; I wore a sarong, only putting on a coat and a helmet when I went out in the sunlight or at night when it was cool....

## 2

We drifted away from Vien-Tiane in a burn of reflected sunlight that lay sluggishly on the Mé-Kong. The river was a great vein of silence, heavy with midday, and it seemed to release its heat into my own veins. When I looked into the glare illusory scars spread over the pupils of my eyes.

The coolies rowed lazily, now and then breaking into song that seemed to send the silence coiling away viscidly as the scum on a torpid pool parts before a clean stone. I lay under the shelter watching the gauzy tattooing take life upon their thighs and waists as they paddled.... One was a gay young fellow with a face like a Rajput; he had stuck a flower over his ear. Often he would rest his oar and undulate his arms and shoulders in a strange dance. Then the other coolies would laugh indolently and pause in their rowing; and the fellow, noticing my interest, would stop with a shy laugh....

About mid-afternoon we stopped beside a high bank.

Leung suggested that we get some chickens, so I gave Deng a piaster and told him to buy a couple in the village.... He returned with four chickens, some eggs and coconuts.... Toward late afternoon the heat rode off on a faint breeze. The clouds were tumbled hydrangeas that filled the bowl of the east. A drum was beating in a monastery somewhere in the thickets along the river, and it made a ghost prance on the silence.

That night the raft was moored beside a low bank where trees tongued the river with gaunt roots. Now and then the leaves shivered heavily as though in sensual ecstasy. The boatmen made a fire in a little clearing and crouched over it darkly. The night was restless with the intermittent stirring of drums. Do they never sleep, these yellow monks of the Mé-Kong? For their drums shudder under the moon as well as after dawn.... Presently one of the coolies got a *khène* and commenced to play. The gay fellow undulated his hips, and laughing, swung into a dance. One by one silent figures appeared in the surrounding darkness, and after a while, their shyness gone, they clapped their hands. There were about twenty Laotians, men and women, gathered on the edge of the clearing. The men sang; the women laughed, clinging to their babies which straddled their hips. The gay fellow from the raft hovered about the blaze, like a priest of an ancient cult dancing about a symbolic fire.

The next morning we were under way with the dawn wind. The day was the usual tawny mood: brown river, brown raft and brown men. Spouts of bamboo softened the shores, but in the sunlight their branches seemed tipped with yellow. I lay sprawled on the rattan mats, my consciousness suspended from my inert body and languidly adventuring across the broad stream. Deng amused himself by stroking the shining barrel of my rifle. Now and then he addressed me in Laotian, and although I hadn't the faintest idea what he was saying, I nodded. He was probably telling me his greatest passion was for a gun, but he couldn't afford one, and even if he could, the French government wouldn't allow him to have it.... Leung was

"He was the *délégué* of Paksane, a little village a few yards up the bank."

"We went up on the sagging veranda, and in the next five minutes a fantastic group gathered."

studying English. The coolies drowsed and paddled. A richness of physical being thickened my blood.

In the afternoon we passed several long pirogues crowded with women. In the bow of each sat a gilded image. Deng gestured toward them and poured forth a volume of Laotian in which I caught the name "Vien-Tiane." Finally he made motions with his hands and hummed a Laotian air; and I came to understand they were dancers going to Vien-Tiane. Then for a while he amused me by trying to teach me to count in Laotian. "*Nung, song, sam, si, ha, hok, chet...*" Until I became drowsy and went to sleep.

Leung awakened me with tea. Great mountains, their slopes mottled with shadows of clouds and their summits coifed with mist, rolled down to the forest-twisted shore. Ahead where the stream gleamed like soft platinum a peak rose sharply purple against the luminous yellow sky, and clouds of orange kindled in preparation for the sunset.

The next afternoon we tied up in a little pocket of green off the soiled current of the Mé-Kong. The water was lucent-clear for a few feet away from the shore, then it tapered into cloudy brown coils. It was the custom of the boatmen to swim at every stop, and I had fallen into the habit. I was stroking about in gelatinous green when I looked up and saw a white man standing on the bank.

He was a most startling discovery, first because I didn't expect to see a white man anywhere about, and second because of his attire. A plaid sarong was bound about his plump hips, and his great torso filled a stiff white jacket fastened with brass buttons. He was carrying a cane; bare ankles gleamed above dancing-pumps. It was a costume I had seen several Frenchmen affect in the jungle, but it never ceased to surprise me.

"*Pardonnez-moi, monsieur,*" he commenced, lifting his helmet politely from a face red and friendly.

He was the *délégué* of Paksane, a little village a few yards up the bank, and his *planton* had reported a raft moored here with a foreigner on it. Naturally, he had come to see.

For a few minutes we talked, he leaning on his cane, I treading water in the pocket of green. Then he asked me if I would dine with him, and I accepted, retiring into the shelter to put on a sarong and a jacket.

A mud path oozed between wet foliage, taking us along the embankment into a village of native huts. The *délégué* talked quickly and excitedly, now and then lapsing into awkward silences as though suddenly afraid he would betray his enthusiasm at the arrival of someone from beyond his lonely horizon. He pointed out a whitewashed building which was the Catholic Mission, where two priests stayed.

We came to the end of our walk at the *sala*, or local rest house, a ramshackle hut leaning wearily on poles. A sallow shaven head appeared in the window. At first I thought it belonged to a monk, but when I saw the shirt and sarong that followed, I knew he was either a very sunburned Frenchman or a half-caste.

"*Un américain!*" shouted the *délégué*.

We went up on the sagging veranda, and in the next five minutes a fantastic group gathered. The fat little Frenchman with his curly black hair and merry eyes; the sallow baldheaded man, who was half Siamese and half French; and the two priests from the mission. The older of these priests, with his long gray beard and his gaze, which made me want to look behind to see what he found there, was like a genial old saint who had become distracted trying to fulfill his sterile duties faithfully; the younger was very blond, with electric-blue eyes—like a mad peasant monk from Russia.

Grenadine and cognac were brought by a servant. The half-caste produced an accordion; played Laotian music, squatting on his chair and swaying with the tune. Then he called to some little native children in the *sala*, and while they danced he sang lustily. The young peasant monk stamped his feet to the barbaric tune in a manner that made me think of blunt-limbed muzhiks[16] dancing to "The Red Sarafin." The *délégué* waved his glass of cognac and thumped the table. The older priest looked on with dazed amusement. It was all very mad and contagious. I found myself beating on the floor with bare heels and humming. The *sala* shook resiliently as though accustomed to this revelry of lonely men.

The dusk came down with a heavy, humid quality. The *délégué* suggested that we move to his house and dine. And so we all squashed along the muddy path singing "Madelon" accompanied by the half-caste, who marched ahead swaying with his accordion.

---

[16] Also spelled *mujik*, this term evokes an image of peasants from pre-1917 Imperial Russia. The word became known in the West through the works of Tolstoy and Dostoyevsky.

**LAOS**
Fille de Mandarin du Moyen-Laos (Savannaket)

"In the house sat a slim tawny-lovely Laotian girl...
He introduced her as his wife, smilingly adding 'temporary.'"

The *délégué*'s house was on a quadrangle facing the quarters of his native escort, and flanked on one side by a long bungalow that served as a supply depot and on the other by the fence of the compound. In the enclosure were tall palms, their crests like bushes of Spanish bayonet raised to torture the sky.

In the house sat a slim tawny-lovely Laotian girl, moving rhythmically over a crude loom where a blue and silver scarf was taking shape. He introduced her as his wife, smilingly adding "temporary." The priests spoke to her with that degree of friendliness which marks a natural human acceptance of what ecclesiastical tradition discountenances; and she vanished, not to return during the evening.

Dinner, being French, was in many courses and accompanied by *vin rouge* and *vin blanc*. With coffee and cognac, the half-caste brought forth his accordion and squatted cross-legged on his chair. As he played, the older priest looked more distracted; a mad blue light danced in the eyes of the

"The *délégué* gave his idea of how Mistinguett would sing a Laotian air."

younger one. The *délégué* gave his idea of how Mistinguett[17] would sing a Laotian air. Then we all yelled the *Marseillaise* until I thought my lungs and ear-drums would burst.

Suddenly the *délégué* called loudly, "*Planton!*" A moment later a barefoot orderly in a khaki uniform appeared, then disappeared to return with five bewildered-looking native soldiers, who marched up on the veranda and stood at attention before us. This, the Frenchman explained, was the *Armée de la République Française* at Paksane. Then he dismissed them and began to sing "*Clair de Lune.*"

Later on, when a bugle sent the six soldiers of Paksane to their quarters, I departed for the raft. The priests walked as far as the mission but the *délégué* and the half-caste accompanied me to the river-bank, begging me to remain at least a day longer in spite of my protests that I had to get under way in the morning. Finally, with consoling shrugs and many "*au revoirs*," they squelched off along the muddy path, shrieking "*Très Moutarde*" to the springing notes of the accordion.

## 3

Those last few days on the raft were days of flame and fragrance—sunlight and warm air spiced with the odors of green things. And they were days of singing. The lyric of native life had an exquisite simplicity. It was pleasant to wake in the morning and think only of a sarong. Meals meant something more than food. They meant we should have to go questing in the villages to find it, there to mingle with brown humanity and experience some adventure, emotional if not physical. Sometimes we stopped on the Siamese side, sometimes on the Laotian. The people were always friendly.

Twice we arrived at little towns where a *boun*, or festival, was in progress. No timid colors for celebration in Laos! Brilliant orange, purples, blues, and shades of rose and magenta, all against the sienna and ocher of native skins. Always drums beat at these festivals, and bonzes moved about in files accompanied by the crash of cymbals. Paper flowers decorated the

---

[17] Hervey's astute reference to French culture was quite *à propos*. Mistinguett was the stage name of a 20-year-old French actress and singer who débuted at *the Casino de Paris* in 1895, later appearing in risqué routines at the *Folies Bergère, Moulin Rouge*, and *Eldorado*. She captivated Paris, becoming the most popular French entertainer of her time and the highest paid female entertainer in the world. In 1919 her legs were insured for the then astounding amount of 500,000 francs. Her birth name was Jeanne Bourgeois (1875-1956).

"The *phu-baos* were very proud as they strode about..."

"The *phu-saos* wore gay sinhs woven with silver, and their scarves were savage with broad stripes of undiluted colors."

little pagodas where dead gods slept; but on these living people the flowers were real, blushing or pale against glossy black hair. The *phu-saos* wore gay *sinhs* woven with silver, and their scarves were savage with broad stripes of undiluted colors. The *phu-baos* were very proud as they strode about with their tattooed flanks a-ripple like wind-stroked satin.

There was festival in the forest too. Bell-shaped crimson flowers drooped their silent chimes along the banks, and tremulous shadows of green lay speared with slender lilies. Always the bamboo exulted on the shore, and against it iridescent flies made carnival. At night the wind beat on the white gong of the moon.... There was something phallic and primitive about this life. It seemed to spring up with shameless song, making lyrics of its birth.

One afternoon just before sunset, while a brazen glare cast its brightness upon the forest, ,a wooden cross appeared incongruously in the midst of a wild, rank clump of palms. The white plaster mission-house and the church, seeming cut into the incredibly blue sky, stared as we floated past. On the bank was one priest, a tall bearded old man in black robes and a white sun-helmet, standing in the midst of many native children. He had a very benignant face and he waved. There was something wistful in that gesture. Then, for some sudden reason, he turned and kicked one of the little boys; and he made me think of a kindly old archangel abruptly yielding to his repressed annoyance with the Cosmic Prefect who had designated him for such isolated duty.

At night, while we were moored beside the dark shore, some young Laotian was sure to come down to the raft, salute, squat and begin a pleasant conversation in bad French. Their questions always went beyond the horizon. Soft-eyed young men, naively concerned with mad little dreams which a few French words had started brewing in their minds. Often I would play my gramophone for them, and in turn they would play on the *khène*, and then figures would multiply on the shore. Gauzy nights, haunted by restless, laughing brown people, and music from the lips of young men dreaming mad little dreams, which were not quite mad enough fortunately to take them out of their forests....

On the seventh day we stopped at a large Siamese village. Numerous pirogues lay along the bank, and above them just as many houses peered between the drooping palms. Our advent was the signal for a crowd of natives to gather on the shore where the raft was tied up. As I climbed the embankment they receded cautiously, as if to inform me that my sarong did not conceal the fact of white skin. So I turned back and started the gramophone. The music was stronger than my bleached complexion. They swarmed about the raft and laughed. When I stopped playing and approached again they did not recede but made way for me to pass, and one savagely handsome fellow ran ahead with a villainous smile, motioning as though to lead me somewhere.

From the path along the embankment a road plunged through the middle of the village between dirty whitewashed shops and gutters where dogs lay sleeping amidst swill and blue mud. The Siamese who had appointed himself guide gestured toward various shops, speaking in his own tongue; evidently explaining what wares were sold there.

This road approached two stone *garudas*, creatures half bird and half man, and then crossed a brick causeway over swampy ground. The sky was gray, threatening rain, and the spire of a *prachedee*, or conical religious memorial, rising out of the trees ahead, made a swan-white taper against the soiled down of the clouds, A little stream flowed under the farther end of the causeway, and built about it were houses tottering on poles. The place ahead evidently was a Wat, or Buddhist enclosure containing temple and monastery.

A very old wall surrounded it, and by the gate were several mutilated statues of Buddha. Inside, a walk led to a little open building where the monks held services. A number of yellow-clad bonzes lounged about, and one came forward to meet us, holding out his hand to me with a smile.

On the right was the house of the monks, and on the other side a small yellow pavilion with two red and gold thrones under its roof of upturned, horned eaves. The young Siamese continued to explain things I couldn't understand.... We walked through cool, pale halls and courtyards dusty with peeled whitewash. In the rear were many small conical mounds of stone and a great *prachedee* decorated with ancient carving and inset with faded tiles of blue, green and yellow; all standing blanched in the motionless shade of palms.

The monks gave me tea, and then I returned to the raft, followed by my Siamese guide, who accepted a few pennies with that charmingly villainous smile of his.

" 'Savan...' said Deng, affectionately abbreviating Savannakhet..."
The local office of the Messageries Fluviales boat service pictured above.

The rest of the afternoon we drifted idly in breathless heat. Daylight was smothered in a fume of rain. After dusk lightning seemed to fray the silken dark and release sounds like the stampede of cattle. Under the bamboo floor the river fussed succulently....

Daylight came with the sight of blue mountains on the Siamese side.

"Savan..." said Deng, affectionately abbreviating Savannakhet; and I looked with something like depression at the thatched roofs that were appearing above the Laotian shore.

That afternoon, moored beside a slippery clay bank, I shaved and put on a stiff twill suit. My black tie seemed to shrink about my throat; my shoes pinched; my face burned with a flush half of annoyance and half of heat. From Savannakhet I planned to travel by motor-lorry to Tchepone, then by pirogue for several days to Lao-Bao, and from there by road down to the coast. I had letters to the *commissaire* of Savannakhet requesting him to assist me; for his benefit I was dressing, somewhat resentfully.

Climbing the bank, I set out along a thickly palmed road. Hedges of crimson hibiscus smoldered in the late afternoon. Beyond them were plaster houses where French people lived. I saw signs in French. "*Douanes et Régies.*"... The white walls of the barracks of the *Garde Indigène* gleamed through the trees, streaked with green mold. A few soldiers wandered past; a coolie trotting with an empty rickshaw. In the pale roadway ahead a peacock spread its tail luxuriously. It made me think of all I was leaving....

Suddenly realizing I didn't know exactly where I was going, and noticing a khaki-clad figure standing on the bank, obviously a Frenchman, I halted to address him and find out the way to the *commissaire's*.

"*Pardonnez-moi, monsieur*,' I said. "*Parlez-vous anglais?*"

He turned a brown grin upon me, resting his hands on his hips in a carelessly arrogant attitude that was suddenly familiar.

"I sure do," he responded with a New England accent.

I knew then, unmistakably, that I had reached the edge of what we are pleased to call Civilization.

# Chapter IX
# I Am the Forest
## *Tells of Nham*
## *and the Suitors of Madame Guillotine*

"It must be understood immediately that Nham was a person of no importance.
I dare say he was a savage."

# Jungle

## 1

ET THESE few pages be dedicated to Nham.

Nham was not his name. Undoubtedly he had a name, but he was one of those insignificant creatures who answer to George or Tom or whatever one chooses to call them. Only, of course, being in Indo-China the equivalents of Nguyen and Nham are more appropriate. So Nham he was to me.

It must be understood immediately that Nham was a person of no importance. I dare say he was a savage. Inasmuch as we had no common tongue in which to exchange confidences, and considering that he deported himself very mildly while I knew him, I cannot truthfully testify that he was a savage. I shall, therefore, give him the benefit of the doubt and say merely, he was a native.

Some people seem to have been born without family or any antecedents whatever; they appear suddenly in our midst with a very authentic air of being alone in the world, and then depart, leaving no clue to their beginning and only a suspicion of their end.

Nham was such a person.

Perhaps some twenty years before I saw him, a peasant woman of Laos paused in her daily routine of rice-planting to deliver him, and immediately returned to her simple duties, leaving him to meet life with his own natural resources. Or perhaps by some inexplicable alchemy he was created out of thin air, to perch upon the stern of my pirogue for a few days and thereafter perch upon the rim of my memory, significant yet insoluble. It does not matter.

Put away all romantic persuasions concerning Nham. He was not a mystery. That is to say, he was not complicated. He was mysterious only in so far as something simple and uninvolved is mysterious. Perhaps, after all, he was a savage.

I became aware of him several hours after leaving Tchepone. I was lying in the bottom of the pirogue, trying to amuse myself by counting the laths in the bamboo shelter, when it occurred to me to look at the native who propelled the craft.

He was squatting in the stern, a few feet from my head. My first sensation was amazement that he was able to maintain his equilibrium. Then I observed his toes—long prehensile toes that gripped the edge of the dugout canoe—and his easy balance as he crouched there, buttocks slung between his legs, sinewy arms working rhythmically with the paddle. Presently my amazement became annoyance. It was irritating to realize that he, a savage, could do naturally what I, with my civilized intelligence, could never accomplish.

Sunlight poured down brutally upon his bare head. It was, I remarked, a singularly unlovely head, with the exception of his hair, shining like rich black plumage, and his dark eyes, which looked at the world with a curious supplication in them. His body, on the other hand, was quite remarkable. The muscles of his stomach were as carefully molded as a bas-relief, and his entire body seemed sheathed in skin-tight silk, which wove quick shadows as he moved.

He was not even perspiring.

I became incensed at his apparent invulnerability to heat, and returned to counting the bamboo laths.

Two days before, having spent a week with the *commissaire* of Savannakhet, I had left in a motor-lorry for Tchepone. By starting from Savannakhet at five in the morning, according to the *commissaire*, I should reach Tchepone in the late afternoon. However, *Monsieur le Commissaire*, with fine French optimism, had not counted upon the idiosyncrasies of a Paris motor and a Laotian road. The lorry broke down three times during the morning, and just before sunset it sank to the hubs in a very innocent-looking mire.

For several hours we struggled with the huge truck. Coolies were inducted into service from the rice-fields; they built an improvised bamboo incline from the front wheels to the end of the mire. But the lorry would not stir. Finally the chauffeur, a Laotian, hunted up a bonze in a near-by village and had him burn a taper in the pagoda. Singularly enough, about half an hour later the lorry heaved out of the mud and across the crackling bamboo.

In consequence, instead of spending that night at Tchepone, I stayed in some nameless little village in a *sala* lifted on poles over the local latrine.

At dawn we started again, and shortly after daylight, halted in a green pocket in the forest where a natural incline dipped into a rushing stream. Here all my luggage was put into a couple of pirogues, Leung and myself in another, and we raced madly with the current toward Tchepone.

I shall never forget that brief ride. My canoe was badly constructed, and the water sent little ripples over the imperfect sides. A single movement would have upset the fragile craft. Leung, sitting in the bottom, did not dare to lift himself to a seat when the boat rapidly filled with water, but sat there clutching the sides, grinning to hide his terror. Being the one white man, I felt it necessary to uphold the dignity of the race by maintaining a casual and fearless manner. After that experience I am sure I observed a new admiration in Leung's gaze.

Within an hour we reached Tchepone. Safely on the bank, I celebrated by falling flat in the mud, and then retreated to the house of the *délégué* to take a bath.

After many months in Indo-China I was surprised at nothing. Therefore I accepted without emotion or change of expression the discovery that the *délégué* of Tchepone was a very black Senegalese. With him and his ample wife I enjoyed *petit-déjeuner* on a veranda facing the jungle and a long blue mountain. A *boun* or festival was in progress, and streams of brightly clad natives gathered at a near-by pagoda where bonzes beat drums and cymbals.

The *commissaire*, that optimistic gentleman presiding over the district of Savannaket, had assured me I could purchase food at Tchepone. He was mistaken. Tchepone did not boast even a Chinese shop. And I did not have so much as a knife and fork!

When I confessed my dilemma to the Senegalese *délégué*, he and his wife grew hilarious and said that, as a matter of fact, their own supplies were late in coming and consequently they could let me have very little. They managed,

"The pirogue in which I traveled warrants some description."

however, to gather together two cans of French peas, a can of *cassoulet*, a can of soup, a loaf of bread and a bottle of wine. Undoubtedly they believed in the popular idea that all Americans are barbarians, for they neglected to add a knife, fork, or spoon.

Leung appeared later with a roast chicken which he had bought from another Chinese. This, with the supplies the *délégué* had given me, I thought would be sufficient for the two-day journey to Lao-Bao.

Just before noon we left, a caravan of six pirogues; four for my baggage, one for Leung and one for myself.

We did not reach Lao-Bao in two days.

## 2

The pirogue in which I traveled warrants some description.

As native canoes go, it was not mean. It was hewn from a tree-trunk and measured about twelve feet in length. It was not more than three feet wide. The half-moon-shaped shelter almost covered it, leaving only a small space fore and aft for the boatmen. This shelter was of bamboo and thatch, and the center lath was less than three feet from the gunwales. Inasmuch as it was impossible to sit comfortably under it—the low top forced one to bend forward until the chin almost touched the knees—the only alternative was to lie flat, and then the uneven floor printed a replica of its defects upon the back and rump.

Such craft, it will be perceived, are not designed to give any great pleasure to the unaccustomed traveler. On the other hand they offer a certain amount of simple diversion. For instance, one unconsciously goes through a few languid calisthenics. First you crouch under the thatch until that position grows tiresome; then, exerting great care not to capsize the boat, you slide the legs forward, occasionally getting a splinter in the posterior, and slowly lower the torso until head and shoulders rest upon the floor. After lying there for an hour or so, you decide that crouching is more acceptable. Accordingly, you raise yourself and bend forward until the chin rests on the knees.

This, it will be seen plainly, is very good for the abdominal-and shoulder-muscles when repeated often throughout the day.

An afternoon nap becomes a novelty in a pirogue. To lie there in the hot shade and watch a spider or some other insect weave across the thatch induces a pleasurable drowsiness not unmixed with mild concern. You wonder indolently whether the spider will drop on your face after you are asleep or whether he will be more cunning and steal inside one of your pockets, to lie there in wait for the first intruding finger. After a while you doze. Suddenly a loud grunt from one of the boatmen arouses you; that grunt is a hint that, unless you sleep without turning over, you are likely to have an unexpected bath. You smile apologetically and return to slumber, feeling very agreeable in the knowledge that when you awaken there is always the amusement of looking for bugs or marveling at the new and intricate pattern the rough floor has modeled into your skin.

Not the least of these diversions made possible by a pirogue is a game which I invented as a means of maintaining balanced reason through the sun-tortured day. It is a game that stimulates the mind and can be quite exciting at the same time. It is also a very whimsical game; indeed, I took a childish delight in it after hours of mad thinking. To play it you must lie on your stomach and concentrate on the bottom of the boat. Presently you will see little streams of water seeping in through the cracks, bringing with them grains of sand. The object is to try to count those grains of sand. At the end of five minutes—or you can make it ten if you like— you take a mental note

"Here the Moi, aboriginal tribes of ancient Champa, mingle with the Laotians and the Annamites against a background unspoiled and aggressively primitive."

of the number. Then you bail out the water and guess whether more or fewer grains of sand will filter in during the next five—or ten—minutes.

In those days of travel between Tchepone and Lao-Bao I developed a strong affinity with the manners of barbarian Rome. While my feasts were not sumptuous, they did not lack for abandon. My breakfast I always took on the bank. Leung would invariably conjure up a number of coconuts which Nham halved with his savage-looking knife, and I would squat with the two of them, this Chinese and this Laotian, and drink the cool milk. The second morning Leung, remembering my civilized tastes while in the hotels on the coast, sliced a banana and served it in coconut-milk in a halved shell.

Luncheon was even more pagan. Lying propped upon my elbows under the shelter of the pirogue, I would dip into a can of French peas or *cassoulet* with my fingers, rend a loaf of bread and wash down the morsels with diluted *vin rouge*. The meal over, I would carefully lean over the side, wash my hands and dry them on the thatch.

Dinner usually was more of an event. The chicken which Leung bought at Tchepone lasted for two evenings. It was served to me on a banana-leaf, with shredded coconut and rice which the coolies had cooked.

At night we moored by the bank, and often I awakened to hear a stealthy rustle in the foliage near-by or the more definite sounds of beasts crying to one another in the solitude.

The customary morning bath was unnecessary, for invariably it rained sometime between dark and dawn, and the thatch shelter served as a primitive shower.

This crude means of travel altered many of my habits. It created new ones as well. But inasmuch as these pages are designed for print in our enlightened republic I must resort to deletion, as the only method of suggesting the less delicate phases of my complete relapse from evolved society.

# 3

I had thought at Savannakhet that I was on the edge of civilization. But in doing so I had neglected to inquire into the physical aspect of that territory between the Mé-Kong and the coast of Annam.

It is as densely forested and wild as any part of Indo-China. Here the Moi, aboriginal tribes of ancient Champa, mingle with the Laotians and the Annamites against a background unspoiled and aggressively primitive. The French have made but one passage through this jungle—this trail, partly by road and partly by river, which I was traveling from Savannakhet to the prison colony of Lao-Bao.

Immediately after leaving Tchepone, the narrow stream steals into a forest of bamboo as obscenely luxurious as the thickest forests of the Mé-Kong. The bushes ascend in green fog on either bank, seeming to sift their color into the atmosphere and create a faintly luminous nebula on the surface of the river. The heavy silence vibrates with insect life. Whirring wings sound gently in the foliage, and brilliant butterflies splash the air like drippings of flame.

Here one feels the solitude and scorn of the jungle. It is not entirely unfriendly, this forest; instead it proudly asserts its superiority and challenges the intruder to share it. It becomes the spirit of aboriginal man, guarding the secret of its simple, enduring life. "I am the Forest," it proclaims; and its authentic tone exposes the hollow chanting of a civilization that pretends to have mastered the forest.

I had been quietly proud of the scaling buildings of my native country, of its groping tunnels and brave viaducts, all those synthetic intestines where machinery digests our dreams of progress. Often I had stood over New York and marveled at the exotic growths of skyscrapers sinking their roots so deep into the earth. Now it all seemed very silly.

No matter how mean our individual and conscious impulses, the one subconscious impulse behind our lives is a desperate desire to perpetuate—not the world but ourselves. It is an impulse which, viewed sanely, is not grossly selfish.

Immortality is a word abused by loquacious clerics. Evangelical hysteria and the mysticism of more dignified but equally theatrical sects have sometimes made it appear either a grandiose wheeze or the tenuous promise of anemic old men. The word immortality has suffered the rape of the bourgeoisie. Nevertheless, I must use it. For underneath all our elaborate civilizations is the simple yearning for that thing—immortality.

And here was the forest accomplishing it without effort.

I realized I was very close to something I had always wanted to understand. It was in this forest. I knew the mental and physical equipment bequeathed me by my race was no fitting instrument with which to sense it, and my intelligence, searching frenziedly for a translator, fastened upon Nham— Nham, the piroguer, the naked savage squatting so near me.

A few months before I could not have understood this native. He would have been merely grist for my literary mill or an enigma to be regarded with that variety of supercilious sympathy current in missionary and tourist circles. I did not pretend to understand him fully now.

But at least I could share with him his freedom of thought and physical being.

This was a very alarming discovery. Such a relaxation of racial and national integrity excluded the slim possibility that I might someday be a constructive citizen or an acceptable American. Without knowing it, I had slipped into the ranks of the damned.

Looking back, I could see that this assignation between myself and the country had put me in the proper mood for my arrival at Wat Phu. Subconsciously I had approached it without archeological interest or any romantic fervor. I was simply part of the primitive come to look upon the wreck of an empire that had been one of its tragic gestures.

I did not now think of the jungle as *jungle* or the river as *river*. Nor did I feel I was in the midst of a strange , people. All were natural elements in a world which had accepted me so easily I seemed to belong. Had I been aware of this transition, it would have been the cue for emotional dramatics; I should have been merely an analytical intelligence caricaturing itself.

For a moment it seemed I was about to acquire my inheritance.

## 4

All afternoon we moved so close to the bank that sprays of bamboo seemed to drip upon us. We were charging a swift current and by keeping near the shore progress was easier. Ahead, seen from my half-moon shelter, the leaders of my little caravan of pirogues glided over the swirling brown water.

In mid-afternoon we halted for a moment by a great sandbank. A *boun* was being celebrated, and natives in savagely bright *panungs* moved about to the cadence of a drum in an adjacent monastery. These garments, of heliotrope,

Groupe de Khas Lovés dans la Forêt (Bas-Laos)
LAOS - Série D, n° 22

"A *boun* was being celebrated, and natives in savagely bright *panungs* moved about to the cadence of a drum…"

Collection Raquez - LAOS - Série E, n° 7
Femmes Lovés buvant le Vin de Riz

"When I climbed the bank…the natives were surprisingly shy, almost frightened: they all moved away… A white man had come: there could be no more celebration while he was there."

of scarlet and of salmon-pink, seemed to stir a hot breath of lust against the virginal sand.

When I climbed the bank to buy a few coconuts, the natives were surprisingly shy, almost frightened: they all moved away, and some of the children scattered into the jungle. Even the drum ceased beating.

It was very significant. A white man had come: there could be no more celebration while he was there.

As we left the village, a low thrumming started again in the unseen monastery. I could hear voices lifted shrilly as the festival was resumed. Then the forest gloom in our wake thickened stealthily across the stream, seeming to shut out all life but its own.

There was something abysmal in the depth of humid shadow. The dip of the paddles, the drip, drip of the water, the faint gurgles under the pirogue, all took on the same quality of turgid green, as though every sound that trickled into this immense quiet became clabbered and verdant, like the seepage in an unused pool.

At dusk we moored beside a thicket. The beat of a drum somewhere in the falling night—always a drum! —and the laughing chatter of the piroguers as they splashed in the river. Amazing children, these brown fellows. All through the hot day they crouched at their paddles, silent, somber, working with a quiet intensity that seemed to occupy all their thoughts; but with sunset this mood slipped from them, and they became troubadours, dancing and singing with a gaiety strangely wistful.

I plunged into the water with them, half afraid my presence would subdue them, but they continued laughing and joking among themselves in a manner that did not exclude me. This manner implied that( during the day I had been the white man, master of the pirogues; but now the dark adjusted this social difference, and I became, not one of them, but an outsider to whom they were hospitable and friendly.

After their bath, the porters kindled fires along the bank, and set to preparing the evening meal. All these tiny blazes made a bloody tattoo on the night. It was a picture barbaric yet intimate. It was like a fragment of boyhood dreams become real; and I realized, proudly, that I was not an onlooker: I belonged.

As the evening drowsed on, the forest lay in moon-shadow. One of the men got out his *khène*, and through the air roved faint, wild notes that died regretfully. All the fires but one had fallen to embers; in its light I could see Nham amusing his comrades with a dance. Even the forest contributed: from the thicket came the shuddering tremolo of night-birds.

In the early morning we moved on. Still those amazing and prolific jungles of bamboo that seemed to overflow the banks. They depressed me now. I found myself trying to remember incidents which threaded elusively into a filmy though none the less secure texture of green. Green. Green. Green. I was infected with the color! Suddenly I wanted to jump up and shout: "Damn the green, damn the green!" A senseless fury snapped my nerves... "Rikki-tikki-tavi." Mongoose shaking a cobra.... Something cold, it seemed, had pounced upon my neck and was shaking me, violently.

The quiet figure of Nham hovering over me added to that enervating rage. How could he be so calm in the midst of this obscene greenness? And the other boatmen?

The river itself was a dark throat drinking in the shadow of the forest with sensual ardor.

Damn the green....

For what seemed hours I lay there cursing that color. Then a moment of sanity showed me I was nagging myself into a condition I had been warned against. I must have something to occupy my mind. As it was impossible to read, I decided to think about the Khmers. ... To hell with the Khmers, I thought. At that instant they were an entirely uninteresting people.

On a sudden I discovered the glaring sunlight outside was filled with black rings that expanded and contracted. I lay in a hot flush.... Quinine... you need quinine.... "Oh, say can you see . . Why the devil should I think of the "Star Spangled Banner"? Damfool.

Damn ... I solemnly contemplated the word damn. I could, I decided, think of expressions much more vehement. For instance, goddamn.... You're sick. You're alone in the jungle and you're sick. You're alone in the damned jungle and you're sick. You're alone in the goddamn jungle and you're sick. Sick—sick—sick...

"Oh, say can you see . . Stop it. ... I switched my thoughts to Saigon, remembering an Indian merchant who had cheated me on the price of some

"Who wrote that?
Henri Mouhot…just before he died of fever somewhere near Luang Prabang."

tussur-silk. I became incensed about it.... Saigon. Rue Catinat. . . Wish I were there.... *Arc-en-ciel*....What's that cool blue street that goes wandering north from the Place de la Cathédrale? The rue... rue... Now why can't I remember? A silly name. O'Dwyer. Idiot. Would a street in a Cochin-Chinese city have an Irish name? O'Dwyer—O'Dwyer... Doesn't matter. But I should remember, I should...

"Oh, say can you see ..." A patriot, aren't you? Well...

I commenced to sing at the top of my voice. Nham looked at me with stupid surprise, and I began insulting him in English. He continued to stare. His brown foot was very near. I was possessed of an insane desire to tickle it....

Fever.... And you need quinine.... Maybe you'll die. Die in the jungle. You'd better think of some classic line to write; you know, something ridiculously sentimental, which, if it's ever read, will be dignified by the fact of your death.... "*Ô mon Dieu, pitié de moi!*" Who wrote that? Prince Henri d'Orléans? No, no. Henri—Henri Mouhot. Just before he died of fever— somewhere near Luang Prabang.[18]

"*Ô mon Dieu, pitié de moi!*" Died of fever—died of fever.

---

[18] French naturalist Henri Mouhot (May 15, 1826—Nov. 10, 1861) explored Indochina and is credited with popularizing Angkor in the West. He died of malaria near Naphan, Laos and today his tomb is to the east of Luang Prabang.

Good stuff for the newspapers. "Novelist succumbs in jungles of Indo-China." Perhaps some of those fellows who wrote rotten reviews of your books will feel a tremor of conscience—for a moment....

Rue Garcerie. That's the name of the nice blue street that goes wandering off the Place de la Cathédrale. Sounds quite like O'Dwyer, doesn't it? I wish I were on the rue Garcerie now—going to Monsieur Poulet's. What excellent *cocktails rouges* he makes!....

Look at that fellow squatting in the stern, look at Nham. He's watching you; watching you as you lie in the bottom of the pirogue sick; sick with fever. What does that expression mean? Pity? Scorn? Dark eyes. Dark as the jungle. They are the jungle. Looking at you, pitying you. I am the Forest, they say; I took you to bed with me—now look at yourself. Lousy white man sick with fever....

Suddenly I was aware the pirogue had stopped, and Nham was motioning me to get out; he was standing knee-deep in the stream.

I crawled from under the thatch.

We were at the foot of a stretch of shallow rapids. Several of the boats had already started up, drawn by the taut, knotted figures of the coolies.

I stepped into the river, too ill to care about shoes or socks, wading after Nham and the other boatmen as they pulled their craft over the rapids. At the end I sat down on a rock and vomited.

When I had crept back into the pirogue, Leung poked his head under the shelter and asked if I wanted anything. As he saw me, he looked frightened and rushed away, to return immediately with the medicine kit....

With midday the sunlight smote the thatch pitilessly. It seemed to penetrate to where I lay, creating a brassy dusk in which the one clear object was the figure of Nham, paddling, paddling. The ceaseless motion of his arms made me drowsy, but those dark, watchful eyes disturbed me and kept me awake. I could not dismiss the illusion that he was the forest crouching there; and if I lost consciousness, this forest would steal over me and smother me.

I remember it commenced to rain: I could feel the drops seeping through the shelter. At length I realized I was wet, and someone—Nham—was wrapping me in a blanket. As he bent over me I had a sensation of complete obliteration. His body became many bodies, brown bodies, sinuous as the roots of trees, that imparted a sense of warmth, of strength creeping into me and growing, stretching like awakening limbs. I seemed caught in mingled hot breaths and intoxicated with an illusion of numberless people. Yet I felt all these people were in reality trees; hundreds of trees, growing, growing, up, up, out of me. It was as though I had died a thousand times and from the accumulated decay a whole forest was rising. Brown limbs of trees and brown limbs of people, all intermingled and entwined; and where the branches broke in orgasms of green were just as many faces; faces that looked at me with dark eyes in which there was something ancient and hidden.

I am the Forest—I am the Forest.

Words beating, beating in my brain.

I rot and bloom. My limbs are the limbs of men, and from the groin of me comes God. I am Man and Woman. I am inception and conception. The prehistoric gods sprang from my phallus. My womb is a temple where Mohammed preached, where Buddha preached, where Jesus preached; where Confucius spoke, where Ananda spoke, where the Twelve Apostles spoke.... "There is no God but the Forest, and men are my prophets...." "O thou jewel in the Forest, hail!" "I believe in the Forest as my Son, the Forest as my Father, and the Forest as the Holy Ghost....

I am the Forest.

I am Life.

...All that afternoon we traveled through the rain, and that night we halted in the rain. Part of the time I was conscious, most of the time delirious. I recall the drip, drip of the water as it fell through the shelter; I recall the dim shape of Nham bending over me, now and then placing his cool hands on my forehead or forcing me to drink some bitter liquid, which, for all I knew or cared, might have killed me. The rest is nebulous. We moved. Figures came and went. I recognized Leung. I caught glimpses of the wet forest or the ugly brown of the river. But I was conscious primarily of a feeling of utter unreality: it was as though I moved through a dream in which these fluid details dissolved.

Nham had appointed himself my nurse. In the intervals between delirium I could see him always near, and even when I was semiconscious I was aware of his watchful eyes or those deft brown hands cooling my forehead or administering that bitter native medicine.

On the third day I was considerably better. We were moored beside a spit of sand that dazzled in the glare; mounting the banks were those seemingly endless forests of bamboo. With my illness Leung had assumed command of the pirogues, and instead of urging the porters on, he had called a halt.

Now the fever was passing, I decided it would be wise to reach Lao-Bao as soon as possible, so at midday we resumed travel.

That evening the jungle was thinner. After dusk we stopped by a great mudbank. I was weak but I had no temperature.

For a long while I sat propped up in the stern watching the twinkling ballet of the stars. From the surrounding darkness came the trilling moan of birds; the stream was very quiet. This repose in the air suggested that the forest, having taken my strength and humbled me, was now offering to share its omniscient calm.

The next afternoon late the river journey ended beneath a green embankment. Just beyond that embankment was Lao-Bao.

When all my baggage was removed from the boats, the coolies squatted in a line in the road, waiting to be paid. One by one they came up to where I sat counting out the money, knelt as they received their wages, saluted, and then moved down the bank to their craft.

Near the last was Nham. After I had paid him I gave him an extra sum. He looked stupidly surprised and spoke to Leung.

"He wants to know what the money is for," Leung translated.

I told him to tell Nham it was for the medicine he had given me.

Nham squatted there a moment, seeming to turn the matter over in his mind, then he returned the extra piasters to me, saluted, and moved off toward his pirogue with simple dignity.

## 5

At Lao-Bao, France maintains a penal colony where some hundred or more native criminals are in the charge of a guard of Annamite troops and one white man; and as I had been told there was no decent rest-house in the vicinity, I made my way immediately to the prison, hoping the *délégué* would be disposed to give me quarters.

As I approached the building, there was a feeling of drama about the place that re-created a mood I had not encountered since leaving Pnom Penh. For the first time in several months I was aware of France as a somber influence.

I remember that scene so well.... Fireflies stitched the dusk like luminous needles, and behind them a few bats reeled in drunken embroidery. The evening had a soft, fantastic quality. Suddenly a bugle-call seemed to inject a momentary glitter in the quiet. Ahead, where the red road entered a stockade, a native soldier appeared, and following him was an irregular line of half-naked prisoners, chained and some wearing the cangue.[19] In the background rose the whitewashed prison building, grim as a medieval fortress.

When I reached the gate I saw more convicts. It was the hour when they were-called in from work in the surrounding jungle; from all directions they came, walking with difficulty because of the linked rods joining their ankle-bands. All had their hair closely cropped and wore ragged clothing. Some glanced at me, but the majority passed with stolid disinterest.

The soldier in the sentry-box merely gave me an inquisitive look.

At closer range, the prison building was even more formidable. Instead of windows there were slits for loopholes, and an upper veranda, open at the front, gave the effect of a covered sentry-walk. Over the entrance-way was a plaque commemorating the bravery of the prison guards during a mutiny of convicts in 1915.

At my approach a whiskered face appeared in the semi-darkness of the upper veranda, shouting: *"Allo!"*

I asked if he was *Monsieur le Délégué*.

"I am," he replied. "Are you *Monsieur le* Américain whom the *commissaire* telegraphed me would be here several days ago?"

A few moments later I was on the upper veranda, with a Picon-grenadine at my elbow.

*Monsieur le Délégué* was a most agreeable gentleman, with comically ferocious whiskers which paradoxically gave him the appearance of excessive good humor.

---

[19] Invented in China, the cangue—derived from the Portuguese "canga" meaning yoke—is a wood or bamboo device clamped around a prisoner's neck to restrict movement.

"...following him was an irregular line of half-naked prisoners, chained and some wearing the cangue."

"We use the guillotine," said *Monsieur le Délégué*; then he added apologetically, "I am sorry but I'm afraid we won't have an execution while you're here."

"You are ill," he pronounced pleasantly. Indeed I must have presented a very miserable figure, unshaven and fever-splotched. "You must go to bed," he added.

I told him I could see no good reason why I hadn't died two days ago; nevertheless, I had no intention of going to bed, or for that matter, dieting. What I wanted most of all was a decent meal, regardless of the consequences.

"Khao!" he shouted.

Immediately a shy Laotian girl of about fifteen came soundlessly on bare feet. This was his wife, he informed me—temporarily, at least. She shook hands timidly, then, having received elaborate instructions for dinner, hurried to the rear.

"You will die undoubtedly," said *Monsieur le Délégué* amiably.

I agreed that undoubtedly I would; then we had another Picon-grenadine, and I recounted all the gossip of the coast.

Obviously a guest was a rare novelty in the prison of Lao-Bao: the dinner was in seven courses, with interludes of wine and champagne. And *Monsieur le Délégué* could not be charming enough. The Laotian girl sat across from me, staring with naive curiosity at the disreputable stranger whom her lord and master was entertaining so splendidly.

All through the meal I could hear the clank-clank of chains in the quadrangle as the prisoners were being put up for the night.

"Afterward, *Monsieur le Délégué* showed me a huge ledger, which he designated as his "guest-book." In it were photographs of shaven, narrow-eyed natives, whose faces showed a mingling of stupidity and dull surprise, as though snapped at a moment when their primitive minds were trying to discover a reason for the predicament in which they found themselves.

"*Tran moi Hop*, murder.... *Lang von Do*, treason.... *Hoang Long*, grand larceny.... *Le Loi*, rape. ..." A long list of names, with descriptions under them, and a few brief words recording the nature of their crimes and their penalties. Beside a few was written "executed,' and a date.

"We use the guillotine," said *Monsieur le Délégué*; then he added apologetically, "I am sorry but I'm afraid we won't have an execution while you're here."

Later he took me down through the quadrangle and into the actual prison rooms.

Prisonnier Chinois

"…there was a rattling of chains and curious eyes peered at us."

The convicts lay in rows on broad wooden slabs built against the walls, with cangues about their necks and their feet thrust into stocks. Smoky lamps half illuminated the two great wards, casting a soiled reflection upon the many faces. I caught the gleam of numerous bare, sweaty bodies. Here and there an oily torso, arresting the light, stood out in sharp relief upon a confusion of dim arms and legs, or a single head or a shoulder seemed to lift itself from the generally vague background of figures like a separate member. The whole scene swam in a nauseating stench.

"Regard," said the *délégué*, "the suitors of Madame Guillotine."

As we passed down the aisle between the prisoners, there was a rattling of chains and curious eyes peered at us. One of the wretches muttered to himself; several of his neighbors laughed. The *délégué* appeared not to notice it.

"That fellow," he said smilingly when we were outside, "hinted that my grandmother was not all she should have been."

I asked him if he would punish the convict.

"No," he replied. "It is best to ignore such things. They are children, these natives—even the worst criminals."

He chuckled.

"I'll give you an example.... About a year ago there was considerable excitement in the village. Every other day or so some native would find his pet dog or goat with his head cut off—as neatly as if it had been done with the guillotine! This went on for about two weeks. I was really concerned, because the natives were terrified. Of course they all said it was done by a devil. Anything unpleasant in this country is always caused by a devil.... Well, finally we caught this particular devil. It was one of my troopers. He had been doing it with a bayonet. When I called him up before the court—I am the court, you know—he said he had been doing it for the government! 'For the government?' I demanded. 'And why?' 'Well,' he said, 'the government cuts off the heads of criminals, so I was practicing so that when I became proficient I could be of use to monsieur and the government.' " He chuckled again. "Now what could I do about that?"

"What did you do about it?" I asked.

"I fined him and had him locked up," he answered, "and then later, when there was an execution, I let him do the job...."

When I went up to my room I could still hear a faint clank-clank of chains from the prison wards; and down in the quadrangle the sentinel beat a bamboo clapper and called the hour.

In the morning I was awakened by the rattle of chains.

An orderly brought coffee, and following him came *Monsieur le Délégué*. He insisted on taking my temperature, reporting that I had no fever. Nevertheless, he forced a dose of medicine upon me.

He seemed distressed when I told him it was necessary for me to leave as soon as possible; he had hoped I should stay at least a week, but if I must go, then he would telegraph to Dong-Ha for a motor-lorry, and it would arrive the next morning.

I spent most of the day in my room taking notes. From my window I had an excellent view of the quadrangle. On the right was the barracks of the guard, a long white structure with black doors and black trimmings.

Opposite this were the prisoners' quarters in a building with windows high from the ground and a run-around where sentinels were posted at night. Hot sunlight smote this stark enclosure, and the few trees, so luxuriantly green, seemed feeble attempts at ribaldry.

I could not get away from a feeling of intense drama. The place was fantastic, yet there was no disputing its oppressive reality. It was a perfect setting for grim and imaginary happenings, much more gruesome than the actual events and circumstances that created this atmosphere. The very fact of Lao-Bao, a penal colony where France punished the children of her protectorate, was in itself sufficiently somber. But it had an added and even more sinister power over my fancy.

It promised numerous engrossing possibilities for a creative mind turned loose to wander in its atmosphere and devise an uncompromising tragedy to be put down on paper.

Instantly I could see a number of arresting ideas that might be worked out against this background. For instance—there was Nham, Nham who so eloquently expressed the simplicity of the forest. Give him the somewhat startling ambition of the native soldier in the *délégué's* story, the trooper who practiced decapitation on domestic animals. Such a trait, transferred to Nham, would not be inconsistent. Place him in Lao-Bao, and add three other characters to this proposed story: a young French *délégué*, his wife—and another man. This other man would also be French, a colonial officer perhaps, charming and slightly iniquitous. Thrust them all, figuratively speaking, into the shadow of Madame Guillotine —and, with these primary elements, the story would tell itself.

Immediately I capitulated to the idea, and began to work it out.... The title? ... I would call it... "The Suitors of Madame Guillotine"... No, better, "The Lover of Madame Guillotine."[20] Nham would be that lover, an uninvolved native with a passion for shiny steel. Around him the other three characters would revolve. It would be a conventional triangle with an unconventional solution. I could visualize Nham daily polishing the blade of the guillotine—waiting—waiting for the first head to fall. And the first head to fall would be... Nham's.

As my thoughts browsed about in the nebulous beginning of "The Lover of Madame Guillotine" I realized that growing out of it was another story—a study done in the same mood and upon the same general theme but more comprehensive and significant.

This story, like the other, was suggested by Lao-Bao.

Actually, Lao-Bao was simply a penal colony established by the "protectors" to punish the delinquent among their "children"; but in spirit it was more universal—it symbolized the tyranny inherent in white men. The story of this tyranny with its attendant problems, set in Indo-China, would be a tragedy more terrific than the tragedy of disastrous incidents.

Lao-Bao, I felt, expressed the inevitable brutality resulting from a civilized temperament brought into contact with a temperament not complicated by a surfeit of acquired knowledge. France, the protector, was definitely masculine, Indo-China, the conquered, definitely feminine.

If I were to personify these elements in a story, I should, I realized, choose for the first a French soldier and for the latter a native *congai*. Obviously the odds were against the *congai*. Yet she had certain insidious weapons.

---

[20] Hervey's story inspired by this encounter appears in the appendices of this book.

"Such a girl necessarily would be destined to become a mistress."

This girl—I was swiftly crystallizing the protagonists of my study—might consistently be a half-caste. Indeed, the more I thought about it the more I was convinced she would better symbolize the country if she had mixed blood.

The opposing force, my French soldier, multiplied: he became several soldiers. Then these miraculously begotten Frenchmen began to change their professional identities. Only one remained a soldier; another was a writer; another a man with his finger in the colony's finances; another a government official, a resident superior or a governor. ... By virtue of their diverse trades they represented France more authentically.

It required no great perception to see immediately that it would not be a short story but a novel. Nor would the physical background be Lao-Bao. That was too restricted. It would commence in a jungle town, perhaps similar to Lao-Bao, but in a locality along the Mé-Kong, and from there it would shift into the midst of French colonial life in some city like Saigon.

As for my *congai*, she would have all the primitive instincts of her Annamite mother and all the civilized intelligence of her French father. Such a girl necessarily would be destined to become a mistress. She would pass from one man to another—in body a courtesan, in spirit a nun. There would have been a native lover in the beginning, a boy by whom she had a child. It was fitting this child should be sired by one of her mother's people, for then that blood would pass through the girl herself back into Indo-China. Her love for this native boy would make it possible for her to retain a spiritual chastity more vital than actual virginity. To each of the white men she would give something, but within herself would remain a spirit untouched to the very end. And that end...?

Suddenly I knew. For had not I seen the end one late afternoon in Saigon when a magnificent tawny creature, suave in French clothes, swept out of the Cafe Continental and into her waiting motorcar?

And a Frenchman sitting at a near-by table had remarked: "I wonder how long that will last?"[21]

---

[21] Hervey's vision of colonial relationships between French men and the indigenous women of Southeast Asia manifested in his 1927 book, *Congaï*, which was released just before *King Cobra*. *Congaï* later became a popular play starring Humphry Bogart's future wife, Helen Mencken. In 2013, DatAsia Press republished *Congaï* as the companion to this new edition of *King Cobra*.

## 7

The next day at noon the motor-lorry from Donga-Ha arrived.

Into it was piled my luggage—instead of decreasing, it had assumed amazing proportions—Leung, a nondescript native who was there for no purpose I could see, a mechanic, the driver and myself. *Monsieur le Délégué* and his shy little mistress stood on the steps of the prison to wave us good-by; the Frenchman shouted that he hoped I would come back to see him soon.

I felt singularly gay as we whirled out of Lao-Bao. My stay at the prison had been most productive, but the atmosphere of the place had oppressed me. Ahead was the coast, Hanoi. In a few days I could sit in a sidewalk cafe and enjoy the novelty of many people. Although I loved the jungle and its simple natives, I discovered I was not displeased with the prospect of sea winds and the comforts of a semi-civilized town.

Soon after leaving the village of Lao-Bao, we were spinning through a cool green forest utterly unlike the humid jungles farther inland. Tall ferns sprayed the aromatic gloom, and rays of sunlight, penetrating the closely woven foliage, glowed behind immense fronds with an effect of tremulous and limpid green.

The people we passed, like the scenery, were different. These natives were the Moi, aborigines of the mountains of Annam. They seemed gentle, half-frightened savages, with their wide, guileless eyes and long hair. Some were carrying bales of thatch or long strips of bamboo; one or two had crude bows slung over their shoulders.

I had thought it impossible for a people to wear less clothing than the Laotians without being entirely naked, but the Moi achieve this feat. Instead of a loin-cloth, their one garment, if it may be called that, is a narrow though adequate strip of cloth passed under the crotch and fastened to a string about the waist.

Beyond the border defining the end of Laos and the beginning of Annam, the road was cut into the side of a mountain. High above, great boulders were bedded in slopes of mud and shale, which, soaked by the constant rains, seemed incapable of sustaining the weight of all those tons of rock. This, the one road, climbed on over the vertebrae of a mighty range, down to the sea.

There were stretches of forest tangled in creepers; sudden sheer precipices that dropped into fronded gorges; now and then a waterfall tumbling soundlessly in white fire; and always ahead, seen at intervals above the winding road and the tops of trees, far blue mountains that seemed to drink their color from the sky.

Suddenly I found the increasing perilousness of that narrow road intruding upon my enthusiastic admiration of the scenery. On one side was a mass of dripping, mossy stone, a veritable cliff; on the other, the mountain lowered its perpendicular side into rapids fully two hundred feet below.

We were racing along this ledge at a ridiculously high speed when, as we approached a turn, several natives ran out from behind the rocks and waved their hats. The brakes screamed; I pitched forward into the midst of the baggage.

As I picked myself up and got out, I heard the natives chattering excitedly with the driver. He swung down from his seat, and the two of us followed them around the bend.

A few yards ahead, the road was buried under what appeared to me to be the entire side of the mountain. Instantly it was obvious what had happened.

The rains, loosening the soil, had caused part of the embankment to collapse, and tons of dirt and rock, tufted with foliage and splintered branches, lay over the road.

Just beyond this impassable stretch, tantalizingly bright in the sunlight, was a concrete viaduct spanning the chasm—connecting the mountain road with the road to Dong-Ha.

An hour later I crawled weakly out of the lorry in front of the prison. *Monsieur le Délégué*, appearing suddenly on the veranda, stared at me.

I announced as pleasantly as possible that he had got his wish.... Then I explained what had happened.

He looked relieved and shrugged. "That happens once or twice a year," he said comfortingly.

"When will the road be cleared?" I asked.

"Oh, perhaps in three days, four days," he replied amiably. "Or maybe in a week. Come, we'll have a Picon-grenadine."

As I followed him upstairs I felt a familiar, ominous chill creeping over me. At the top my knees seemed to dissolve; I realized, rather sheepishly, that I couldn't make it to a chair.

Evidently, I remember thinking, the fever, too, has encountered a landslide and been forced to come back.

## CHAPTER X
# The Chinese Inn
*Tells Why This Book is Called King Cobra*

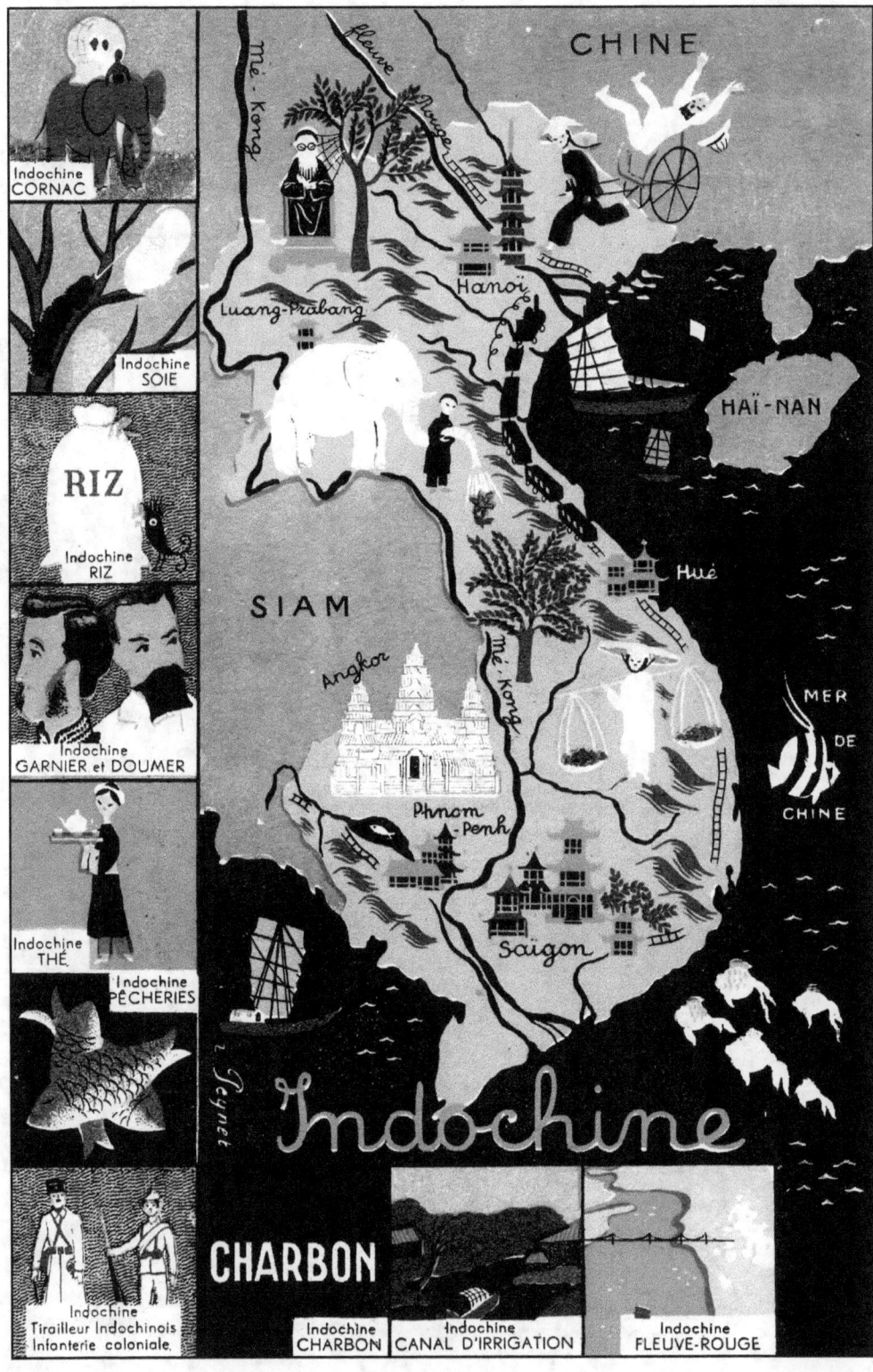

# Ha-Tinh

## 1

A BOOK of personal adventures, no matter what vulgar levels it pursues at times, should always end on some glorious peak, or at least in a mood equally exalted.

This one ends in a dirty Chinese inn at Ha-Tinh.

Fever is not a pleasant companion. After two weeks with it, I was in no condition, either mentally or physically, for further adventures that involved any degree of uncertainty. This was not a flattering admission to make, even to myself. Yet I felt for a while I should be content with expected happenings and all the comforts which, in sentimental moments, I had pretended to scorn.

Accordingly, I set out by motor from Dong-Ha—not so many kilometers from Lao-Bao—to travel up the coast of Annam and Tongkin to Hanoi. After a while in Tongkin, I would take the boat from Hai-Phong to Saigon, and then—home.

That word "home," with all its implications, had a curiously unfriendly aspect. For I realized the place I called "home" seemed, suddenly, very alien to me. With vague trepidation—vague because this trepidation was no more than a gesture to my Nordic heritage—I discovered that I had been poisoned by a heathen land; I had no desire to return to this place which birth and circumstances had designated as "home." Such an attitude, I realized, was little short of treason. In fact, it was heresy—but of a rather agreeable sort.

I had capitulated to Indo-China as I had never done to any other country.

This both troubled and pleased me. It seemed, on first glance, a bit unpatriotic—yet it suggested I was being emancipated from provincialism. I felt somewhat encouraged; there is a certain charming iconoclasm about liking a foreign country more than your own. It gives the impression that you have graduated from the tourist class and belong to an eminently aristocratic group, a sort of traveler's intelligentsia. For surely only the very intellectual and evolved can enjoy the role of renegade without qualms.

This affinity between Indo-China and myself could not be attributed wholly to sentimental association or to the gaudy enchantment of a part of the world publicly classified as exotic. Nor would I credit any esoteric explanation. I was half persuaded it was due to the fact that I was becoming quite cosmopolitan, when I made the alarming discovery that instead here was proof that I was definitely provincial and eloquently American.

For was not I merely absorbing the psychology and philosophy of another land? And the only element that made me in any way different from the majority of my countrymen was my willingness to admit my susceptibility to outside influence.

The Hindus have an expression, "*gnanam*," which means, loosely, the submersion of the personal Self in the universal Self.

During all this analysis I was, then, not brazenly intent upon a study of my own temperament but upon a study of the reaction of this section of the East upon an individual raised in antithetical surroundings. I was trying to accomplish "*gnanam*," so to speak, by regarding myself as a general instrument.

It is the habit of writers, and a sorry habit, to practice literary surgery upon their associates, no matter how casual. Inasmuch as this deplorable tendency cannot be overcome, it seems to me that after a writer has dissected those around him the one chivalrous thing he can do is to turn the scalpel upon himself.

By which it will be perceived, at least by the discerning, that a momentary blush of apology colors the latter pages of this hitherto unabashed chronicle of personal persuasions.

## 2

That I should spend a night in a Chinese inn at Ha-Tinh was entirely unexpected.

At noon we had left Dong-Ha by motor, expecting to reach Vinh after dark and continue in the morning.

Certainly the scenery along the way did not portend misadventure. Beyond Dong-Ha, flat plains sprawled between the mountains and the sea, the latter not yet visible. The soft dun-color of the soil was restful after so many months of constant green. At the side of the road were numerous weather-stained shrines and little temples of faded tiles. The road itself was dyked, and on either side land was being cultivated by *nhaques*, or peasants; small brown people plowing with bullocks or working knee-deep in flooded areas. In the air was a smell of wet mud, sharpened by intermittent salty whiffs.

Under the smooth whiteness of this French-made road sleeps the ghost of the old Mandarin Road. Here, in the days of Annam's glory, sedan-chairs bearing court dignitaries traveled laboriously between Hue and Hanoi, and imperial corteges, bright with royal yellow and purple, swung along with a distressing amount of ceremony.

Few traces of those days have remained. Now the Mandarin Road is a highway of commerce; autobuses and smart French roadsters race between Hue and Hanoi. Yet the natural grandeur of the country is unaltered. A mighty range flows westward, sinking its slopes into a sea whose intense purity of blue hurts the eyes. In many places, high above the road, slender waterfalls powder the rocks; below, white beaches slumber in the glare; and far out in the sea dim islands seem to breathe over the horizon.

Toward mid-afternoon we reached Dong-Hoi. Dong-Hoi is characteristic of Annamite coast towns: staring, sun-steeped houses; narrow streets astir with indolent life; and beside the beach fleets of sampans moored in the midst of nets and fishing-traps. From the native part the main road plunges between the dark, scarred walls of the French fortress.

Here I noticed the types were more robust than farther south. Gaunt women in cinnamon-colored tunics moved through the streets, carrying unbelievable loads and balancing immense straw shades on their heads. There

"One tawny gallant who wore a tunic of flowered black grenadine…"

On the Azure Coast.

was an even more pronounced Tongkinese influence in the dress of the men. All bound their hair in the tight folds of a band-like turban. Some were attired very elegantly. I particularly remember one tawny gallant who wore a tunic of flowered black grenadine over white silk and patent-leather sandals that dropped flippantly from his heels as he walked.

As late afternoon crept down, we climbed the range that marks the boundary between Annam and Tongkin. Below, the rice-fields were verdant patches sewn with silver where tiny streams wound inland; the sea was a deep mauve burned with rose. Before complete darkness came we descended from the pass—the Gate of Annam it is called—into Tongkin. Lights twinkled by as we rushed through an increasing number of hamlets. The chauffeur, determined to reach Vinh in time for dinner, drove at a mad speed. Once or twice I suggested that I might enjoy the ride more if we traveled with less abandon, but evidently he considered these feeble protests unworthy of a white gentleman or accepted them as high humor, for we dashed on with increasing recklessness.

Suddenly many lights sprayed past; through the dust I caught glimpses of shop-fronts and people. The chauffeur muttered, "Ha-Tinh."

A few minutes later the headlights of another car advanced out of the darkness ahead. As we approached, they swerved abruptly and our car jerked to a halt not six inches from them.

Considerably unnerved, I shouted profane denunciations at the other driver. I could not see him, but when I had finished swearing, a very polite French voice announced it was fortunate for us that he had blocked the way. The road to Ben-Thuy, he explained, was completely under water; if we were headed for Vinh, it would be impossible to go farther tonight. He would suggest, therefore, that we return to Ha-Tinh and telegraph the Resident at Ben-Thuy, who would arrange for a *bac* to transport us across the flooded district in the morning.

Then, before I could thank him, this unseen driver threw in his clutch and shot ahead toward Ha-Tinh.

"And this was the end. I would go on to Hanoi…
but whatever experiences I might have would be in the nature of an epilogue."

Harry Hervey in a Hanoi garden at the end of his adventure.

# 3

There was no hotel at Ha-Tinh, only the Chinese inn.[22]

This inn was a low, white building facing an *épicerie* across the street owned by the same Chinaman. To reach the rooms, one had to pass through a storeroom and climb a disreputable stairway to an upper veranda. Below this veranda was a courtyard that smelled like a latrine. The same odor soiled the air of the rooms; small, cell-like rooms, furnished only with battered chairs and beds that sagged under yellowed mosquito-nets.

I had dinner downstairs in the storeroom. A torn *punkah* flapped over the table, worked by a little Chinese boy who pulled the cord with his toe. Odds and ends of furniture were piled about the room; in one corner stood a broken rickshaw. As I ate, groups of curious natives shifted back and forth in the doorway. Among them were beggars, filthy with sores, who whined for alms until the serving-boy chased them away with kicks. Finally I abandoned trying to eat and went upstairs.

The room was hot, oppressive. Blurred sounds drifted up from the street; clacking of sandals, voices and the beating of a drum somewhere nearby. I was obsessed by the feeling that I was in a cell.

What a sorry end for adventure! And this was the end. I would go on to Hanoi and elsewhere in Indo-China, but whatever experiences I might have would be in the nature of an epilogue. For many months I had been living a book. Now that book, the book of my adventures in quest of a dead city, was being finished, here in Ha-Tinh, tonight.

In the light of this realization, our enforced halt seemed significant: I was being called upon by my conscience to account for what I had learned in Indo-China. And I must find a fitting conclusion for this book I had lived.

Well...

"Sometime during the ninth century," said my notebook, "Wat-Phu was built... and between the latter part of the sixteenth century and the eighteenth century it was given over to the forest...."

And as to the Khmers... "After 1297 the whirlwind came.... Siam seized Angkor many times, on one occasion killing thirty thousand and on another

---

[22] Hervey used the "Chinese inn" as a dramatic venue in his companion novel, *Congaï*.

removing ninety thousand prisoners.... The Karen kingdom of Tchen-Tching rose and took revenge. The Mon Shans shared the spoils. Nor were the Annamites inactive.... Even Laos joined in the succession of terrible wars upon *Tevada Nagkon*. ... In 1570 Angkor was reported deserted. The vengeance of the jungle, more dreadful than the reprisals of once vassal kingdoms, had overtaken the Khmers; the thin stream of people left were engulfed in stronger races. . .

But to use these details as the end of my book of experiences seemed too academic.

Of course, there was the very imminent fact of my novel "*Congaï*." But no—it would be indelicate to end one book with the threat of another. Moreover, this story I had lived required a conclusion less personal—something symbolical of the country, Indo-China.

Outside, that drum was still beating. It seemed to half translate some sorrow concealed in the darkness.

It was upon such a note, I decided, my book must end.

Glad of any excuse to leave the room, I went downstairs to follow that drum-beat.

The street was abnormally alive. Crowds of natives wandered about aimlessly; others squatted inside lighted doorways drinking *choum-choum* or eating roasted rice-cakes and sweetmeats. Women sat on the doorsteps, chatting and spitting betel-juice. Rickshaw coolies shouted to clear the way, panting obscenely as they trotted. From the stores came the mingled smells of garlic and liquor; the air was thick with dust and with the odor of sweaty skins. I could no longer hear the drum, but a Chinese fiddle, played in some brothel, whined a maddening obbligato to the rasping of many voices, the lisp of bare feet and the clack-clack of sandals.

Hastily I turned off into a side street; I could never formulate the end of my story amidst such confusion.

Suddenly a figure stepped out from a black doorway.

"*Bonsoir, monsieur*," said a young voice.

"*Bonsoir*," I returned.

Sandals clattered after me.

"*Pardonnez-moi, monsieur. Vous avez une allumette?*"

I paused and handed the boy a box of matches. As he struck a light he smiled; his face was very white, his clothing absurdly French.

"*Merci, monsieur,*" he murmured; and I could feel him still smiling in the darkness....

# 4

As I walked back to the Chinese inn I felt depressed and not a little disturbed. I knew my ending. Certainly the grotesque, pathetic figure of that Annamite boy was eloquent. But how could I put him into words? It would not be easy. Yet I could try. For instance, I might write:

*History repeats itself.*

*Again a king has come from the West*
*and married a cobra's daughter;*

*And their children—are they the gods of modern Indo-China?*

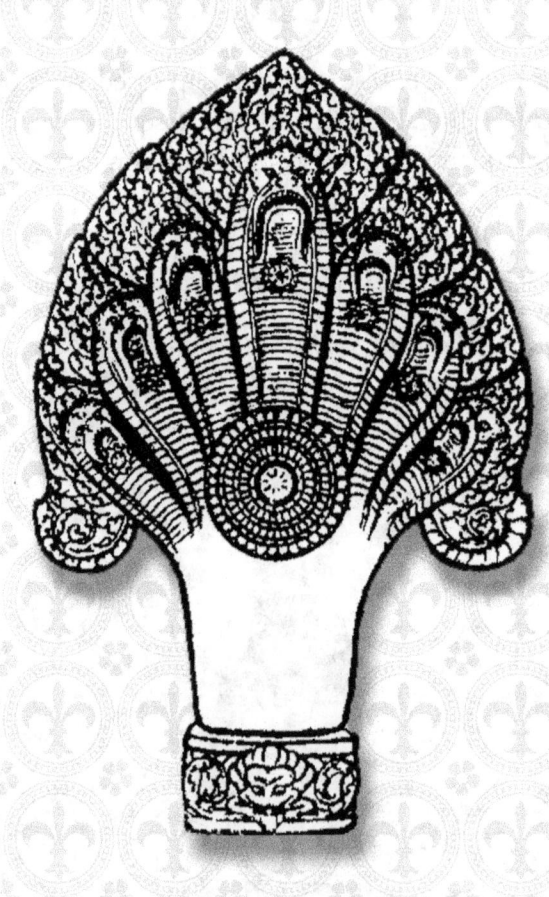

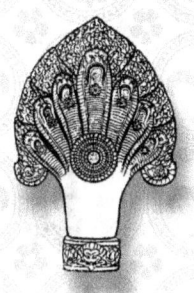

# Appendices

---

### *Harry Hervey: The Charmer Behind the Cobra*
Harlan Greene

### Harry Hervey Bibliography
Kent Davis & Harlan Greene

### *King Cobra* 1928 Review
Margaret Mead

### *The Lover of Madame Guillotine*
Harry Hervey

### List of Illustrations

**Harry Hervey**
November 5, 1900—August 12, 1951

# Harry Hervey:
## *The Charmer Behind the Cobra*

### By Harlan Greene

Today Harry Hervey might be as obscure as the lost city he once set out to find as a young man: but in his prime, he captivated the public with an alluring, self-made persona of a world traveler, serious author, dare devil explorer and "Orientalist." He packed his writing with so much color, drama, danger, and unbridled emotion that readers couldn't help but believe that the man himself embodied these traits. And they were right, for Harry's life was as fantastic and melodramatic as the leading characters he invented.

Coming of age in the 1920s, he began publishing his pulsating stories in the popular pulp magazines that help pioneer *noir* fiction. Switching quickly to novels and nonfiction, he moved on to Broadway and Hollywood, producing a total of 12 books and 13 films before his premature death at age 50.

Now, some six decades later, people are rediscovering Harry Hervey. His unique travel experiences, his vibrant literary style and his rather flamboyant no-apologies lifestyle are inspiring new interest. While his films, starring the likes of Marlene Dietrich, Gary Cooper, Bob Hope and Bing Crosby have continually been watched, his books are only now reappearing as cultural critics and social historians embrace Harry once more. If any argument arises as to what his greatest work might be, however, the answer, hands down, has to be Harry Hervey himself. Blurring the boundaries between fact and fiction, Harry became his art.

His start, however, was rather, prosaic—a problem to overcome, because he inhaled a taste for exoticism, color and splendor with his first breath. Harry hated admitting having been born November 5, 1900 in Beaumont, near Houston, Texas to a family that was definitely middle class. His father, Harry Clay Hervey, Sr. was one of four brothers who had followed the *pater familias* into the hotel business; his mother, Jane, or Jennie, Davis, was a local belle, barely 20 when her son and only child was born. Jennie told him that the birth scar above his eye, an injury later to impact his eyesight, was "where the fairies kissed you when you were born." [1]

His birth came just after the great Galveston hurricane that had obliterated that part of the country, and the feeling of having missed a great adventure haunted him from his early youth on. Making it worse was the adventure all around him. He lived in a world of arrivals and departures, around ziggurats of suitcases and steamer trunks plastered with labels of faraway lands. But the destinations, the glamor and the adventures were never his, but those of the guests passing through the chain of Hervey Hotels.

It was quite galling for the boy who dreamed of romance to witness it happening for others, but not himself. Dragged behind his failing father from one hotel to the next, Harry, the only youngster in an extended family, pined for escape, and he found it through his voracious reading.

It's easy to picture the dreamy boy sitting in palm decked lobbies, perusing "piles of books" and "yellowed geographic journal[s] containing pictures of far-off places and people". (He'd give this part of his childhood to the eponymous hero of his third novel *Ethan Quest*.) One image in particular, a photograph of "queerly dressed" men he found "quite astonishing." Again and again, he stole away to peruse that image of "men in long flowing garments with turbans on their heads, and others who were nearly naked." [2]

Leaning over the pictures, "[h]e struggled with the names. Tangier. Nairobi; Cambodia. He rather liked the sound of Cambodia. 'Cam-bo-d-uh,' he pronounced, wistfully...."[3]

He loved the image of a "great causeway…flung across a marshy stretch, tapering to the foot of …tremendous stairways and monstrous cone–shaped towers, above the black jungle…. The hugeness, the utter newness, trapped and held him." Again there were those "dark, naked men moving among the galleries…. [B]eneath the picture was a line that he read slowly. 'The Ancient Ruins of Angkor…' Angkor. What a splendorous word! …When he became a man he would go there. He knew he would." He'd be among "[j]ungles and strange, dark men…."[4]

And he would. In the future, he'd go off to Southeast Asia, the lands now Vietnam, Laos and Cambodia and write *King Cobra,* claiming to have found a lost city, becoming one of the first Americans fascinated with this part of the world. But, even before then, years before he left North America, he started fantasizing and fibbing about his globetrotting life. Reporters and readers were told he had started his peripatetic adventures even before he reached his teens—something that never happened. Did he lie about traveling to exotic lands with his father to cover the fact that he was left behind when Harry Sr. vanished, abandoning his wife and son?[5] Making up lies (about his past, his father and himself) bothered Harry Jr. not a jot. He, at least, was truthful in acknowledging that "the fact that he had deliberately falsified [stories and events] troubled him—slightly. He found it disturbing that he did not regret it more. It showed him that he had a capacity for violating the fringe of ethics without leaving more than a transient sediment of his conscience."[6]

Harry had apparently realized at a very early age that he was gay, and despite the censorious attitudes of the times, he seemed to have no conflicts over it; in fact, he often flirted with "outing" himself in his works. As a young boy, he dressed up in outlandish Mardi Gras outfits in celebrations held in cities around the Gulf; other lads in that time and place may have imagined fighting with Stonewall Jackson or Robert E. Lee, but young Harry poured over images of scantily dressed dark men in front of tall phallic towers in far off-lands.[7] Sensitive critics would detect his eventual conflating of desire for exotic scenes with desire for the erotic life. "Don't miss 'King Cobra'," W.E. Seabrook would write. "Beginning mildly as any other travel book then changing into a series of time-fused explosions as definitely sex-inspired as anything in the Wagner score of Tristan and Isolde, King Cobra is a panic. I use that word in its original sense. To me, it is not decadent; it is powerful, beautiful, and more than a little mad."[8]

Jennie apparently felt that her dreamy boy, who drew and sketched in charcoal, with no father, needed discipline and a role model, so she enrolled him in a military school in Sewanee, TN. A short time later, however, the boy and his mother had moved on—to Atlanta, where he attended the Georgia

Military Academy, and Jennie worked in a nearby hotel. A report card shows 90 in Composition, (good for a future writer) but 58 in Math (he'd always be in debt and harassed by the IRS). In English, however, another 90.[9]

He continued to live in a parallel world—now that he was reading the works of Joseph Conrad and those of the French writer Pierre Loti, wherein the boy found a mirror of his own dreams; Loti's "*Un Pelerin d'Angkor*, and its depictions of Angkor, a dead city buried in a living tomb of jungle, filled [him] with the anguish of dissatisfaction." [10] The first chapter shows a boy dreaming over pictures of Angkor, just as Harry had; the rest of the book recounts the author's sojourn there as an adult. If Loti could achieve his childhood dreams of reaching Cambodia so perhaps could a boy named Harry Hervey.

He began channeling his fantasies into stories he wrote. "Slinky words, like colored panthers" prowled his mind and lured him on with their savage loveliness, he reported. [11]

"Your work is very puzzling," the editor of a poetry journal writes to Harry's fictional alter ego, Ethan Quest. "It is not poetry and it is not prose. …You feel color and emotion, but you cannot harness them in the necessary technique." [12]

He despaired of ever being published, till one day the impossible happened. At the age of 16 (an anecdote to be told again and again, grace many of his dust jackets and even be mentioned in his *New York Times* obituary), pre-eminent critic of the day, Henry Louis Mencken, accepted a short story Harry wrote. Everyone knew that inclusion of teen work in Mencken's *The Smart Set* was almost too good to be true, as indeed it was; for it never happened. Mencken *had* written to the school boy to acquire one of his fabulous tales, but it was not for the highbrow *The Smart Set*, intended instead for one of the lurid lowbrow magazines Mencken secretly published.[13]

Even though the fledgling author had graduated from the Georgia Military Academy, the teenager lacked any sort of military bearing (as his photo, slightly pudgy and monocled, attests). Yet somehow, again, he managed a sleight of hand. When America entered WWI, he passed a physical (conning people into believing he could see out of an eye that would soon become virtually sightless). He was still in training when the war ended, forcing him to face civilian life, a job in a boring office, living with his mother in Texas.[14]

"...but it was not for the highbrow *The Smart Set*, intended instead for one of the lurid lowbrow magazines Mencken secretly published.

Desperate to find a way out, he escaped into his alternate parallel world of writing. In 1920, Harry published a story called "Drums of Doom".[15] "Devil's Business" followed soon after. In it the hero is overpowered by a woman and kidnapped. In a country like Cambodia, in a temple like Angkor Wat, Eric witnesses a devil dance where women sway like cobras while attended by white apes, who are really emaciated men, enslaved and virtually emasculated by their seductress. The evil female sets her eyes on the hero, but he kills her, freeing his enslaved male friend from the castrating clutches of a woman.[16]

Eight more of these hard to believe and slightly homoerotic stories would end up in *Black Mask Magazine*, considered by many as the best pulp magazines ever to allow young writers (Dashiell Hammett being one of them) to hone their craft. [17]

This Harry was definitely doing. He seized on two of his early stories and expanded them into novels. One became *Caravans by Night* (1922). "The author knows his India," a reviewer wrote glowingly of the book, set on the sub-continent and in Tibet. "He has fairly wallowed in its

"Finally (at the ripe old age of 22), flush with royalties from his books, he acquired a passport and set off to see the world."

mysteries and seems to have caught the philosophy of this ancient people and woven it into his tale with rare skill." [18] A mere year later, his second book came out, *The Black Parrot*. The books sold well (and were translated into various languages going in and out of print for decades); Harry was acclaimed a *wunderkind* and the best rising young romantic writer of his day. He let everyone believe he had had used his own experience in foreign lands to write those books; that he had just done his research in books read in hotel lobbies no one would ever guess.

Finally (at the ripe old age of 22), flush with royalties from his books, he acquired a passport and set off to see the world, leaving from the West Coast in early 1923.[19] This voyage (and a second one, which he silently emended into his first) served him as the basis of his first nonfiction book, *Where Strange Gods Call* (1924).

Invoking a metaphor he would often use, the story unrolls with the vividness of an unspooling bolt of bright fabric. (Beautiful textiles would obsess him, witness his story of a man seduced not by a woman, by but the color of her dress).[20] His first stop was Hawaii, where he despaired of what missionaries had done to the natives; in Japan, he obsessed on the sex life of nearly every one he met (including male priests), visited the brothels (careful to note he just came to *talk* to the women), fixated on the males dressed as women in dramas, and giggled with his readers as to how he managed to elude a woman who had romantic designs on him. One adventure after another took him further down "the blue road of romance," as he called it, "blue" as in blue movies. If there was any doubt of that, Hervey dispelled it, telling, in very easy to decode prose, of his assignation with "a British soldier, a tall bare-kneed chap in kilt and sporran" who spent the night with him in a temple in moonlit beauty, a place, Hervey winked at his readers, "where the fairies danced." [21]

Having spent all his funds on travel, Harry soon found himself grounded in Savannah, Georgia where his mother was working in that city's landmark DeSoto Hotel. He finagled a room up under the eaves, and adorned it with souvenirs of his travel, including idols, incense on altars and billowing bolts of barbaric colored fabric. A visiting journalist insinuated that the kimono or sarong he often wore would have been more fitting on the glamorous vamp and silent film actress Pola Negri. [22]

It was here, in a hotel named for explorer Hernando DeSoto that Harry Hervey began his autobiographical novel, *Ethan Quest*, about a boy abandoned by his father, dreaming of foreign travel and wanting to write. Ethan, "not the marrying kind", influenced by a "Gay Sarong" as a talisman, escapes to Hawaii, where he meets a handsome half naked dark man, with whom he bonds. He and Ilio, the young man, go off to spend their life together, priest and disciple, on their own blue road of romance.[23]

Reviewers could not help but notice the similarity between the created and creator and how their lives overlapped. [24] But what they didn't realize was that, just like Ethan, Harry was setting off on his own lifetime journey, with his own underage lover, from whom he'd never part. The novel was not just autobiographical, but prophetic.

**Harry the explorer as featured in *McCall's Magazine*, replete with pith helmet.**

Harry's Ilio was a boy named Carleton Hildreth. It was probably in a little theatre production, just as he writing *Ethan Quest*, that they met. Carleton Hildreth, (born in 1908) was a handsome high school lad, interested in drama and intent on shaking off his Alabama origins and accent. [25] Harry, a world traveler with three books to his credit and the fourth about to be published, must have seemed very glamorous.

Looking older than his 25 years, Harry managed to convince the 17 year old Carleton's parents that he needed a secretary; he'd pay for everything—his passage abroad, housing and the rest—in exchange for secretarial duties from their son. The Hildreths agreed, and in fact, Harry, on the voyage out, as well as for the rest of his life, would dictate his stories to Carleton, who'd also research, punctuate, and proof. [26]

*King Cobra* is dedicated to Carleton, and every footstep Harry took was matched by Carleton's. But Harry erased his lover/travelling companion/secretary entirely from its pages. Perhaps it would be hard to explain why he had a boy with him as a companion. Or maybe publishers and Harry himself believed it would look better if he were portrayed facing danger alone, with no one there to help him. (Carleton, as if to compensate for that slight, later told reporters he'd saved Harry's life, chartering an airplane to pluck him from certain death. [27])

Deception had been embedded in the project from the very start. Just as his plans were gelling, author and *Titanic* survivor Helen Candee published *Angkor the Magnificent*, thus preventing Harry from becoming the first American author to bring Angkor Wat to the public. [28] So perhaps a new "hook" was necessary to attract both readers and a publisher. In this era still excited over Howard Carter's discovery of Tutankhamen, he concocted a fanciful tale (lifted, if anyone cared to notice, directly from his novel *The Black Parrot*) of having encountered a derelict adventurer who passed on rumors of ruins similar to those at Angkor lost in the jungle unseen by civilized people for centuries.[29] "This young man," *The Bookman* soon dutifully reported, "who is an authority of many Far Eastern subjects…believes that hidden somewhere in the fastness of the Indo-Chinese jungle are broken piles of sun bleached stones that may add another chapter to the story of the Khmers, the lost builders of mysterious and magnificent city of Angkor in Cambodia."[30]

Harry was going to set off into the jungles, single-handedly slice his way through them and find those ruins of that lost city and use them to decode the riddle of who had built the civilization that had mysteriously vanished. Cosmopolitan Book Corporation accepted the proposal; it would publish the book that *McCalls Magazine* would first excerpt in three installments. "The McCall Expedition to Indo-China" (the name patterned after scientific expeditions by the Smithsonian, the American Museum of Natural History, and the like) was what Harry, naming himself as director, called it.

"We landed at Saigon, a prominent seaport and the capital of Conchin-China," Carleton would write introducing the magazine installments and inserting himself into the story;

> then followed months of journeying through strange towns, in the midst of ancient forests, and long jungle rivers; traveling in small river-boats, in canoes, on rafts; in motor cars, in bullock-carts, on horseback and on elephants – every means of conveyance from poles of rattan lashed firmly

together into a floating platform to the latest model of a luxurious automobile.... All this, the adventures, the hardships, the intimate life of a dead race and a living one—and something of that soul—Harry Hervey has put into his papers with an emotional intensity that gives him the right among those who know the Far East, to be hailed as one of its faithful interpreters.[31]

Despite the purple prose and overblown rhetoric, Harry *was* faithful to his mission and his vision, sharing his clear sighted opinions and insights. Sitting at a café tables in Saigon, he watched the pretty *congais*, temporary wives of the European men, and "painted boys" pass. As he had in his earlier travel book, he dissected the foreign country he was visiting through the lens of sex, zeroing in on the relationships between the subdued natives and the occupying French. Behind the fine words of colonialism, as behind the fancy facades of French colonial buildings, lay the gutter truth that "one who offers protection…. [s]ubstitutes exploitation." He was certainly no Kipling, assuming the white man's burden. "In every country where the white man is 'protector' I have found that democracy, the gallant cry of those of paler skins, is a mere rhetorical term, to be recited by children and used by politicians."[32]

After a while in Saigon, Hervey and Carleton set out for Angkor Wat, finally achieving his life-time quest. "Angkor!" he wrote a Savannah friend.

> After fifteen years of dreaming (from a little boy over the map of the world, like 'Ethan [Quest]'!) I am here. And it leaves me a little incredulous, a little breathless…. Imagine five square miles of ruined temples and palaces, all locked in the green grip of the jungle; imagine it if you can; and you will have a faint picture of Angkor. Great gray towers; mighty cruciform stairways flung up from dusky courts; tremendous cloisters; miles of bas-reliefs; ancient walls cracked and ripped part by the sinuous tenacles [sic] of vines …. But there is no use trying to tell you of Angkor in a letter.

Even so, he went on,

> I must tell you of one experience I've had here. Night before last I saw eight Cambodian dancers performing by torchlight on the great terrace of Angkor Wat. There was a half-moon out, too, and lightening [sic] in the distance that presaged a tropic storm. Fifty native boys held torches (sweet torches of damar-gum) and the *danseueses* did their pantomimes in their tremulous half-light. They were the same dances that were done in the same spot over a thousand years ago. And the girls wore the same kind of headdress, the same jeweled robes of silk and gold cloth. When it was over the rain came down suddenly, like a dark, glittering curtain at the end of an amazing performance."[33]

Making the visit more intriguing was a handsome male guide who hinted of strange phallic ceremonies that had taken placed there. Hervey, unlike most travelers, did not fixate on the countless sculpted images of women adorning the walls, but referred instead constantly to the towers as "the lingam of Siva," using a Sanskrit word as a substitute for the possibly censored "penis."

"I had a new picture of Angkor," he wrote, "Angkor in the shadow of lingam;" In an apotheosis of civilization, he saw all cultures, "Brahma the Creator and Siva the Destroyer.… Relentlessly chanting the creed of the phallus."[34]

He broke a taboo of the day, actually using the word "homosexuality" in his text and commenting on the homosexual in history, but almost as if fearing he had said something too positive, he backtracked, but not before noting that he detected male lovers carved in the stones around him. "On the great bas-relief stretching around the lower terrace of Angkor Wat is a section which shows Khmer warriors marching to battle, and the profile of each figure is rimmed with the profile of another, suggesting – and not fantastically – that there existed among the soldiers of ancient Cambodia, a comradeship not entirely Platonic and similar to that of the Dorian Greeks." [35] Perhaps being there with his lover Carleton prompted him to see their love as a link with others from the past.

Going upstream and then across land, Harry grew infatuated with the land and its people. Watching the men and women, but mostly men, walk on the roads and bathe in the river, he had an epiphany, noting how he "wanted to go down from the deck, into the torrid swarm of the roadway, and mingle with them, bare and unashamed."

> It was an emotion stark, utterly naked. There could be, I realized, no mistaking the implication. For what could I…. have in common with this people… except the same basic sensuality?
>
> In the past I had been much in the East, wandering through city and jungle, across desert and mountains, but always the East itself had been in the background. I was the self-conscious writer surveying the scene. Now…this little village by the Me-Kong had reached out and drawn me in. Through it I had felt the warm body of the East. My fingers had strayed amorously in the hair of the East. The East was inviting me to bed with it.

"I was definitely disturbed by this suggestion of assignation," he wrote rather disingenuously, continuing in an apostrophe, about the boatmen taking him upriver.

> Look at those fellows aft, you white man. You pursue beauty through a studio, in a lecture hall… Look at those [male] bodies, at the flexing of their muscles as they move; the dark, tragic mystery of their eyes… Make that live, you writer.… Here is the East offering her lips to you, ….Drink the incense, white man. Musk of a wild beauty. [36]

Harry apparently consummated his dream of desire with half naked dark men.

When he finally "discovered" Wat Phu, the hidden ruins supposedly no one has seen for centuries, he noted, not the carvings of women, but again "the blunt stones resembling phallic symbols; indeed they were almost identical with lingams I had found in some of the ruins at Angkor." [37] With some easy speculations, and arm chair archeology, comparing photos he had taken at Angkor, and with other images in books, he came to the glib conclusion that the ruins had indeed been built by the same civilization. So, mission accomplished, he pressed on despite his fever, never mentioning Carleton by his side to nurse him; or that he was never too sick not to relay bulletins on his condition to the obliging New York press.[38]

Despite deceptions like these, Harry wrote honestly of a land he saw and of the times in which he lived. Both have so vastly changed that his perceptions bear witness and his descriptions are important. While we may be amused by his some of his antics, we can only applaud his analysis of practices destroying the people and their culture. Not a Cassandra exactly, he, nevertheless, was sounding a warning bell of the deadly effects of imperialism in a land soon to change its name from Annam to Vietnam. And he wrote as honestly as he could as a gay man, telling his truths, not very subtly at that, in between the lines of his text.

When he left Indochina, having spent less than six months on the entire trip from start to finish, Harry came back, changed and recharged. Even before publishing *King Cobra*, he brought out the novel *Congai* (1927), which he and Carleton later adapted as a successful Broadway play.[39] It is the story of Thi Linh, a half-caste woman, with whom Harry obviously identified, a woman who, not being European, not being Asian, does not fit within precise categories, the way a gay man did not fit specific expected gender roles in the 1920s. He followed her path from village to Saigon, using her sexual wiles to triumph and be trapped simultaneously.

In *King Cobra*, the vision of chained and sweating half-naked men he had seen in the penal colony Lao Bao, "where France punished the children of the protectorate," also fired his imagination, as did the real-life woman in Saigon who had inspired *Congai*. [40] To bring the men's world before the public, he wrote a play based on a similar camp, but it was too overtly gay to pass the censors and so it was never produced. Harry turned it instead into the novel *The Iron Widow* (1932), a slang term for a guillotine (and another version of castrating womanhood). Harry also turned *King Cobra*'s chapter that "Tells of Nham and the Suitors of Madame Guillotine" into a short story, "The Lover of Madame Guillotine" which later served as the basis of one of his Hollywood films. [41]

When *King Cobra* was published in 1927, the critics were almost unanimous in their praise of it. While a few objected to the "descriptions… rather flamboyant and… metaphors somewhat luxuriant", others commended him for the deft and cool observations and commentary beneath, praising the author for his critique of the colonial government's control of the opium trade, and his condemnation of colonialism itself, naming it for the fraud it was. [42] His focus on sex was not just for sensation's sake, but for highlighting how flesh, too, became a commodity in which both the natives and the French traded.

When it was published in the United Kingdom the next year, with the more sedate and less phallic title, *Travels in French Indo-China*, one scholarly journal called his bluff, noting that the ruins at Wat Phu had been known for decades, with archeological reports dating back to 1914. [43] As if anticipating being found out, Harry had put the following words in the mouth of a skeptic he supposedly encountered just before finding Wat Phu, "'Some Frenchman, or an American, or anybody finds a big pile of stone and some rotten carvings and gets all excited because he thinks he's the first white man that ever saw the glorious ruin of the What-not Empire; and then he suddenly discovers that an Englishman or a German has been there two hundred years before …. When you get to Wat Phu you will probably find that… the whole French Annamite army camped there at one time.'"[44]

So Hervey had shown his hand, laughing into his long kimono-like sleeve, admitting what he knew to be the truth about Wat Phu all along, but coming up with an evocative and often trenchant narrative nonetheless. A few parochial scholars may have doubted him, but to the public, the book confirmed Harry as an expert on "the Orient." The belief was so great that

Original 1927 cover of *King Cobra*.

he was called upon for his expertise in the kingdom of make believe. Movie producer Samuel Goldwyn, not a stickler for the truth himself, summoned Harry to Hollywood for his help in "The Devil Dancer," (drawn from Harry's own short story "The Young Men Go Down").[45] "Entirely aside from his standing as a novelist and a dramatist, Hervey has a high academic standing as an Orientalist," Goldwyn told the press, promoting the first film ostensibly set in Tibet. "Naturally, we depended on him a great deal, not only for the continuity, but also for the local color."[46]

When the Great Depression hit, Harry was saved from penury by continuing his film work in Hollywood, where he supposedly earned enough money to pay off the $60,000 debt he said he owed *McCalls* for overspending on his *King Cobra* trip.[47] He put touches of the East in his script for *The Cheat* (soon to be pulled from theaters by censors), *The Devil's in Love*, *Prestige* and other stories. His greatest success, by far, however, was with another Eastern vehicle (literally) for Marlene Dietrich, the film classic, for which Harry supplied the scenario, *Shanghai Express*.

Hollywood was good for Harry, until his belief in needing a high lifestyle to match his fabled life caught up with him. His drinking grew, his film work fell off, and he found himself blackmailed by a devilish man with whom he had a sexual liaison. In debt to the IRS, with all jewelry pawned, he and Carleton fled back to Savannah where Hervey's mother offered some help. He was so broke, he said, that he could not even afford cigarettes.

Here Harry would eventually mend and produce some of his most entertaining works, including *The Damned Don't Cry* (1939), a naturalistic, albeit melodramatic, novel of a girl from the wrong side of the tracks trying to prove to Savannah that she could transcend her past, and *School for Eternity* (1941), a sophisticated and wise tale of strangers and lovers crossing paths and destinies in an out-of-the way West Indian Island.

In 1943 he was called back to Hollywood for his knowledge of the Far East when developments in China turned timely in World War II. The film he worked on was never produced, and back to Georgia he went.[49] Yet other films bearing his mark would appear. The initial story he had crafted for *Shanghai Express* (again of wanderers having their fates cross in remote places) proved successful enough to be timeless, being filmed again in 1943 (as *Night Plane from Chunking*) and 1951 (as *Peking Express*.)

Supporting himself and Carleton, just barely, from his writing, always late on the rent and borrowing small sums from neighbors and friends, Harry dreamed of getting out of Savannah, but he never managed it. He became a familiar figure instead in the DeSoto Hotel lobby, telling stories of his fabulous life for a drink, or a cadged cigarette, to hotel guests. It was a sad decline in many a way: the boy who had spent his time in lobbies dreaming of adventures to come had become a man, still in hotel lobbies, recalling the adventures he had lost.

The end was sadder still. His years of constant smoking led to cancer of the larynx, and after a series of gruesome operations, he died in New York City on August 12, 1951 and was buried in Savannah's Bonaventure Cemetery.

As the years went on, the stories he had published went out of print, and the stories he had told about himself languished. Carleton Hildreth, in a homophobic era and a conservative city, prevaricated about his past. In interviews, he was described only as Mr. Hervey's secretary and not the love of his life. [50] The few things left to Carleton, who died in 1977, of their fabulous past—some carvings and art—were sold, and the photos of them together in strange and foreign lands, with some of their correspondence, went out one day in the trash.

But Harry had been too colorful, too flamboyant and, in fact, too truthful, to be forgotten. His films still appear from time to time on classic film channels; his novel about Savannah has been republished. Scholars are now peppering their articles and dissertations with references to Harry Hervey and his works on Indochina. A biography is going to press, and perhaps he will be claimed as a lost gay writer next. Like Angkor Wat, and Wat Phu, Harry Hervey is slowing being rediscovered, and is on the verge of being restored to us.

In *King Cobra*, he closes his book on a puzzling character, surely meant to symbolize the assimilated nature of a place no longer East or West. He focuses not on a *congai*, or a half caste woman, but a young Asian man, "his clothing absurdly French," his face powdered white, assailing the author from a doorway, begging a light for his cigarette. Perhaps that image, suggestive of a possible assignation, will do for Harry himself. As more time passes and recognition comes to him—or not—it remains to be seen if he will be beckoned from the shadows, or if he'll just stay smiling at us, alluringly from the darkness. [51]

## Notes

1. Harry Hervey, *Ethan Quest: His Saga*. (New York: Cosmopolitan Book Corporation, 1925), 13.

2. Hervey, *Ethan Quest*, 16.

3. Hervey, *Ethan Quest*, 16–17.

4. Hervey, *Ethan Quest*, 17.

5. No letters have surfaced discussing this disappearance, or why. But newspaper advertisements and articles re the Hervey hotel chain list various brothers being in charge of various properties. One newspaper article by 1913, however, notes that Harry Clay Hervey, Sr. was no longer listed as a partner or a member. See: "Hervey Hotels" (advertisement), *Times Picayune*, September 1, 1909; "Middleton Taken to Mobile Hospital," *The Montgomery Advertiser*, November 3, 1913.

When Harry Jr. registered for the draft, he would use his father's address at a Hervey hotel in Florida, different from his mother's address; and Harry Clay Hervey, Sr. and his wife are listed as living at separate addresses in Texas after World War I. There is no mention anywhere of the fact that Harry Hervey, Sr. remarried and ended his life in a hotel room in San Francisco in the 1920s. The sole manner one can see of the writer taking note of the death of his father is in his dropping of "Jr." from his name.

Missing and/or despicable fathers are a staple of many of his books. Despite this, he told those tales, perhaps in compensation, for heroic events with his father. In a 1930 interview he said he went abroad with both his parents when he was twelve. ("Making the Grade in Gotham," *Dallas Morning News*, August 19, 1930.) A few years later, he said he went to the Orient first with his father when he was about nine. "Harry Hervey in Demand for China Stories," Robin Coons, undated (ca. 1932) clipping from unknown newspaper, Carleton Hildreth/Harry Hervey Papers, Georgia Historical Society (hereinafter cited as CH/HH Papers/GHS.) Jennie Hervey would not apply for a passport until 1923 and there is no record of one for Harry Hervey, Sr.

6. Hervey, *Ethan Quest*, 73.

7. Harry's grandfather, Frank A. Hervey enlisted in the Confederate infantry as a second sergeant in Company A, Tochman's Polish Brigade. Wounded in combat, he was eventually promoted to chief of artillery on the staff of General John Baylor and was captured by the enemy, languishing in a Union prison. After the war, he joined the United Confederate Veterans, achieving the rank of General. ("Gen. F. A. Hervey Dead," *The Montgomery [AL] Advertiser*, September 18, 1910.)

8. Seabrook review quoted in William B. Richardson, Jr., "Harry Hervey: A Bio-Bibliography," thesis Florida State University, 1958, 16.

9. Hervey often told people that he had attended the University of the South, at Sewanee, TN, but it was only the preparatory military school – and that only briefly. (Email communication from Elizabeth Duncan, St. Andrew's-Sewanee School, to author, December 12, 2006.) A copy of Hervey's Sophomore Georgia Military Academy report card is on file Woodward Academy, Atlanta Georgia. Copy, author's files.

10. Hervey, *Ethan Quest*, 43.

11. Hervey, *Ethan Quest*, 124.

12. Hervey, *Ethan Quest*, 123.

13. The same thing had happened to playwright S. N. Behrman, who was contacted by Mencken who called the pulp a "sister" publication. "I had never heard of this sister," he recalled more truthfully, "but I was happy to be admitted to the family." Marion Elizabeth Rodgers, *Mencken: The American Iconoclast*. (Cary, NC: Oxford University Press, Inc., 2005), 149. On the back of the dust jacket of *The Veiled Fountain*, published in 1947, there is this author note, "My first sale of a story was when I was sixteen – to H.L. Mencken. Fortunately for me, I didn't sell another for three years. Then I wrote steadily for pulp-paper magazines." A survey of *The Smart Set* shows no stories by Harry Hervey. For obituaries, see the August 20, 1951 issue of *Time Magazine*. "Harry Hervey, 50, Author of Novels," *New York Times*, August 13, 1951.

14. When it was time to register for the draft, Hervey was working in Greenville, South Carolina, at the Imperial Hotel. There was just the matter of his age to lie about. Born in 1900, he first wrote "1899" on the line asking for his birth year. In doing the math, however, he saw that did not make him the desired age. Hervey then crossed that out and changed it to 1897 to make himself twenty-one. (For good reason he had only scored a 58 in Math in his first term at the Georgia Military Academy.) Across the top of the card, he noted that he was a student at Sewanee. (Harry Hervey, Jr. World War I Draft Registration Card, 1917-1918, AncestryPlus database.) Even that was not totally true. He had enrolled instead as a special student in 1918 to join the Student Army Training Corps. (Email communication from Elizabeth Duncan, St. Andrew's-Sewanee School, to author December 12, 2006.)

15. Richardson, "A Bio-Bibliography," 5.

16. Published in a magazine called *The Follies*. Undated clipping (ca. 1921), CH/HH Papers, GHS.

17. Harry Hervey, "Piracy," *Black Mask*, 1, 1 (April 1920), 65-78. Mention of his second story "The Black Menace" is noted in *Black Mask*, 1, 2 (May 1920), 24, 55. Harry Hervey, "More Deadly than the Viper," *Black Mask*, 1, 5 (August 1920), 49-64. Harry Hervey, "The Devil at the Helm," *Black Mask*, 5, 4 (July 1922), 3-23. Harry Hervey, "Mr. Sin," *Black Mask*, 2, 6 (March 1921), 3–42.

18. "A Romance of the East," *Los Angeles Times*, June 11, 1922.

19. When he had applied for his passport to go abroad, Hervey put down his profession as novelist. As for why he was traveling, he answered, "pleasure," and enumerated the places he'd go and for how long – the next six months. They included Japan, Hong Kong, Palestine, Java, Singapore, British India, Egypt, Italy, Constantinople and France. He left San Francisco on *The Emperor of France* in February 1923. (United States Passport Applications, 1795-1925, Harry Hervey. AncestryLibrary database.)

20. A copy of his never-published story "The Conquering Magenta" exists in the Carleton Hildreth/Harry Hervey Papers at the Georgia Historical Society, Box 3, folder 11. See also Hervey, *Ethan Quest*, 17–18, 123–124.

21. Hervey Hervey, *Where Strange Gods Call* (New York: The Century Co., 1924), 7. He uses the term "blue movie" in Harry Hervey, *The Iron Widow*, (New York: Horace Liveright, 1931), 26. Hervey, *Where Strange Gods Call*, 320-323.

22. A New York journalist seeking Harry in his lair wrote, that he found his "studio hung deeply with oriental rugs and…a scent of incense in the air." She noted that "Hervey is a dark young man who wears on his hand a ruby ring presented to him by a beneficent oriental potentate. He showed us a white robe embroidered with a golden peacock and lined with saffron, that should be worn by [silent film actress] Pola Negri. We forgot to ask him if he ever wears it himself." ("The Gossip Shop," *The Bookman*, Vol. 6, no. 6 February 1925, 799.)

23. Hervey, *Ethan Quest*, 144–145, 184.

24. At least one reviewer caught this fact and remarked on how the author's and Ethan's life "curiously" crossed. "For Lovers of Words," *Overland Monthly and Out West Magazine*, Vol. LXXXIII, Number 8 (August 1925), 307.

25. "Youth in search of high adventure" *The Hartford Courant*, April 7, 1929. Carleton mentioned his desire to shed his accent in an interview, "The Whitaker Bay Bugle," the newsletter (?) of the *Savannah News-Press, Inc.*, undated copy in CH/HH Papers, GHS.

26. As soon as they set sail together, Harry realized that Carleton was "a marvelous choice. Aside from being an excellent companion, he is quite a help in my work. He's the first person I've ever been able to dictate to on the typewriter; and doing my stories in that manner expedites matters a lot." (Harry Hervey to Pauline Corson, "Tuesday, May 26 [1925]", Eugene Rollin Corson Collection, GHS.)

27. "Novelist Here to Write Book," *Charleston Evening Post*, January 15, 1926.

28. An expanded and annotated edition of Helen Churchill Candee's 1924 book *Angkor the Magnificent - Wonder City of Ancient Cambodia* was published in 2010 by DatASIA Press.

29. Hervey, *The Black Parrot*, 151–153. "'[W]hat I saw was worth all the agony of the journey[']" the character says. "'Of course, it wasn't as large as Angkor Thom, but there were the same conical towers, the same exterior cloisters; the huge stairways, the carved Nagas and lotus-buds, the daring relief work. And such decay! I can't describe it! The ruins were being devoured by the jungle, a cruel bestial jungle….'"

30. "The Gossip Shop," *The Bookman*, Volume LXI, Number 4 (June 1925), 504.

31. Harry Hervey, "Discovering a Lost City, Introduction by Carleton Hildreth who accompanied Mr. Hervey on this expedition," *McCalls*, Volume LIV, Number 4 (January 1927), 8–9, 63. 8.

32. Harry Hervey, *King Cobra: An Autobiography of Travel in French Indo-China* (New York: Cosmopolitan Book Corporation, 1927), 47.

33. Harry Hervey to Pauline Corson, August 1, 1925, CH/HH Papers, GHS.

34. Hervey, *King Cobra*, 89, 92.

35. Hervey, *King Cobra*, 95.

36. Hervey, *King Cobra*, 131-132, 147-148.

37. Hervey, *King Cobra*, 199.

38. He passed on information to a friend in Savannah, who passed on information to the press. "The Gossip Shop" column of *The Bookman* included the tidbit that he was "ill with fever at Angkor… He has been exploring Siam and China and Cambodia in Indo-China. To see the ruins of Angkor has been the dream of fifteen years, and his letters express no

disillusionment." "The Gossip Shop," *The Bookman*, Volume LVII, No. 3 (November 1925), 359.

39. Written by Harry and Carleton, the play opened in New York at the Belasco Theatre on November 27, 1928. The sexual aspect of the play created quite a stir, and it had a very successful run for its time, running for 137 performances and closing on March 23, 1929.

40. Hervey, *King Cobra*, 283.

41. Harry Hervey, "The Lover of Madame Guillotine," *McClures: The Magazine of Romance*, Volume 58, No. 1 (January 1927), 49 – 51, 80 – 81.

42. "Travels in French Indo-China by Harry Hervey," *Pacific Affairs*, Volume 2, number 6, 375.

43. "Reviews," *Geographical Journal*, Volume 73, Number 2, 169. Hervey conceded that others had been there before him in an interview wherein he described his and Carleton's adventure: "Further research has convinced us that we were not the first white men to see the city of Wat Phu; that probably seven or eight members of the French forestry service have run across the ruins." This article is the most direct admission on Hervey's part that Carleton was an integral part of the mission. "Lost Indo-China City Described," *Los Angeles Times*, January 9, 1927, 20.

44. Hervey, *King Cobra*, 159.

45. The story was originally published in the *Nation* in January 1924 and later collected and reprinted. Harry Hervey, "The Young Men Go Down," in Edward J. O'Brien, ed., *The Best Short Stories of 1924* (Boston: Small, Maynard & Company, 1924), 110 – 118.

46. "Gilda Gray Excellent in Story of Tibetan Dancer, New Orleans *Times-Picayune*, January 1, 1928.

47. "Harry Hervey Makes Profound Impression in Local Lecture" Unidentified Savannah Newspaper, November 30, 1939, CH/HH Papers, GHS.

48. "You must understand one thing," Hervey wrote to the man with whom he had been having an affair and who wanted money from him, "I have no money, and no way of getting any right away. Mother pays my bills, and that is all—she can do no more. I have scarcely enough change for cigarettes; certainly not for drinks like I used to. Please don't ask me for any money—I haven't any now. When I get it, I'll help you." (Harry Hervey to Lester Brack ([August 27, 1938], CH/HH Papers. Attached to the letter is a newspaper clipping of a news story of how Lester Brack, just arrived three days before from California, was arrested for shoplifting a radio in North Miami Beach.)

49. Hervey went to Hollywood in May 1943, having sold a story called "Saigon." He stayed for several months rewriting, but his option was not renewed and the film not produced. The script is in the Georgia Historical Society.

50. An interview appeared in "The Whitaker Bay Bugle," the newsletter (?) of the *Savannah News-Press, Inc.*, undated copy in CH/HH Papers, GHS.

51. Hervey, *King Cobra*, 301.

## About the biographer

Harlan Greene was born and educated in Charleston SC. He has served as assistant director of the South Carolina Historical Society, director of the North Carolina Preservation Consortium, director of Archives at Avery Research Center for African American History and Culture, at the College of Charleston, where he is now Head of Addlestone Library's Special Collections. He has received awards for his archival and historical work and for his fiction. Some of his publications include *Mr. Skylark: John Bennett and the Charleston Renaissance*; *Slave Badges and the Slave Hire System in Charleston, SC, 1783 – 1865* (with Harry S. Hutchins, Jr. and Brian E. Hutchins); and the novels *Why We Never Danced the Charleston*, his Lambda Literary Award-winning *What the Dead Remember*, and *The German Officer's Boy*. He is a frequent contributor to scholarly and popular journals on topics related to Charleston history, and is author of a forthcoming biography of Harry Hervey.

# Harry Hervey Bibliography

### by Kent Davis and Harlan Greene

This chronological bibliography documents Harry Hervey's major creative works. More detailed information will appear in Harlan Greene's forthcoming biography, *The Damned Don't Cry: They Just Disappear. The Life of Harry Hervey.*

## BOOKS

### 1922

*Caravans by Night: A Romance of India*

New York; The Century Co.

An exuberant first novel. A tale of jewel thieves and political intrigue in India, Burma, and Tibet. Along the way, the heroine, Dana Charteris, is torn between two men, Arnold Kent and Euan Kerth.

### 1923

*The Black Parrot; A Tale of the Golden Chersonese*

New York; The Century Co.

Based on his earlier short story, "The Black Panther," the book describes the exploits of adventuress Lhassa Camber in the wilds of Borneo, the Malay peninsula and Southeast Asia. Lhassa is kidnapped by Stephen Conquest and becomes involved in a plot to steal the priceless Emerald Buddha, along with other twists and turns along the way.

### 1924

*Where Strange Gods Call; Pages Out of the East.*

New York; The Century Co. Illustrated by Christopher Murphy.

An account of the author's travels in Hawaii, Japan, China, the Malay Archipelago, Indonesia and the South Seas with vignettes portraying the exotic people, sights and cultures he found there. The book is based on two Pacific voyages Hervey made.

## 1925

*Ethan Quest : His Saga.*
New York; The Cosmopolitan Book Co.

This tale's namesake and artistic hero hails from Savannah, GA and moves to Tennessee to attend Sewanee University. There, he loses his closest male friend and leaves his wife, before embarking to travel the world. Prophetically paralleling the life the author adopted for himself, the protagonist is joined by a male companion at his side; a native Hawaiian named Illio. Ethan never quite becomes the artist he wanted to be, but never gives up his idealistic quest for romance. In the United Kingdom the book was published under the title of *The Gay Sarong*, exemplifying Hervey's fascination with exotic fabrics.

## 1927

*Congaï*
New York; The Cosmopolitan Book Co.
London; Thornton Butterworth – 1928.

An emotional novel of a young French-Cambodian girl seeking survival as the mistress to a series of increasingly powerful French colonial men. This culturally and historically accurate novel provides unique American perspectives of the often painful interaction between French colonialism and Southeast Asian lifestyles. The book is the basis of the successful Broadway play of the same name, co-written with Carleton Hildreth, that cast Helen Menken (Humphrey Bogart's first wife) in the starring role.

*King Cobra; an Autobiography of Travel in French Indo-China.*
New York; The Cosmopolitan Book Co.
London; Thornton Butterworth – 1928.

Hervey's non-fiction account of his travels in French Indochina with vivid descriptions of colonial Saigon, a French prison camp in the Vietnamese Highlands, the temple of Angkor Wat and a trip up the Mekong river to search for the "lost" ruins of Wat Phu to help him decipher the mystery of the disappearance of the Khmer civilization. In the United Kingdom the book was published as *Travels in French Indo-China*.

## 1929

*Red Ending*
New York; Horace Liveright, Inc.

A tale of two brothers, Belano and Dominy Farrell, during the jazz age in Charleston, SC. Contriving a "not quite romance" with a young flapper named Marianne, Belano tries to escape his mother, his Charleston life, and the fiendishly handsome Charles Semprez. It's a bleak view of a decadent culture where appearances are more important than the truth that lies beneath.

## 1931

*The Iron Widow*
New York: Horace Liveright. (Re-released as *She Devil* in 1953)

Delphine—a half-caste, sexually voracious woman—wreaks havoc on the men imprisoned in a French prison camp. Captain Lesesne, the dashing new administrator, resists her wiles, and is instead drawn to the same young boy, Jacquot, whom Delphine desires. Originally written as a play, it's overstated homoerotic overtones prevented production, so Hervey rewrote it as a novel. Published as *The Red Hotel* in the United Kingdom.

## 1939

*The Damned Don't Cry*
New York; The Greystone Press.

Born on the wrong side of the tracks in Savannah, Zelda O'Brien grows up unsullied in a dismal and sordid world. She falls in love with the aristocratic Dan Carter, and nearly succeeds in breaking with her squalid past until it catches up with her. Years later, she returns to the city to try to get her revenge, with tragic consequences. Powerful in spots, this naturalistic novel upset Savannah and has recently been returned to print.

## 1941

*School for Eternity*
New York: G. P. Putnam's Sons.

Lives and fates intertwine on a fateful Easter weekend on a Caribbean island. A band of disparate characters are suddenly invited to accept the hospitality of a mysterious count, who lives in a mountaintop mansion overlooking the city. While some characters are more types than individuals, the novel is highly polished, witty and well written. This was among Hervey's best received and best-selling works.

## 1947

*The Veiled Fountain*
New York: G. P. Putnam's Sons.

Two brothers in the Kimberly family, a composer named Brian and an English civil servant named Buzzy, inadvertently pursue the same mysterious woman with tragic results. Set mostly in India, the novel explores Eastern mysticism and is infused with music. A sophisticated tone offsets some of the soap-opera like plot twists.

## 1950

*Barracoon*
New York; G. P. Putnam's Sons.

Set in mid 19th century Portugal and Southwest Africa, the story revolves around Maria de Castro's realization of her husband's brutal role in the horrors of slave-trading. It is, as noted on the dust jacket, "the case history of a crime, but… also the story of a tender love and a spiritual victory over the powers of darkness."

## SHORT STORIES

In the 1920s, Hervey sold dozens of short stories to publications of the "pulp fiction" genre. While he returned to many of these themes in his novels, his early efforts—most hard to track down being in ephemeral publications that have not survived—should be counted more as his juvenilia rather than serious attempts at fiction.

### *The Parisienne* magazine.

*(Title and plot unknown)*. When Harry was only 16 and still attending school, renowned author and critic Henry Louis Mencken purchased one of his short stories. Mencken was editor and publisher of prestigious literary magazine, *The Smart Set*. The story he purchased from Hervey, however, actually appeared in his less prestigious, but more popular, "sister publication" *The Parisienne*. Mencken's co-editors soon used this formula to launch two other pulp magazines; *Spicy Stories* (1916) and *Black Mask* (1920).

*The Drums of Doom*. The first of Hervey's many works focusing on the devil, damnation and doom. (publication date unknown)

### *Black Mask* magazine.

From the first issue of *Black Mask* (April 1920), Hervey was a regular contributor with eight stories published between then and July 1922.

*Piracy*. A tale set in Burma with an American college boy becoming involved with a stowaway and pirates. April 1920, pp. 65-78.

*The Black Menace*. "A complete novelette of romantic adventure…in the African wilds…in the manner of Rider Haggard's famous stories." June 1920, pp. 3-37. Henry Rider Haggard (1856-1925) was an English writer who specialized in African adventures.

*More Deadly than the Viper*. A mystery set in Tibet with an American trying to help a friend who is trapped by a vampire-like woman seducer who dooms her male victims to oblivion by tossing them into the Valley of the Vanishing Men. August 1920, pp. 49-64.

*Daughter of the Pigeon*. Plot unknown. September 1920, pp. 61-71.

*Two Bells*. Plot unknown. November 1920, pp. 97-113.

*Can This Thing Be?* Plot unknown. February 1921, pp. 95-110.

*Mr. Sin (Complete Mystery Novelette).* A London-based mystery with "Scotland Yard detectives, séances by an Egyptian girl, an opium addicted baronet, a brother and sister set, a hunchback, a man named Quest, switched bodies, and a turbaned Hindu." March 1921, pp. 3-42.

*The Devil at the Helm (Complete Mystery Novelette).* Another tale with a demonic theme. July 1922, pp. 3-23.

**The Follies magazine (successor to *The Parisienne*).**

*Devil's Business.* A romantic adventure in Siam with a hero similar to the partially autobiographical protagonist in *Ethan Quest* and a temple similar to Cambodia's Angkor Wat. Published circa 1921.

**Saucy Stories magazine.**

*Monsieur Satan.* Set on Bluebeard's Typhoon Island, Hervey's heroine later became the basis for one of his most famous characters, Shanghai Lilly, whom Marlene Dietrich later portrayed in the 1932 film, *Shanghai Express*. May 1921.

**Fascinating Fiction magazine.**

*The Black Leopard.* Plot unknown. Circa 1923.

**Other short stories:**

*The Young Men Go Down.* A young man watches beautiful men pass him in droves. He follows their path, to discover "the Golden One," a half-caste Magdalene who teaches him a different sort of salvation that changes his life. Edward J. O'Brien included this in *The Best Short Stories of 1924* and became the basis for the film *The Devil Dancer*. *The Nation*, January 30, 1924.

*The Lover of Madame Guillotine.* In a remote French prison camp in Indochina, the commander's wife unexpectedly joins him and begins an affair with another officer. Based on Hervey's experience visiting the Lao Bao camp during his trip described in *King Cobra*, this story provided the basis for Hervey's film script for *Prestige*. *McClure's*, January 1927. [Included in the appendices of this book.]

*Pulaski Adventure*. In this cross between a rumination and a short story, Hervey rewrites history in a love story set in the environs of Civil War era Savannah, GA. *The Georgia Review*, Vol. 5, #2, Summer 1951, pp. 157–161.

*On the Wall*. Told in a hotel bar in the Far East, this weaves the tale of the unfaithful Marcia Cleverdon, whose husband tries to punish her by making his suicide seem like murder, framing Marcia as the primary suspect. Published posthumously. *The Georgia Review*, Vol. 7, #4, Winter 1953, pp. 390–402.

## **MOVIE SCRIPTS**

### **1927**

*The Devil Dancer* (story). This silent film with screen play by Alice Duer Miller, is now lost. Miller based the film on Hervey's short story, "The Young Men Go Down," but changed much of the narrative, making the film into a vehicle for actress Gilda Gray. Gilda is credited by some for the invention of the dance, "The Shimmy."

### **1931**

*The Cheat* (screenplay). Originally produced twice as a silent film by screenwriter Hector Turnbull, Hervey adapted the concept into a talking film. He added his own touches to the story of a woman who loses at gambling and borrows money from a mysterious Oriental. Her benefactor surmises he was cheated and punishes the woman, played by Tallulah Bankhead, by actually branding her. Released just before the 1931 Hollywood censorship codes were enforced, the shocking film was withdrawn and unavailable for years. It has been re-issued as a "Pre-Code" classic.

### **1932**

*A Passport to Hell* (story). About to banished from an English colony in Africa, the story's heroine, played by Elissa Landi, marries a German, who is sent off to into a remote part of the continent, leaving her to drive other men to their doom. It was also released under the name *Burnt Offering* and *Dangerous Lady*.

*Devil and the Deep* (story). Charles Laughton made his American film debut in this film playing a naval submarine commender who is insanely jealous over his wife, played by Tallulah Bankhead. He incorrectly suspects her of having an affair with his subordinate, a lieutenant played by Cary Grant. His irrational and abusive behavior instead drives her into an affair with another lieutenant, played by Gary Cooper, leading the commander to plan a violent act of revenge.

*The Wiser Sex* (screenplay, co-written with Caroline Francke). Based on the Clyde Fitch play, *Her Confessions*, the plot centers on a woman framing a man for a crime he did not commit while another woman, knowing the evil women can do, tries to exonerate her victim.

*Shanghai Express* (story). A jilted woman in China, played by Marlene Dietrich, becomes a "coaster" known as Shanghai Lily, who earns a reputation as a notorious adventuress. Then, on a train to Shanghai during the Chinese civil war, she meets her past lover as other lives and fates intersect. Directed by Erich von Stroheim, the film is considered a cinema classic. Many people collaborated on the film, and although Hervey's contributions are clear, his work has largely been ignored in critical discussions. The film was remade twice, first as *Night Plane from Chunking* (1943) and then as *Peking Express* (1951).

*Prestige* (story). Partially based on Hervey's short story, "The Lover of Madame Guillotine." Therese Verlaine travels to the French prison camp run by her husband, the commandant, to find that his morals have degenerated. As in the original short story, she plans to flee with another man, but her plans fall apart in unexpected acts of violence. Her husband is then challenged to stabilize the situation, which will only be possible if he can regain his discipline and his personal prestige.

## 1933

*The Devil's in Love* (story). A wholesome young missionary woman, played by Loretta Young, becomes involved in the case of a dissolute outcast of the French Foreign legion when he is unjustly accused of a murder he didn't commit.

## 1934

*His Greatest Gamble* (screenplay). In an unusual twist for Hervey, this plot centers on male protagonist instead of a *femme fatale*. The central character, unjustly jailed, escapes prison to help his daughter who was raised to be neurotic and weak. Her father's positive influence restores her strength, but then he must decide how to deal with his own status as a fugitive.

## 1936

*A Son Comes Home* (story). A woman running a San Francisco chowder house rushes to defend her son when he is accused of a crime. She soon realizes it was another woman's son, and not her own, who is charged with the crime. As she works to clear the other boy, she encounters a moral dilemma when she realizes that her son was, in fact, complicit in the crime.

## 1940

*Green Hell* (additional dialogue). Hervey assisted his friend Frances Marion, once one the few leading women Hollywood screenwriters. The film's plot is of a woman wreaking havoc among adventurers seeking Incan treasure in the jungles of South America.

*Road to Singapore* (story). This was the first Bob Hope and Bing Crosby "Road" movie, a successful formula that became a series. Although Hervey originally intended this as a legitimate drama, the comedy duo played for laughs in the exotic setting, acting in playboy roles while oogling the glamorous Dorothy Lamour.

## 1942

*So's Your Aunt Emma!* (story). Also know as *Aunt Emma Paints the Town* or *Married to the Mob*, the plot features an unsophisticated country woman (played by Zazu Pitts) who comes to town to save her prize fighter nephew, who has become involved with big city crooks. She is mistaken as another mobster while fighting the criminals with her innocence.

## Critical Biographical Studies of Harry Hervey

### 1954

*Harry Hervey, Savannah Novelist*

Anna C. Hunter. *Georgia Review*, Vol. 8 #2, Summer 1954, pp. 151–156.

### 1958

*Harry Hervey: a bio-bibliography*

William B. Richardson. Master's thesis, Florida State University, 80 pgs.

### 2014

*The Life of Harry Hervey* (Final title to be announced)

Harlan Greene.

Forthcoming from the University of South Carolina Press.

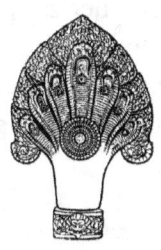

# KING COBRA - A Travel Journal

By Harry Hervey

New York: Cosmopolitan Book Corporation. $4.[1]

**Book Review by Margaret Mead**

"For many months I had been living in a book — the book of my adventures in quest of a dead city," says Harry Hervey, and it is his peculiar quality of always seeing the present as part of a book, a book half-written, partly obliterated, filled with unread, half decipherable paragraphs, which gives "King Cobra" much of its undoubted charm.

Of great service also is Mr. Hervey's unswerving and complete enthusiasm which made the name of Angkor a satisfactory symbol of romance from the atlas on the nursery floor to the actuality of the ruined temples in the heart of Indo-China. And there is still one other item of his special equipment for this kind of storytelling which Mr. Hervey shares with children and the primitive peoples whom he describes so sympathetically. His thinking draws no line between the animate and the inanimate, images from one order of experience serve perfectly in a different order. It is without effort that he sees the jungle one moment as a vindictive monster, the next as an annihilating river beneath which a whole civilization drowns.

The book is given form and climax by the search for an un-chronicled, ruined city, Wat Phu, whose tale he heard from the lips of a stranger in a bar in Singapore. But three-quarters of the volume deals with the journey, with Saigon and its ghostly reminiscences of Paris, and the spiritual miscegenation of Indo-China and the French, with Angkor Thom, and the long trip up the Me-Kong, punctuated with disaster because the coolie smoked too much opium at the wheel. No smallest detail is recorded for itself alone. All are symbols, of the decay of one regime, the slow torturous birth of another, the triumph of one people over another, the substitution of a religion of peace for a religion of death, of the bitter landmarks which strew the path of western empire; each present fact trails behind it a train upon which its past or future implications are delicately, unpedantically traced.

---

1 $4 in 1927 is the equivalent of $49.78 in 2010.

It is an exciting background, the history of the Khmers and their great mushroom kingdom in Cambodia which vanished in the course of three centuries; this kingdom which a Chinese ambassador describes in the zenith of its power in 1295, and a Portuguese explorer found a heap of ruins in 1570. Mr. Hervey knows his history, or quite enough of it to make each step in his journey significant. His book is the tale of what one man, and he an exceedingly romantic one, saw and thought.

This is a record for those who wish the kingdoms of fantasy bodied forth in terms of history and geography, built upon the data of actual experience, but stripped of all dullness and infused with the spirit of unflagging romance.

### About the reviewer

When Margaret Mead (Dec. 16, 1901 – Nov. 15, 1978) penned this 1928 review she had already begun her career as an American cultural anthropologist. After earning her Master's Degree at Columbia in 1924, Margaret headed to Samoa in 1925 to do fieldwork. In 1926 the American Museum of Natural History hired her as an assistant curator. She returned to Columbia to complete her doctorate in 1929.

Mead established herself as an expert on sexuality and gender roles in native cultures. In 1928, she released her first book on the topic, *Coming of Age in Samoa*, followed by *Growing up in New Guinea* (1930) and *Sex and Temperament in Three Primitive Societies* (1935). Her research, books and opinions reached their peak in the 1960s and 1970s when she gained praise as a writer and speaker.

All this made her an ideal reviewer for Hervey's societal observations of Indochina. In *Coming of Age in Samoa* she expressed her empathetic viewpoint in this quote:

"As the traveler who has once been from home is wiser than he who has never left his own doorstep, so a knowledge of one other culture should sharpen our ability to scrutinize more steadily, to appreciate more lovingly, our own."

Guillotine executions in Indochine. Tonkin (top) and Haiphong (below).
For a detailed history of the guillotine visit www.BoisDeJustice.com

# The Lover of Madame Guillotine

## By Harry Hervey

"OF LATE," remarked Pierre Lochard, brooding lazily over a rainbow cocktail,[1] "Madame Guillotine has been fasting...."

We sat at a sidewalk table just below the enclosing-rail of the Continental Cafe, in Saigon; Pierre Lochard, (who, some say, will be the next Governor of Laos), Deschanel, Captain in the French Colonial Army, and I, who have nothing to distinguish me but a few more or less desultory books.

Inside, an orchestra played the latest airs from Paris while the groups at the various tables talked and laughed and drank, in a vain attempt to forget the heat. A most cosmopolitan crowd indeed, Including, in addition to the many types of Frenchmen, a few British, a few Americans, the inevitable Russians, and the equally inevitable half-castes. Except for the natives wandering lazily by and the passing rickshaws, one never would have suspected that this was a sun-tired heathen land.

"The guillotine," I observed, "belongs to a barbarous age."

Deschanel laughed.

"Ah!" said Pierre Lochard, "the American speaks! Well, do not we live in a barbarous age? And is not this, our Indo-China, a most barbarous country? Ask any Frenchman!" And he smiled, whether ironically or not, I was not sure. "My friend," he confided leaning across the table, a faint twinkle in his eyes, "we who rule these millions of brown 'brothers,' as the Church is pleased to call them, must preserve the legend of our superiority and what better means than fear? ... Which reminds me of a story...."

---

1 Judging by Harry's numerous mentions, the "rainbow" cocktail—*pousse-café* in French—was quite popular in Indochina. The drink is made with a variety of colorful liqueurs that form separate layers in the glass due to differences in their specific gravities. Liqueurs with the most sugar and least alcohol are denser and rest at the bottom of the glass. Those with the most alcohol and least water are floated on the top.

"It is not, I hope," ventured Deschanel most discourteously, "the story of the Resident Superior who was affected by the heat and went to the. Governor General's reception in only a sarong?"

"It is not," said Pierre Lochard unperturbed.

"Then pray continue, my dear Pierre."

"It is quite a different sort of story," maintained Pierre Lochard, "with little humor in it—unless you perceive the grim humor of the justice which overtook the main characters. It is. in fact, the story of one of the 'barbarous savages' which it is our duty as good Colonials to discipline into acceptable French citizens—exteriorly, at least. A stupid brown fellow whose Annamite mother stopped planting rice only long enough to deliver him: thereafter paying very little attention to him and leaving him to face the world with no particular intelligence', no virtues to speak of, and no background except a heritage of thousands of years of unrefined instincts.

"It is interesting to observe," Pierre Lochard interpolated, smiling slyly at Deschanel, "and quite significant, that being thus unequipped mentally and socially, he became a soldier when he was very young... But that is getting ahead of the story.

"He was, you must understand," Pierre Lochard continued in his grandiose manner, "of a very low order of human life; one of thousands of his kind in this fecund land, as ugly as an Annamite can be, with narrow little eyes, high cheekbones, and a broad, flat nose-no redeeming features whatever, nor any mental qualities to make up for these deficiencies in appearance. Just ... well, just another dog of a native.

"My story begins after he had been in the Tirailleurs Annamites[2] for some time—a slow, dull soldier with nothing to his credit but a number of years of faithful if unintelligent service. Of his life between the time when that coolie mother so carelessly cast him out upon the world and the time when he was detailed, with a small detachment of native troops, to the prison colony at Lao-ban, nothing need be said. For what is there to tell about in the life of such an insignificant creature as Nham?

---

[2] In French, *tirailleur* means a shooting fighter and designated light infantry troops. In the 19th and 20th centuries, the French Army used the term for indigenous soldiers recruited in French colonies and protectorates, Annam in the example cited above.

That was his name, Nham—a name as common among the Annamites as Jacques among the French or George among the English...

Who knows why he became a soldier? Perhaps because he liked the shiny bayonets or-well, there is no use conjecturing. He had never married, due, it was rumored, to the very sound reason that he believed all women unfaithful! It seems his mother, who was a bit indiscreet, was punished in the manner common among her people when a woman commits such an indiscretion; she was tied to a tree and gored, literally stripped to ribbons, by an elephant that had 'gone musth,' as we say.[3]

"It was at Lao-Bao, with that handful of troops who guard those brown devils sent there, that Nham's rise began-and quite by accident.

"The Délégué[4] in charge of the prison colony was not an entirely admirable character, either in appearance or morals, nor, on the other hand, was he wholly disreputable. As a matter of fact, for some reason the Colonial Government considered him a valuable man-except, of course, when he was filled with absinthe.[5] That was Verlaine's great fault, absinthe. Of course Verlaine wasn't his name. The story is too intimate, to... well, you understand... for that.

"When Verlaine had absinthe in him he was crazy; indeed, he was quite capable of throwing either an empty bottle or a chair at the first dirty, slant-eyed dog of a native that came near him.... Yes, that was his opinion of the particular mixture of the brown and yellow races that inhabits Indo-China... Inasmuch as he was the only white man at Lao-Bao, he was often lonely. And it is natural, as well as courteous, to assume that this was the reason he forgot, at times, that he was a Frenchman and a gentleman.

"One morning when Verlaine had been hurling bottles, an important message came from Hue. His orderly, who bore a number of scars already and had no desire to add to these very realistic service stripes, gave the telegram to Nham to take to Monsieur le Délégué. And so it was that

---

3 Musth is a periodic hormonal condition in male elephants characterized by highly aggressive behavior towards humans and other elephants.
4 A general French title for a lieutenant or an authorized agent.
5 Absinthe is a distilled, highly alcoholic drink distilled from botanicals, including the flowers and leaves of the wormwood tree (*Atremisia absinthium*). Especially popular in late 19th- and early 20th-century France, the potent (45-75% alcohol) beverage incapacitated users and led to rampant alcoholism.

Nham, the stupid, the utterly inconsequential, came under the observation of Verlaine; came, I assure you, dodging a rain of bottles and glasses, some of which will not miss their mark. But—the message was delivered.

And Nham, credited with the virtue of courage when, in reality, it was only unreasoning obedience, became the personal orderly of Monsieur le Délégué. Thus does Fate play her little jokes!

"Now this Verlaine was not exactly an agreeable person even when he was free of the devil of absinthe; and had Nham been a human being, instead of the low, unfeeling creature that he was, this story might have had an entirely different end. As it was, when Verlaine struck him or kicked him, he only grinned, chin and buttocks slung a few inches from the ground—a stupid, senseless grin. Why should not Monsieur le Délégué strike or kick him? Monsieur le Délégué belonged to the Superior Race; that race which had demonstrated its transcendent virtues by conquering his people and then, with that benevolence peculiar to evolved human beings, bestowing upon them the blessings of civilization. So, Nham must have reasoned—if, indeed, he reasoned at all!

"Well, after a few months, Nham became a *doi*, that is to say, a corporal; and instead of nightly parading about among the Laotian and Annamite girls of the village, as all his brother soldiers did, he spent his evenings squatting outside the barracks, most of the time merely chewing betel but sometimes polishing and sharpening his bayonet. It seemed to have an unholy fascination for him, that bayonet. Perhaps because in some way his dull brain grasped the fact that it was a symbol of power, but more likely because he was pleased with the shining metal. At any rate, he would squat there when off duty, nursing that steel as though it were a baby....

"Have you ever noticed the way natives squat? No? Well, this way... knees thrust up almost to the chin and buttocks slung a few inches from the ground, balancing by God—and they—only know what freak of equilibrium. Picture him squatting there like that, a perfect monkey, and then you have a good idea of Nham... a monkey... absolutely....

"About that time curious things were happening in the jungle around Lao-Bao. The natives said a devil was abroad. Every few days some peasant, going through the forest, would find the carcass of a dog or a goat, with its head neatly severed.... The Délégué was appealed to, but—well, clearly you can see that exorcising a devil was not in line with his duty as a servant of the Colonial Government so long as that devil did not meddle with politics!

"Eventually, of course, Nham was caught. Some peasant came to Verlaine with the story... Nham was called before Monsieur le Délégué. Monsieur le Délégué was very annoyed. 'What do you mean by slaughtering all those dogs and goats?' he demanded of Nham... Well, the explanation is a very good illustration of Nham himself. He said he had done it in the service of the Government! Yes! Imagine that! He went on to explain that the heads of certain criminals were cut off by order of the Government. and that such executions required the services of an experienced executioner; therefore, ill view of the fact that he was only practicing so that when his skill was recognized he would be thoroughly competent, he had done nothing wrong, you see? Just like a monkey—only a little worse.

"Savages, these natives," growled Pierre Lochard with a curiously ironic gleam in his eyes, "nothing but savages—as you will see by this story....

"Well, Verlaine had a sense of humor—he must have had or he never would have acted as he did. He told Nham he would have to use his pay for the next few months to compensate the peasants for the loss of their goats, and then he kicked him out of his office... The next week Nham had another duty added to his routine work: he became *l'homme de mort*; in other words, the next time a head came off at Lao-Bao, it would he Nham who would lower the blade of the guillotine.

"And now." said Pierre Lochard, pausing to mop his flushed, perspiring face, "the woman enters the story..."

"It is time," remarked Deschanel, affecting a yawn, "I suppose your dull native fellow falls in love with some lovely *congai* —"

"As usual, my dear Andre." interrupted Pierre Lochard agreeably, "you are wrong. But first let us have another drink—and also observe the lady in question more closely. If you both will turn you will see her sitting at a table up there in the café—that table in the corner, looking out over the Rue Catinat."

Both Deschanel and I turned and stared rudely in the direction he indicated.

"Which one?" I asked; then added incredulously. "You mean the woman *herself* is actually up there?"

"Why not?" returned Pierre Lochard shrugging, "Why would I have thought of this story if I had not seen one of the principal characters? A woman's eyes are the keyholes to many a closed affair."

"Your metaphor is extremely bad," commented Deschanel. "Nevertheless, which one is she?"

"The one with her back this way with the blond hair."

Again Deschanel and I stared in an ill-mannered fashion.

Although the woman's back was toward us, I had the impression that she was extremely well poised. Perhaps it was the very patrician manner in which she held her cigarette, fingers clasping it easily and gracefully, as though both cigarette and hand were part of a delicate design. Women who smoke in that manner are born to privileges. Virtue, with them, is a matter of discrimination.

Above the concerted discord of mingled voices, clinking glasses, and the thud of bare feet as "boys" rushed back and forth with drinks, I heard a quick, tense laugh. It was a voice of such vibrance that, low as it was pitched, it wove tremulously above the other sounds.

"Can you imagine such a laugh echoing in the gloomy silence of Lao-Bao" Pierre Lochard asked smiling slightly. "Add to it the clanking obbligato of chains as the prisoners moved about the compound, and you have the sense of incongruity that her presence created there."

"It is difficult," I ventured, "to picture a woman like that in such a setting."

Pierre Lochard smiled again. "She found it so herself, my friend," he said. "But she made her gesture of duty. After two years of separation, spent in Paris, she joined her husband at Lao-Bao... Yes, the lady of the golden hair is Madame Verlaine....

"Let us pause now, for a moment, to consider Lao-Bao, that dismal spot which she first saw one evening at dusk. The village itself is only a huddle of thatched huts, with a few ancestral shrines and pagodas scattered here and there; a river on one side and the prison on the other. A bulky fortress-like building, that prison, with small slits of windows in the front downstairs, serving the double purpose of admitting light and air and providing loopholes for guns. In this building the Délégué lived: behind it was a sort of quadrangle, with the barracks facing the main building and the prison rooms on either side. Put all this in a jungle setting, with the notes of bugles calling the prisoners to and from work, the eternal rattle of chains, and you have a picture of Lao-Bao as Madame Verlaine saw it that evening at dusk.

"She had not telegraphed her husband that she was coming—it was to be a surprise. Very bad, these surprises, when a husband uses too much absinthe. But how could she know? It was a habit he had acquired in Indo-China. So she arrived in the midst of things; all those half-naked brown fellows filing in, chained and wearing the cangue:[6] and Verlaine sprawled out in his room... But she was spared the sight of him—for Nham met her at the gate. Nham, who recognized her from the photograph in Monsieur le Delegue's room and who, by God, knows what process of reasoning sensed that she should not come upon her husband in that condition."

"But," I interposed, "was that act the act of a 'savage'?"

Pierre Lochard smiled—tolerantly. "Who else but a savage would have done it? The civilized man would have remembered the blows and kicks that Verlaine had given him. But Nham did not—or, if he did, he overlooked them. He told her that Monsieur le Délégué was away for the night... But of course she found out. After she had gone to sleep, he made a devil of a lot of noise. Nham tried to calm him, but he came bursting out into the hall, and there was his wife, terrified to the point of swooning... As a consequence Nham got several kicks from Verlaine for not trying to arouse him the moment his wife arrived. and Therese Verlaine never trusted him because she thought he was in league with her husband to deceive her...."

"You must not conceive the idea that this Verlaine was entirely calloused. I think, underneath, he had a certain affection for that 'yellow

---

6 The cangue was a punishment device commonly used in Asia until the early 20th century. Typically, it consisted of a large flat board with a hole in the center that clamped tightly around a person's neck. Generally, the board was large enough to prevent the prisoner from reaching his mouth with his hands, so assistance eating was needed. The Great Ming Legal Code of 1397 AD specified weights of 25, 20 or 15 *jin* (roughly 12.5, 10 or 7.5 kilograms), depending on crime committed. The French term originates from the Portuguese word *canga*, which means yoke.

dog-of-a-native,' as he called him; but Verlaine, being a Colonial officer, could not lose sight of the fact that he was a member of the Superior Race. That, of course, is very clear....

The "boy" came with drinks, and Pierre Lochard took a sip before he resumed.

"As you may well see, under these circumstances Therese Verlaine was not entirely happy at Lao-Bao. All day *clunk-clunk-clank*, as the prisoners moved about in their chains; and between retreat and reveille, every quarter of an hour, the calls of sentinels guarding those murderers and thieves who were locked almost beneath the room where she slept. And, in addition to that, a husband who used absinthe.... Yes, it is easy to understand how the place got on her nerves. The slightest incident annoyed her—and chief among these muses of annoyance was Nham. In all justice to him, he did nothing to irritate her. But that was not necessary; he himself was sufficient.

"Her aversion to Nham grew out of the incident immediately following her arrival, it was perpetuated by his repulsive appearance, and it became complete when she learned of that particular duty which was the pride of his life. It always made her shudder when she saw him polishing his prize—he kept the guillotine-knife in perfect condition, awaiting the day when he would first use it. Jokingly, among themselves, the other soldiers called him the lover of Madame Guillotine.

"Now," announced Pierre Lochard, gazing introspectively beyond me, "the last of my characters enters—Captain Remy Baudoin we shall call him.

"Verlaine had to go to Hue to see the Governor, and Therese did not feel disposed to make the trip over the mountains, so before he left he called Nham to him and said: 'Nham, you will be responsible for Madame while I am away. See that she has every attention.' And Nham saluted with that stupid grin of his.

"The very evening after Verlaine left, a pirogue came in below the hill, manned by two boatmen, and carrying Captain Remy Baudoin, delirious with fever. Four days before, he had started out from Tchepone on his way to the coast via Lao-Bao; *'fievre-de-bois'* had struck him in the jungle. As soon as the pirogue reached Lao-Bao he was carried up to the prison, and upon Therese Verlaine, who knew nothing about the equatorial sicknesses, fell the responsibility or saving his life....

"It is to her credit that she did—yet had she known the consequences... well, but who can say? After all, even if she had known, it is probable she would have tried to save him; not in the interest of humanity, ah, no! But—and I am not being unkind—because he made quite a charming picture lying there in her husband's bed. Not an entirely handsome fellow, this Baudoin, but sufficiently dissolute-looking to interest a cosmopolitan woman, And Therese was that....

"During the days of Baudoin's illness, when Therese was alone at his bedside, Nham always squatted outside the door, chewing betel and musing upon whatever such sluggish-minded fellows think about. Do not for an instant imagine he suspected anything! Not that dull creature!

"Late afternoon of the day Baudoin got out of bed, Nham wandered down by the river. It is questionable if any aesthetic impulse, challenged by the soft skies or the luminous rain of fireflies that comes with dusk, took him there. More likely he had seen Therese and the convalescent Baudoin go that way, and had followed to thoroughly discharge his self-imposed duty as chaperon.

Nham, of course, had been around the French long enough to know they kissed on the lips, whereas the Annamites rub noses, and it is also highly probable that he was aware that French wives, as well as Annamite wives, could be guilty of indiscretions. Nevertheless, it must have been something of a shock to him to suddenly come upon the wife of Monsieur le Délégué in the arms of an officer of the French Colonial Army.

"That night, as usual, Nham slept outside Madame's door; and some time very late Captain Baudoin came out of his room and, seeing Nham, kicked him and told him to get away. But Nham smiled that idiotic smile of his and said he was obeying the orders of Monsieur le Délégué; whereupon Captain Baudoin became very angry and talked in such a loud voice that Madame was awakened. It must have been a very ridiculous scene: Therese emerging from her room, very frightened, Baudoin confused and apologetic, and Nham squatting there with that silly smile on his face.... The next morning, quite unexpectedly, Verlaine returned.

"He appeared extremely pleased at finding Baudoin there—it was not often that he had visitors at Lao-Bao—and he announced that they would celebrate that night in honor of the occasion, champagne, caviar and *foie gras*—just as though they were in France. Baudoin thanked him, replying that it would be, for him, a farewell dinner, as he was leaving in the morning for Quang-tri.

"That afternoon at dusk Therese and Baudoin met down by the river. They both were very nervous, particularly Therese, who thought several times she heard someone in the bushes. Their plans were laid very carefully:

"In the morning Baudoin would leave, as planned, but he would go only a few kilometers from Lao-baa and return through the forest, hiding in a pirogue which he would have waiting on the river. Then, that night, Therese would see that Verlaine had too much absinthe, and after he had fallen into a stupor, she would go down to the river where Baudoin would be waiting in the pirogue. She would know the pirogue by a white handkerchief tied to the thatch; she would step in, and off they would go! To Tchepone, then Savannakhet, then down the Me-Kong. It was very simple.

"That night they had their banquet, the three of them, and for a few hours that grim place echoed with the music of wine glasses instead of the clank of chains. In the morning Baudoin departed.

"Those hours of waiting were torture for Therese. She tried to go about her daily routine with the usual bored air; she watched the prisoners assemble in the quadrangle; she pretended to read a novel; after dejeuner she retreated to her room ostensibly to take her customary midday rest. But she did not rest.

"Among Nham's few accomplishments was the ability to play a guitar, whether well or not, I cannot say. At any rate, that afternoon he sat on the veranda outside Therese's room and amused himself by picking the strings and singing. As you probably know, Annamite music is not generally appreciated outside Annamite circles. Therese was no exception. She very promptly told Nham to remove himself. Nham apologized—he was very sorry if he had disturbed Madame. It was an old legend he was singing, he explained with that senseless grin; a legend about a man who, finding his wife unfaithful, had her tied to a tree and gored to death by a mad she-elephant.

Very coldly Therese told him she was not interested in his legends.

"Well, night finally came. Therese was frightened. She wondered what Nham knew—if he knew anything. Perhaps he had told her husband about the incident that night in the hall....

But she noticed nothing different in Verlaine's manner at dinner, and that reassured her. After the meal, she had the house-boy bring absinthe and she took a sip with Verlaine. After an hour he was carried to his room.

"Therese got ready... Just before she stole down the stairs and out through the compound, the sentinel in the quadrangle called the hour, and in the prison rooms she heard the rattling of chains as the prisoners were fastened into the stocks for the night. Undoubtedly she shivered and said to herself: 'Thank God I shall hear that no more; tonight I am free of all chains.'

"It was comparatively easy to leave the building unobserved, and once outside, in the dark jungle night, there was no danger whatever. But surely her heart trebled its beat as she hurried down the path to the river. Suppose some part of the plan had miscarried; suppose Baudoin were not there; or suppose, after they had left, her husband discovered their trail and followed...!

"I can imagine with what relief she saw the pirogue, darkly outlined against the river; then an instant of fright, acute, nauseating, before she made out the white spot of the handkerchief tied to the thatch. The boatman squatted in the stern, paddle ready. A moment now, and they would be under way. 'Remy!' she must have called, very softly. Then the boatman motioned her under the thatch shelter amidships.

"Baudoin was there, waiting. As she crawled into that narrow, dark space, she saw him half reclining aft, the squatting boatman visible in the opening behind him. 'Remy!' she must have called again. And then the breathless silence and his motionless attitude combined to thrust upon her a sudden feeling of apprehension. 'Remy!' As she called him this time. in a voice strident with fright, she caught his arm and shook him; and then his head seemed to roll sidewise upon his shoulder, and there followed an ominous splash as something dropped into the river—just as his body slid down into the bottom of the pirogue. She gave one terrific scream before she fainted—a scream that must have chilled even Nham as he squatted in the stern...."

Pierre Lochard paused for breath, a strange, half-satirical look in his eyes. Very deliberately he drained his glass, and then smiled in his charming manner at Deschanel and me.

"Yes," he said, answering our silent interrogation, "it was indeed the stupid Nham squatting there in the back of the pirogue. In the morning the body was found. You may be certain that the night before, when Therese rushed up to the prison half-demented, she did not report it! Naturally, there was no doubt as to who had done it; for who in Lao-Bao but Nham could have so neatly severed a head from a body?"

Deschanel affected a sophisticated air to cover his interest.

"And I suppose." he prompted, "your 'dog-of-a-native' who spent so much time polishing the blade of the guillotine, was the first to go under it?"

Pierre Lochard nodded. "Yes, Nham celebrated a complete union with Madame Guillotine. Such a horrible crime—you can well see the effect it would have upon the natives if he were not speedily punished. At the trial he gave his reason for slaying Captain Baudoin—"

"Then, after all. Verlaine found out about his wife?" I interrupted.

Pierre Lochard shook his head. "That is the grimly amusing part of the story. When asked why he killed Baudoin, Nham said he did it because he was tired of waiting for someone to use the guillotine on!

We were all quiet for a moment after that. In the café, the orchestra was playing a tango, and the ring of silver and glass sounded sharply above the indolent music.

"A gallant lie for this 'un-evolved creature,'" I mused aloud.

"Yes?" said Pierre Lochard. "But was it a lie? Who can understand the brain of a savage? And," he added, with a little glimmer in his eyes. "they are savages, these brown fellows!"

"But," Deschanel pointed out, "your story is incomplete."

"You mean Verlaine and the cosmopolitan Therese? They were divorced some years later."

"Ah! Then she confessed the whole affair?"

Pierre Lochard shrugged. "Who can say? I only know that there she sits," he nodded beyond me at the woman with bright hair, "and he—well, you remember I said that for some reason the Government valued him. Perhaps he is still somewhere in the interior."

"A pretty story," Deschanel commented presently. "I, for one, feel the need of strong drink after hearing it. What shall it be? Absinthe—to be consistent?"

I assented.

Pierre Lochard smiled reminiscently.

"No." he replied. "Another rainbow cocktail for me. I never touch absinthe."

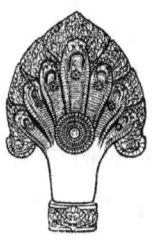

# List of Illustrations

The editor is indebted to Joel Montague for granting access to his extensive archive for this new edition of *King Cobra*. Many of the photos seen here, and hundreds more, are featured in his 2010 book, *Picture Postcards of Cambodia 1900-1950*, published by White Lotus Press.

Photo Credits: Harry Hervey [HH]; Montague Archive [MA];
DatAsia Archive [DA]; Wikipedia [W]

### Front Matters
"There came a King from the West who married a cobra's daughter…" [DA] . . . . . . . . II
Map of French Indo-China and Siam [HH] . . . . . . . . . . . . . . . . . . . . . . . . . . . VI
Pico Iyer [Photo by Derek Shapton] . . . . . . . . . . . . . . . . . . . . . . . . . . . . . . . . . XVI

### I. Bayonets in the Sun
"Indo-China forms an argus-pheasant whose plumes are the jungles…" [MA] . . . . . . . .4
"A ghost of the rue de la Paix has wandered down to the equator." [MA] . . . . . . . . . . .4
"The rue Catinat—that ghost of the rue de la Paix." [HH] . . . . . . . . . . . . . . . . . . . . . .7
Messageries Maritimes mailboat arriving in Saigon in 1921. [MA] . . . . . . . . . . . . . 12
Map of downtown Saigon, circa 1930. [DA] . . . . . . . . . . . . . . . . . . . . . . . . . . . . 12
"…who found an acceptable gentleness in the native *congai*." [MA] . . . . . . . . . . . . 20
The Régie d'Opium on the rue Paul Blanchy. [MA] . . . . . . . . . . . . . . . . . . . . . . . 22
"Very few white men frequent the opium-houses of Cholon." [HH] . . . . . . . . . . . . 22
A facsimile of the Tired Cavalier. [MA] . . . . . . . . . . . . . . . . . . . . . . . . . . . . . . . . 24
Saigon's Rotonde café. [DA] . . . . . . . . . . . . . . . . . . . . . . . . . . . . . . . . . . . . . . . 24
Newell Convers Wyeth's 1913 painting, "The Opium Smoker." [W] . . . . . . . . . . . . 30
"…one lies on his side, with his head resting upon a small block of wood." [MA] . . . . . . 30
"As an attendant prepared two pipes…" [DA] . . . . . . . . . . . . . . . . . . . . . . . . . . . . 32
"Who is the lady?" I asked the Tired Cavalier. [DA] . . . . . . . . . . . . . . . . . . . . . . . . 36
The market at Mytho. [MA] . . . . . . . . . . . . . . . . . . . . . . . . . . . . . . . . . . . . . . . 38
Map of Harry's route from Saigon to Angkor. [DA] . . . . . . . . . . . . . . . . . . . . . . . 38
French Naval personnel relaxing in Saigon [MA] . . . . . . . . . . . . . . . . . . . . . . . . . 44
Résidence Supérieur staff in Cambodia, 1912. [MA] . . . . . . . . . . . . . . . . . . . . . . 44

### II. The City of Serpents
Picture map of Cambodge. [MA] . . . . . . . . . . . . . . . . . . . . . . . . . . . . . . . . . . . . 48

Harry's personal photo of his iconic "King Cobra." [HH]........................48
"I must admit the trip was made in a French motor-car..." [DA] .............50
The tourist bungalow at Angkor [MA]........................................52
"How could I wait, with those black towers inviting me across the moat?" [MA]......52
"The *Apsarases*, according to legend, were dancers and consorts of the gods." [MA]....54
"...*Tevadas* were their earthly reproductions..." [MA]...........................54
"Tall palms that gave the illusion of growing mysteriously out of the stone..." [HH]...58
"Angkor Wat in the daylight is no less stirring than at night." [MA]................58
"...staring up at the prodigious mass of sculptured rock." [MA] ..................60
"On the walls are delicate figures of *Apsarases*..." [MA] .......................62
"On the four sides of the penetralia are shrines..." [MA] ........................62
Group of *Tevadas*. [MA].....................................................64
"They were the dancers of another century..." [MA].............................68
"Ong Kim Khouan, son of the Khmers." [HH]..................................70
1926 map of Angkor..........................................................72
"Galleries...haunted by a ghost of incense burned by some bonze." [MA] ...........74
The Gate of Victory with sacred *naga* serpent balustrades. [MA] ..................74
Tower of Four Faces at the Bayon in Angkor Thom. [MA].......................76
"Trees...with the souls of gods in them—angry gods." [MA].....................80
"...past the torn pyramid of Bayon." [MA] ....................................82
"Buddhas; silhouetted in doorways and windows..." [HH] .......................88
"Courtyards seeming sunk in fountains of plants..." [HH]........................90
"One can fancy those graceful creatures, lily-pale and flame-slim, dancing..." [HH] ...94
"I wandered in the vine-grown cloisters..." [MA]...............................96
"It is a relief to reach Siem Reap." [DA + MA]..................................98

## III. Saramani

His Majesty Sisowath, King of Cambodia. [MA]...............................102
"The hotel, separated from the Mé-Kong by only a road..." [MA] ................104
Mailboat departing for France on November 7, 1924. [MA] .....................104
"Pnom Penh, the town, flows about a gaunt pagoda." [Top-HH, Bottom-MA]......106
"Toward the museum I rode..." [MA].........................................107
"Behold this *congai*—a most enchanting remainder of the Khmer civilization." [MA] 108
The king's royal barge. [MA]..................................................110
"The next day the Tired Cavalier and I went to the palace." [MA] ................110
"She has been designated as a gift to the king, she will dance in the royal ballet." [MA]114

"Soon Saramani learns that life in the palace is very dull." [DA] .................. 114
"She is to be a god, so she wears a *mokot*...a head-dress shaped like a pagoda." [MA] . . 116
"Now when she dances in the ballet she wears more than thirty necklaces." [DA] .... 118
"Grotesque masks glittered above sheening costumes." [DA] ..................... 118
The royal elephants. [HH] ...................................................... 120
The Silver Pagoda. [HH] ....................................................... 120
The Throne Hall. [MA] ........................................................ 122
The *Salle de danse*. [MA] ....................................................... 122
The tomb of King Norodom at the Royal Palace. [MA] ......................... 124
"The *première danseuse* became a fiery vortex around which they swirled." [DA] ...... 126

## IV. Green Serenade

"Merciful God, I wasn't going up the Mé-Kong, was I?" [MA] .................... 130
"Toward dusk we reached Kampong-Cham." [MA] .............................. 130
"And the towns. Names that are savage little poems." [HH] ...................... 142
"A great river, la Mère Mé-Kong. Gentle...yet capable of terrible things." [DA] ..... 142
Moi merchants. [MA] .......................................................... 144

## V. Laos

"Her black hair was done in a flippant knot...circled with flowers..." [HH] ......... 150
"Cambodia was behind; here at Khone was the beginning of Laos." [MA] .......... 152
"The *Garcerie*...jerked through a low jungle of bamboo..." [DA] .................. 158
The waterfalls of Khone where "...yellow mist hung in soiled rainbows." [MA] ...... 162
Map of the Khone waterfalls. [DA] .............................................. 162
"Bassac — finis!" he said with an eloquent wave of his hand." [MA] ................ 170
Supreme Leader of monks in Phnom Penh. [MA] ................................ 178

## VI. The Twilight of the Khmers

"There was a touch of barbarity about these men seen in the flush of torches." [MA] . . 184
"I passed through the middle door into what had been the penetralia." [HH] ....... 192
"...a carved panel with a god seated on a three-headed elephant..." [HH] ........... 194
"These *Apsarases* were different from those at Angkor Wat." [HH] ................. 194
"Each held a lotus-flower in her right hand..." [MA] .............................. 200
"At Prah Khan...*Apsarases* identical with those on the walls of Wat Phu." [HH] ..... 202

## Chapter VII. Sun-Weary Town

"Seven hundred miles up a jungle river, traveling in pirogues and on elephants." [MA] 206

"Oh, You Beautiful Doll." [W] .................................................210
The eponymous pagoda of Vien-Tiane. [top-MA, bottom-HH] ................212
An *épicerie* in Vien-Tiane. [MA] ............................................214
"At night the bugle calls of the *Garde Indigène* have a shuddering echo..." [MA].....214
"Near the rue du Marche I noticed a Laotian theater..." [HH] ..................216
"The morning ended, incongruously, over Picon-grenadines..." [DA]..............220

## Chapter VIII. River and Drum

"Deng, the head man; and five coolies, all blunt Laotians..." [MA] ................228
"Presently one of the coolies got a khène and commenced to play..." [MA].........228
"He was the *délégué* of Paksane, a little village a few yards up the bank." [HH] ......232
"In the next five minutes a fantastic group gathered." [MA].....................232
"In the house sat a slim tawny-lovely Laotian girl..." [DA] ....................235
"The *délégué* gave his idea of how Mistinguett would sing a Laotian air." [DA] ......236
"The *phu-baos* were very proud as they strode about..." [HH] ..................238
"The *phu-saos* wore gay sinhs woven with silver..." [MA] .....................238
Office of the Messageries Fluviales in Savannakhet. [MA]......................241

## Chapter IX. I Am the Forest

"Nham was a person of no importance. I dare say he was a savage." [HH] ..........244
"The pirogue in which I traveled warrants some description." [MA]...............248
"Here the Moi, aboriginal tribes of ancient Champa, mingle..." [HH]..............250
"A *boun* was being celebrated..." [MA] .....................................254
"A white man had come: there could be no more celebration..." [MA].............254
"Who wrote that? Henri Mouhot....just before he died of fever." [W] ............257
"Half-naked prisoners, chained and some wearing the cangue." [MA] ............262
"We use the guillotine," said *Monsieur le Délégué*..." [MA] ....................262
"...there was a rattling of chains and curious eyes peered at us." [MA] ...........264
"Such a girl necessarily would be destined to become a mistress." [MA]............268

## Chapter X. The Chinese Inn

Postcard map of Indochine. [MA]..........................................274
"One tawny gallant who wore a tunic of flowered black grenadine..." [HH] ........278
On the Azure Coast. [HH]..................................................278
"And this was the end. I would go on to Hanoi..." [HH] .......................280
Harry Hervey in a Hanoi garden at the end of his adventure. [HH]...............280

# Exotic Visions of French Indochina

A 1925 adventure in Angkor.
ISBN: 978-1934431023

A jungle temple trek of 1912.
ISBN: 978-1934431900

Paintings of 1920s Indochina.
ISBN: 978-1934431917

Antique postcards of Cambodia.
ISBN: 978-9744801197

# Exotic Visions of French Indochina

Exploring the Mekong in 1929.
ISBN 978-1-934431870

A romance of colonial Cambodia
ISBN: 978-1-934431-94-8

Fantastic folktales from ages past.
ISBN 978-1-934431-21-4

A lost-race romance of Laos
ISBN: 978-1934431764

## Harry Hervey's passionate sequel to *King Cobra*

"My deepest astonishment came with seeing how much *Congai* anticipates perhaps the greatest and most evergreen foreign novel about modern Vietnam, *The Quiet American*, by Graham Greene. Almost ninety years later, even in his wildest moments, Hervey caught something true that those of us more than twice his age can only bow before."  **Foreword by PICO IYER**

www.ingramcontent.com/pod-product-compliance
Lightning Source LLC
Chambersburg PA
CBHW051359070526
44584CB00023B/3222